FAILED TO RETURN

EDITED BY **KEITH C. OGILVIE**

FAILED TO RETURN

CANADA'S BOMBER COMMAND SACRIFICE IN THE SECOND WORLD WAR

Heritage House Publishing Company Ltd.
heritagehouse.ca

Some of the text in this anthology originally appeared in *Bomber Command:
Failed to Return* and *Bomber Command: Failed to Return II*, both published
in the United Kingdom in 2012 by Fighting High Publishing, and have been
edited and reproduced in this volume, with permission from the original
publisher and contributors.

*Cataloguing information available from
Library and Archives Canada*
978-1-77203-381-6 (paperback)
978-1-77203-382-3 (ebook)

Copyedited by Warren Layberry
Proofread by Nandini Thaker
Cover and interior book design by Setareh Ashrafologhalai
Cover photograph: Teddy Blenkinsop in front of an Avro Anson at No. 4
SFTS. With permission from the Blenkinsop family, via John Neroutsos
and Peter Celis.

The interior of this book was produced on 100% post-consumer recycled
paper, recycled chlorine free, and printed with vegetable-based inks.

Heritage House gratefully acknowledges that the land on which we live
and work is within the traditional territories of the Lkwungen (Esquimalt
and Songhees), Malahat, Pacheedaht, Scia'new, T'Sou-ke, and W̱SÁNEĆ
(Pauquachin, Tsartlip, Tsawout, Tseycum) Peoples.

We acknowledge the financial support of the Government of Canada through
the Canada Book Fund (CBF) and the Canada Council for the Arts, and the
Province of British Columbia through the British Columbia Arts Council and
the Book Publishing Tax Credit.

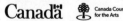

25 24 23 22 21   1 2 3 4 5

Printed in Canada

"One day... it will be recorded that when human society stood at the crossroads and civilization itself was under siege, the Royal Canadian Air Force was there to fill the breach and help give humanity the victory. And all those who had a part in it will have left to posterity a legacy of honour, of courage and of valour that time can never despoil."

FATHER J.P. LARDIE Chaplain for 419, 428 Squadrons, RCAF
Inscribed on the Bomber Command Memorial Wall in Nanton, Alberta

CONTENTS

FOREWORD

MOST OF THE stories related in this book were originally published in the United Kingdom as part of the *Failed to Return* series of books released by Fighting High Publishing. These books chronicled the fates of the unfortunate crews of the Royal Air Force's Bomber Command who did not come back from campaigns on German industrial centres, supporting D-Day operations, with the Dam Busters, against the Nazi V-weapons, and ultimately, against the heart of the Reich, Berlin.

Canada and Canadians made two very significant contributions to Bomber Command: by training about half of Bomber Command's aircrews in Canada and by providing, from Canadian cities, towns, farms, and countryside, a quarter of the men who undertook these dangerous assignments. This volume gathers the stories of individual young Canadians whose names and contributions should not be forgotten.

The authors are acclaimed historians and writers of military history who have drawn from family archives and records, wartime memoirs, logbooks and official combat records, diaries and letters, and on rare occasions, the personal testimony of men who were party to the events described. From these disparate sources, they have stitched together the remarkable and tragic stories set out in this volume. The introduction sets out the Canadian context for these stories, with background on the British Commonwealth Air

Training Plan (BCATP)—under which most of those whose names appear herein were trained for war—and a description of how the RCAF "grew up" from a small, dated, and underequipped force in 1939 to one of the largest air forces in the world by the end of the war. A new chapter, previously unpublished, recounts the story of S/L Teddy Blenkinsop, a native of Victoria, BC, whose tragic fate is not well known in his home province and country.

KEITH C. OGILVIE
November 2021

INTRODUCTION
THE AERODROME
OF DEMOCRACY[1]

FIRST, THE SHOCKING statistics. In the end, over a quarter of the 125,000 aircrew who served in Royal Air Force (RAF) Bomber Command during the Second World War were members of the Royal Canadian Air Force (RCAF), flying with RAF units or increasingly, as the War progressed, in RCAF Squadrons. The horrific rate of loss across Bomber Command—45 percent of aircrew killed outright, 6 percent seriously wounded, and another 8 percent taken as prisoners of war[2]—was equally felt by Canadians, whether they flew in RCAF squadrons or were attached to the RAF. Attrition rates weren't shared with operational aircrews as they flew, fought for their lives, and slowly tallied the missions they survived, but the ones who did return had ample evidence in the heartfelt absence of squadron comrades who had not been so lucky. Squadron Operations Records systematically and impartially recorded the aircraft number, crew names, mission, time of takeoff, and for the unfortunate few, a brief and poignant notation in the column that would normally describe the assessed results: *Failed to return. Nothing heard from this aircraft following takeoff.*

Despite the burden of these tragic losses, night after night, flyers continued to prepare themselves mentally and physically for long and tense combat missions, often on several consecutive nights, repeatedly performing their personal "good luck" rituals and climbing into the narrow airframes that would take them into unforgiving skies over enemy territory.

By 1945, some 40,000 Canadians had served in operational squadrons or training units of RAF Bomber Command. Nearly 10,000 of these young Canadians would give up their lives before the end of hostilities in 1945. They were volunteers, most aged nineteen to twenty-five, with limited experience of life, and none with any idea that he stood only a forty percent chance of coming home whole from the task for which he had volunteered.

Where did they come from, these young men with vague, idealistic, and sometimes romanticized visions of waging a righteous war miles in the air against a dangerous enemy? How were they molded and trained to operate the most complex and lethal weapons of war of the time? How did they learn the essential skills and self-discipline so that, barely out of their teenaged years, they could take command of a state-of-the-art, eighteen-ton, four-engined aircraft along with six other young men and carrying as much as ten tons of bombs and aviation fuel through hostile airspace bristling with flak, enemy fighters, and often, foul weather, to a precise target somewhere in Europe?

Nearly all of them came through a truly extraordinary training program based in Canada that would, by war's end, graduate 131,553 aspiring aircrew into the ranks of professional flyers. It would be the largest training initiative in Commonwealth history. It would cost $2.2 billion, $1.6 billion of which would be contributed by Canada. It would operate from more than 100 aerodromes and emergency landing fields, many built from scratch, across Canada. The British Commonwealth Air Training Plan (BCATP) was the common experience that introduced these young men to each other and to the skills they needed to carry out their deadly profession as wartime flyers.

The BCATP—Laying the Groundwork

By the time Britain formally declared war against Germany on September 3, 1939, there were already several young Canadians flying in operational units in the RAF or undergoing flight training at one of the many facilities in the United Kingdom that were preparing aircrew for service. A week after Britain's entry into the war, Prime Minister William Lyon Mackenzie King's cabinet approved Canada's own declaration of war, opening the door to the greatest contribution to Britain's air defences after that of Britain itself. But it was a fragile beginning.

When war was declared, Canada's air force was in no shape to anticipate the scale of its ultimate contribution. With one eye on events in Europe, air staff of the day had already been working on ambitious plans for supporting the Allied war effort, but the reality was a far cry from the ambition. The RCAF had only eight regular and twelve auxiliary (reserve) squadrons at the start of hostilities. All were understaffed and underequipped. Total service strength was just over 3,000 regulars and another 1,000 reservists. Of these, some 235 pilots[3] were flying what was even then antiquated equipment. Few had any combat experience. Their pre-war flying activities had been largely in support of other government departments, performing tasks like forestry patrols, conducting aerial photography, and assisting police. Of the RCAF's 270 aircraft, only a handful could have been considered modern by the day's standards.

A few of the Canadians serving in the RAF in September of 1939 were combat pilots from the First World War who had elected to remain in service when the RAF was formed in 1918 through the amalgamation of the Royal Flying Corps and the Royal Navy Air Service. Others had followed their flying dreams to pursue opportunities in the United Kingdom during the period between the wars. And as Britain began to build its forces in the pre-war years to meet the anticipated Nazi threat, an increasing number of young men were recruited by RAF enlistment offices in Canada. By the start of the war, when the RCAF assumed responsibility for all Canadian recruitment, it was estimated that more than 440 Canadian pilots or pilot/navigators had already signed up directly with the RAF[4] and had undergone or were undergoing aircrew training in Britain.[5] Interestingly, this meant there were more Canadian pilots serving with the RAF at the time than in the RCAF.

The early commitments Canada was able to make in support of the British war effort were necessarily limited. Long-standing Canadian policy placed the top priority in pre-war military planning on home defence. It was initially planned to mobilize twenty-three squadrons, of which three would constitute an army cooperation wing and three would form a bomber wing to be sent overseas, but without aircraft or equipment. The remaining seventeen would remain in Canada. In the longer term, an additional eighteen squadrons would be added to the first six scheduled for overseas service. All of this would require a concentrated recruitment and training effort.

For their part, planners in Britain quickly recognized the importance of air defences and the imminent need for large numbers of trained aircrew. Realizing the scale of training would be a challenge in the face of actual hostilities, in May 1938, Britain approached the Canadian government asking about creating an air training operation in Canada. The answer reflected Canada's growing sense of itself as an independent nation: Prime Minister Mackenzie King confirmed that Canada could do it, but on its own terms. He was committed to maintaining a sovereign Canadian presence in all the country's support to the British war effort. While he agreed to provide the requested training facilities, he was adamant that they should be under RCAF control and not that of the RAF.

The Canadian commitment was certainly genuine, but as discussions began between the two countries, there were misunderstandings and miscommunication, deliberate or inadvertent, over critical details. In particular: whether training should be for only British or for British *and* Canadian aircrew; and, given the already limited RCAF training capacity, how many trainees could be taken on. The question of scale was further complicated by an early request from the RAF to first provide already trained RCAF personnel to immediately serve in RAF units, an action that could potentially remove many experienced instructors from contributing to the expanding training.

An agreement for the cooperative training scheme was finally concluded in March 1939. It was small, anticipating training of fifty British aircrew, along with some seventy-five pilots for the RCAF to meet Canada's own needs. The training syllabus would be adapted to current RAF standards and elementary training contracted out to civilian flying clubs located across the country. However, the pressures of the imminent war kept the RAF trainees in Britain, and the agreement was never able to be fulfilled.

Nonetheless, this work proved to be a strong foundation for the extraordinary ramping up of aircrew training efforts that would follow, under what ultimately evolved into the British Commonwealth Air Training Plan. The intense discussions leading up to the first agreement and the growing understanding of the scale of effort required meant that, by the time war was declared, Canada fully understood the importance the RAF placed on training large numbers of aircrew for its wartime effort. For their part, the British also understood Canada's insistence on carrying out any training in Canada under its own control.

On September 26, 1939, Britain returned with a proposal that Canada dramatically expand its capacity to be able to train nearly 29,000 aircrew annually. These were orders of magnitude larger than anything conceived of before. Volunteers would enlist in their own air forces in countries throughout the Commonwealth, come to Canada to receive basic and advanced aircrew training following an RAF syllabus, and be seconded directly to the RAF on graduation. Canada would cover the costs of the program, estimated by the RCAF Chief of Staff as being the "equivalent to maintenance of at least 50 squadrons in the field."[6] In return, the British government agreed to fund fifteen RCAF squadrons overseas. Further heavy negotiations followed on funding details, the formation of the RCAF squadrons, and how Canadian graduates from the new training initiative would be deployed. An agreement on the creation of the BCATP was finally signed by Canada, Britain, Australia, and New Zealand on December 17, 1939. It was, not quite coincidentally, the birthday of Canadian prime minister Mackenzie King, and he considered this to be a fine birthday present.

The background issues of distinctive identification of RCAF squadrons and assignment of aircrew to these squadrons would plague RAF-RCAF relations for most of the war. However, for the moment, attention could be turned to making the agreement work.

The Early Days

Finalizing the BCATP agreement was one thing; putting into place all the pieces to make the BCATP function smoothly was entirely another, and it took an extraordinary effort. More than eight times the number of personnel in the whole of the RCAF at the start of the war would be needed just to deliver the BCATP's vision. Whole new cadres of specialists from aircrew to ground support technicians to administrative trades had to be recruited, trained (or if possible, recruited already in possession of the needed qualifications), and organized within Canada. Some of the technical and organizational leadership required was temporarily loaned from the RAF, ultimately about three hundred officers in all. The most senior of these was Air Commodore Robert Leckie, a Canadian in the RAF with a distinguished flying record in the First World War. He would fill the crucial position of RCAF Director of Training, since the RCAF had no one sufficiently senior or experienced to deal with the mind-boggling scale of the training challenge they now faced.[7]

The necessary physical infrastructure had to be built or amassed, and 3,540 aircraft of various types had to be found. Dozens of new training bases and thousands of buildings—hangars, support facilities, and barracks—had to be quickly acquired or constructed with unprecedented speed. Other government organizations also provided badly needed help to the RCAF. The Department of Transport provided critical support in selecting and planning some eighty new airport sites as well as offering another forty existing DoT airfields that could be adapted to the purpose. Civilian flying clubs were contracted to provide elementary level pilot training to RAF and RCAF candidates (Australians and New Zealanders received elementary training in their home countries). Commercial aviation companies operated the air observer schools, with civilian pilots flying the aircraft and RCAF service members providing instruction. Every possible source of professional expertise was tapped.

Meeting the organizational challenge often required no little ingenuity. Procuring the much-needed training aircraft was a particular headache. Initially some came from England, but this supply rapidly dried up as training efforts in that country were ramped up. Canadian manufacturers were quickly enlisted to produce the de Havilland Tiger Moths, Fleet Finches, and Avro Ansons that became the heart of the training program. For more advanced single-engine training, the RCAF had already purchased thirty Harvard trainers just prior to the declaration of war. The first batch had been delivered from the North American Aviation factory in Inglewood, California, by flying them up the Pacific coast to Vancouver. RCAF crews then flew them across the country to training stations in Ontario. However, when war was declared, the US Neutrality Act precluded that country from flying war materials to belligerent nations, of which Canada was now officially one. The solution was to fly the remaining aircraft from the first purchase, and all that followed until the US entered the war, to airfields in locations like Sweetgrass, Montana, just across the border from Coutts, Alberta. The US–Canada border runs right through the middle of the east-west dirt runway shared by the two towns. Aircraft arriving from American factories could be parked on the US side, pushed across

the border, and flown away to RCAF training bases without techni-
cally violating American law.

So, with all the necessary parts of the plan moving into place, the
next and most important piece of the puzzle was to start getting the
young men who would be trained into the system.

The BCATP Experience

And the young men came. When the BCATP was announced to the
nation by Prime Minister Mackenzie King on the day it was signed,
there was already a backlog of applications to join the RCAF. An
additional surge of Canadians flocked to recruitment stations almost
immediately after the announcement was made. The conditions for
applying were many: age had to be between eighteen and twenty-
eight for pilots, observers, or navigators, and eighteen to thirty-two
for air gunners or wireless operators; education to junior matricula-
tion or equivalent was required; and applicants had to be residents
in Canada and, in a reflection of the times, "of pure European
descent." Finally, recruits needed the "right stuff" for aircrew: to
be of good character, intelligent and adaptable, personable, and—
naturally—keen on flying.

Those who passed the basic medical and initial aptitude testing
at local application centres were sent first to the intake manning
depots (initially in Toronto and Brandon, Manitoba) for basic training. These sometimes offered relatively primitive conditions. In
Toronto, the new recruits lived in the cattle barn and comparable facilities on the Canadian National Exhibition grounds. One
wryly noted that when the recruits were temporarily moved out to
house the CNE's annual show "it took seven days to prepare the
grounds to "welcome" back the horses and the cattle for the exhibition, and only one to prepare the grounds for the recruits when
they got back."[8] Individual performance in the face of rigorous
testing provided the basis for sorting the trainees into different
skill streams.

Pilot and observer candidates went from basic training to begin theoretical studies at one of the initial training schools, often under similar living conditions. For example, No. 1 ITS was established on the appropriated grounds of Toronto's Eglington Hunt Club on Avenue Road, where trainees were bunked in converted horse stables. Based on individual aptitudes and performance, a small number of candidates might at this stage find themselves reassigned to the wireless air gunner category. The remainder moved on to elementary training schools to learn to fly with contracted civilian instructors, usually in de Havilland Tiger Moths. Many of those found unsuited to further pilot training but who still wanted to fly were transferred to the observer or navigator stream.

Successful pilot candidates moved on to one of the service flying training schools for advanced flying training. There, most prospective bomber pilots were introduced to the venerable Avro Anson, a stable, durable, and drafty twin engine machine that had started service with the RAF first as a maritime reconnaissance aircraft.[9] They were also given much more exposure to night and instrument flying, vitally important to meeting the kinds of challenges to which they would be exposed in combat. The culmination of all this intense learning was a series of skills tests, covering navigation, formation, and instrument flying; then, finally, the long anticipated (and mostly dreaded) wings test. Here, the testing officer put the aspiring pilot through a comprehensive review of all aspects of flight, the culmination of which—for the lucky and skilful ones—was the awarding of official wings as a qualified pilot.

Students designated for other aircrew trades were posted to specialized schools, similarly scattered across the country: air observer schools; air navigation schools; bombing and gunnery schools; or wireless schools. As for the pilots, their aerial education took a mix of ground study and airborne practice, from night navigation exercises to shooting at drogue targets—in the latter case, making best efforts not to hit the tow plane.[10]

This was as far as they would be taken under the often-frozen Canadian skies. And here one of the sticking points between the

Canadian and British signatories to the Plan reared its head: decid-
ing how many and which of the now qualified graduates would
be offered commissions as officers. The British proposed a quota
system that allowed for only twenty percent of wireless operators
and air gunners to ever reach commissioned rank and disagreed
with Canada's desire to have fifty percent of pilots and observers/
navigators commissioned automatically on graduation from service
flying training schools. The issue would remain a point of conten-
tion throughout the war, with the RAF consistently resisting the
more egalitarian approach adopted by the RCAF.

Nearly all the early pilot graduates of the scheme remained in
Canada, with assignments either to a flight instructor school, where
they would learn to teach their successors in the scheme, or in some
cases, with attachment to home defence squadrons. A small number, along with the first classes of observers and wireless operators/
air gunners, began to head overseas late in 1940 for assignment to
RAF squadrons, mainly in Bomber Command. With the instructor
ranks now filled, the flow overseas of newly qualified aircrew began
in earnest in the following months.

For those headed overseas, the wings graduation parade was
followed by a train ride to Halifax or Montreal and embarkation
on anything from the luxury liner *Queen Elizabeth* to small coastal
steamers for the transatlantic boat trip. These were no easy rides.
Hazards of learning to fly notwithstanding, these voyages were
the first venture for most passengers into a hostile environment.
German U-boats preyed on Atlantic convoys and more than once
cut short the career of an aspiring pilot before it began. The fate
of the small steamer MV *Amerika* offers just one stark example of
the greater hazards of wartime. Not a fast ship, she fell behind her
assigned convoy and was sunk just south of Greenland on April 22,
1943. The lives of thirty-seven of the fifty-three trained pilots and
instructors on board, most with the RCAF, were lost on their way to
join the RAF's war effort.

For the many who successfully completed the crossing, the first
stop in the UK was a personnel reception centre on the coast. Here,

the new arrivals received their battle dress and flying equipment: warm flying suits and boots, gloves, helmets, and goggles. Then, true to military form, they waited. Advanced flying units (AFUs) where newly minted aircrew would go to further develop their flying skills, learn to handle heavier aircraft, and find their way over unfamiliar territory were often overburdened with new arrivals from both the BCATP and the English aircrew training programs. There was nothing to be done but bide one's time, suffering twice daily attendance parades, until an AFU opening appeared. Frustration and boredom became the hallmark of these periods of suspended animation, highlighted only by the weekly hospitality dances put on by the local communities and occasional youthful misbehaviour. But even these holding facilities were not safe havens. Because of their proximity to the continent, many suffered repeated attacks by roving German aircraft, with sometimes fatal results both for the locals and the waiting trainees.

When their hiatus finally ended with an AFU posting, the new airmen were catapulted into an intense and demanding program of advanced training. The English countryside and weather conditions were nothing like those encountered in Canada. Navigation was a particular challenge for the new arrivals. The ancient layout of roads, train tracks, towns, and country lanes was at first indecipherable to those more accustomed to the orderly grid patterns so common in Canada. In winter especially, the weather was often misty or rainy, a stark contrast to the bright blue Canadian skies, making the unfamiliar terrain even more hazardous. By spring of 1943, the pace of training replacement bomber crews was reaching its peak, given the output of BCATP and the frightful Bomber Command average mission loss rate of nearly three percent, an average of four bombers and crews being lost each night. AFU flying continued seven days a week, building experience, introducing pilots to advanced skills of bad weather instrument landing techniques, and extending their exposure to night flying.

The final phase of training took place at an operational training unit, or OTU, where aircrew were now introduced to the complexities of flying a heavy bomber. It was here as well that the actual crew teams—pilot, navigator, bomb aimer, wireless operator, flight engineer, air gunners—were put together, using the most rudimentary and effective of techniques. New arrivals were early on deposited en masse into one location and left to their own devices to form up into a crew. Those who were unable to organize themselves would be crewed up by OTU staff. This process at least offered the sometimes-fragile advantage of self-selection as the basis for the cohesiveness and teamwork that would be required going into active combat.

It quickly became clear that this was a different level of training. Crews familiarized themselves with their future roles through practice bombing runs and air firing. They were exposed to the latest, often highly secret electronic navigation and bombing aids that were being rapidly introduced to the front lines. The final test would be a mission over enemy territory, usually dropping leaflets. A year or more after they first polished their newly issued uniform boots, and with an "official" mission under their belts, the crews finally would be sent on to join an operational squadron.

Canadianization in Bomber Command

As the war progressed and the flow of BCATP graduates increased, so did political pressures for Canadianization of the country's contributions to the war in Europe—that is, clearly identifying RCAF aircrews as Canadian, and wherever possible, bringing them together and putting them directly under Canadian control. In the beginning, there simply weren't enough to create the necessary critical mass. The early cohort of BCATP graduates were all assigned to operational roles in RAF squadrons. As well, throughout the war there were arguments—from both the RAF and the RCAF sides—that mixed crews would provide the best opportunities for sharing experience and strategic perspective. In fact, most crews had some mix of RAF and Commonwealth members right through to the end of the war.

As the war progressed, there was continued pressure from the Canadian government to bring about some form of Canadianization, despite the arguments for full integration. The RCAF did not even have a distinct presence in Bomber Command until April 1941, when 405 "Vancouver" Squadron was formed under Wing Commander P.A. Gilchrist, DFC, a Saskatchewan native who had joined the RAF in 1935. Flying Wellington II aircraft and with (then) predominantly RAF aircrews, 405 Squadron carried out its first operation on the night of June 12, 1941, and would eventually participate in Bomber Command's heaviest efforts through to the end of the war.[11] By the end of 1941, three more RCAF Squadrons—408, 419, and 420—had been established and were regularly engaged in bombing operations, all still integrated within the general structure of RAF Bomber Command.

After another lengthy period of transatlantic political wrangling, the growing proportion of Canadians (and other non-British flyers) in RAF crews, together with Canada's indication of willingness to pay for RCAF squadrons overseas, finally tipped the scales in mid-1942, when it was agreed to form No. 6 Bomber Group, consisting entirely of RCAF Squadrons. Air Vice-Marshal G.E. Brookes moved from his position as Air Officer Commanding No. 1 Training Command in Canada to take over. It was an inspired and appropriate appointment, as the new bomber group would need considerable training before they could become operationally effective. Under Brookes were some distinguished Canadians, including Group Captain C.R. Slemon, who would become Senior Air Staff Officer, and Wing Commander "Johnny" Fauquier, an experienced and highly respected pilot, former Commanding Officer of RCAF 405 Squadron (twice!) and himself a former instructor with the BCATP.[12]

Air Marshal Sir Charles A.T. "Bomber" Harris, chief of Bomber Command and until the last a vociferous opponent of the creation of non-RAF units, officially welcomed the new No. 6 Bomber

Group into its operational career with the following message, on January 1, 1943:

> A happy birthday and a prosperous New Year to the RCAF group. As individuals and as RCAF squadrons you have done fine work already. As the RCAF group I know you will maintain and even surpass your own high standards. We are proud to have you with us.
>
> Hail Canada.
> Hail Hitler, but with bombs![13]

No. 6 Group began with three squadrons—those first three RCAF squadrons formed in Bomber Command—and by March had nine operational squadrons flying out of six separate former RAF stations, all in Yorkshire. However, identification of No. 6 as a Canadian group was still a bit misleading. Just as there remained many Canadians intermingled with RAF and other Commonwealth airmen throughout the system, so too was the initial composition of No. 6 Group crews very much mixed—in fact, initially the minority of flyers were Canadian. But at least the Canadian government was paying the bills.

Initial losses were high for several reasons, not least the lack of experience of many of the crews, who were also caught up in the process of Bomber Command's conversion from two- to four-engined aircraft. As 1943 progressed, the pace and complexity of bombing operations was also increasing significantly. Nonetheless, they adapted, improved, and went on to achieve a distinguished record. At peak strength in the final year of the war, No. 6 Group would comprise sixteen Canadian squadrons. Over the course of the war, some ten OTUs, equipped with experienced and often weary former front-line aircraft, fed crews into No. 6 Bomber Group. By the time No. 6 Group was disbanded in August 1945, it had amassed a strong record of performance within Bomber Command that included some of the war's most challenging missions against targets like the industrialized Ruhr valley, Hamburg, Peen-emünde, and the Allies' ultimate objective, Berlin.

The BCATP Contribution

The first graduates crossing the Atlantic to England in 1941 marked the beginning of a steady stream of aircrew from 97 different schools across Canada, a stream that would ultimately number 131,553 by the closure of the BCATP in spring of 1945. Nearly 50,000 would qualify as pilots. The remainder would fill out the other essential aircrew positions as navigators, bomb aimers, observers, flight engineers, wireless operators, and air gunners.

And BCATP students came from all over, not just the Common-wealth, although trainees had to be associated with one or another Commonwealth air force. In addition to volunteers from the signa-tory countries to the agreement, there were Americans who crossed the border to join the RCAF and fight before the US entered the war in December 1941. RAF trainees came from the United Kingdom, more than 42,000 in all. Among these were some 5,425 expatri-ates from other countries that had been invaded by the Nazis: Poles, Norwegians, Belgians, Dutch, Czechs, and Free French volunteers, who all committed to supporting the war however they could and found a home in the RAF. Overall, nearly half the Commonwealth aircrew who took part in the war in Europe were trained through the BCATP.

It was truly an extraordinary achievement that changed the face of Canada as well as the course of the war. Of the total grad-uates from the training program, more than half—nearly 73,000 Canadians, along with that handful of Americans and others—had joined the RCAF.

The Canadian air minister, Charles "Chubby" Power, who shepherded this program (and the rapid expansion of the RCAF) through the war years, summarized the scale of the contribution in the Canadian parliament in May 1945, when he outlined for the record where the graduates of the program had landed, and how they had performed:

> Some have been ploughed back into the plan as instructors. Some ... were kept for the home war establishment. But the vast majority have gone overseas ... They are in every raid, in every sortie, they are in every attack on Germany. Wherever the British forces are attacking, there you will find graduates of our air training plan.

He went on to rue the human cost to the country, with the high rate of loss among graduates, pointing out that "not a day goes by ... without a very heavy casualty list of young Canadians serving in the Royal Air Force or in our own squadrons."[14]

The Men and Their Stories

There has been much controversy over the destruction wrought by Bomber Command, and how much—indeed, whether at all—Bomber Command operations contributed to advancing the end of the war. Seventy-five years after the conclusion of the war, there is still no end in sight to these discussions, and this book makes no judgements on these issues. The authors have undertaken simply to record for history the stories of some of the young men who believed deeply in what they were doing and who drew the courage night after night to embark on their dangerous missions into enemy airspace.

The men whose experiences are related in these pages served in RAF and Canadian squadrons. Their mates, often the people with whom they died, came from countries around the world. The range of nationalities that made up these close-knit teams clearly reflects the extraordinary commitment each of them had to a common purpose.

The broader history of the air war plays out in these individual stories of the men who fought it, by turns heroic, terror-filled, and tragic. The stories in this book relate the final experiences of just a few of the many Canadians who contributed their skills, bravery, and often their very lives to what they understood as a worthy and principled cause. In one sense they are representative of the experiences of all their unfortunate colleagues; in another, each story is utterly unique. They all lived the noise and vibration of the bomber engines, the shouts in the earphones, sometimes the sudden crash of bullets or shrapnel from exploding flak. They smelled the oil, fuel, and cordite as their gunners fired back on marauding night fighters. They felt the turbulence of the unsteady air as they approached their target zones and the violent pitching, pinning them against the sides or top of the bomber's fuselage as the pilots struggled to evade being "coned" by searchlights. They felt the wash of fear and adrenaline as they went into action. But each would have his own story of the final moments that resulted in that simple, terrible entry in the Squadron log: *Failed to return.*

The telling of these stories will never be fully satisfactory, since so few can be related in the words of the participants themselves. But it is important to put them on the record. It is the best we can do for these men, that each person's short, intense, and individual existence, and their collective contribution to humanity, should never be forgotten.

TOP On the Ramp, No. 19 Elementary Flying Training School, Virden. FROM "VIRDEN DAYS," COURTESY COMMONWEALTH AIR TRAINING PLAN MUSEUM

BOTTOM, LEFT Course #47 Wings Parade, No. 5 Air Observer School, Winnipeg. COURTESY COMMONWEALTH AIR TRAINING PLAN MUSEUM

BOTTOM, RIGHT Fairchild Cornell over Virden, Manitoba EFTS. FROM "VIRDEN DAYS," COURTESY COMMONWEALTH AIR TRAINING PLAN MUSEUM

ABOVE The de Havilland DHC1 Tiger Moth (top) was the biplane in which all prospective pilots were introduced to the joys and discipline of flying. Those with the potential to become fighter pilots went on to train on a more advanced single-engine monoplane, the North American Harvard (bottom). These two iconic aircraft are maintained in flying condition eighty years later by the Commonwealth Air Training Plan Museum in Brandon, Manitoba. COURTESY COMMONWEALTH AIR TRAINING PLAN MUSEUM

Operational training units (OTUs) were the final stage of training for Bomber Command airmen. After completing training courses for their specific crew positions, the airmen were posted to OTUs and trained to fly as a working crew in preparation for joining an operational squadron. The instructors at the OTUs were experienced airmen who had generally completed one or more tours flying on operations. A tour at the time of the episode in this chapter would normally be thirty operations. Being posted to instruct at an OTU was considered by the RAF to give the men a break from the stress and strain of operational flying. However, in some respects it was just as hazardous as flying on operations over enemy-occupied territory, and many lives were lost in training accidents. The crew of Wellington R1646 exemplify the young lives sacrificed and valuable experience lost in these circumstances.

I

FUTURES DENIED

LINZEE DRUCE

THE WINTER OF 1942 was one of the worst that the northeast of Scotland had experienced, with heavy falls of snow and bitterly cold temperatures. In the middle of February, near the village of Braemar, some sixty miles south of Lossiemouth as the crow flies, gamekeeper James Wright was out scanning the snow-covered landscape, checking for deer through his telescope. He noticed something unfamiliar near the top of a steep hillside in Glen Clunie. He couldn't be sure, but to him it looked to be the tail section of an aircraft.

On returning to the village of Braemar, James reported his sighting to the local policeman, Constable Gerrie, who in turn telephoned his headquarters in Aberdeen to enquire if there were any aircraft reported missing in the Braemar area. He was told there were none.

James Wright, however, was convinced that he had seen something that warranted further investigation, and the following day a small search party of four set out from Braemar for Glen Clunie. Joining James and Constable Gerrie in the search were William Brown, a member of the local Home Guard, and his fifteen-year-old son, Andy.

A truck with a snow plough was used to drive as far along the road as possible, but the last mile and a half had to be covered on foot up a very steep hillside, the men sinking at times waist deep into the snow.

The party finally reached the wreckage and could see that what James had spied through his telescope had indeed been the tail section of an aircraft, the glass of the rear gun turret glinting in the light. The rest of the aircraft was buried under the snow, and it was obvious that it had been there for some weeks. There was no sign of life, and they were not able to identify the aircraft as so little was above the snow. They could do nothing but return to Braemar, where Constable Gerrie again telephoned his HQ and reported that the wreckage of an aircraft indeed had been found.

The RAF sent a surveying unit from No. 56 Maintenance Unit to the scene a few days later to investigate. The weather was extreme, making it incredibly difficult even to access the wreckage. Steps and paths had to be cut out of the ice- and snow-covered hillside to reach the wreckage. It was eventually identified as being that of Vickers Wellington R1646, missing since January 19, 1942, on a training flight from its base at No. 20 OTU, RAF Lossiemouth, on the northeast coast of Scotland. For the past month, the aircraft and the eight young men aboard had been presumed to be lost at sea.

It took a further two months to complete the recovery of the crew, who were subsequently buried side by side in Dyce Old Churchyard near Aberdeen. They were named as:

Flying Officer James Williamson Thomson, DFC, RNZAF, age 25, Pilot/Instructor

Sergeant Robert James Jackson, RCAF, age 21, Pilot

Sergeant Michael Henry John Kilburn, RAFVR, age 19, Pilot

Flight Sergeant Harry Joseph Kelley, RCAF, age 23, Air Observer

Sergeant John Bernard Riley, RAFVR, age 23, Wireless Operator/ Air Gunner/Instructor

Sergeant Beaumont Churchill Dickson, RAAF, age 22, Wireless Operator/Air Gunner

Sergeant Roy Alistair Milliken, RAAF, age 22, Wireless Operator/ Air Gunner

Sergeant William Morphet Greenbank, RAFVR, age 20, Air Gunner

Eight young lives had been wiped out in a training accident. Two of the young men had already completed tours over enemy-occupied Europe and were introducing their charges to the challenges of wartime flying. The crew members in the last stages of their training came from Australia, Canada, New Zealand, America, and England. Before the outbreak of war, they had been embarking on the start of their adult lives, completing their education, and going on to work as accountants, bank clerks, scientists, salesmen. The war changed the direction they were to take with their lives and was to deny them the futures they deserved.

JAMES "JIM" Thomson was from Oamaru, Otago, in New Zealand. He was a member of the New Zealand Territorial Force for two years, studied accountancy at college, and went on to work as a clerk with the Justice Department in Blenheim. In 1939, he applied to enrol with the Royal New Zealand Air Force Civil Reserve of Pilots, who, in the event of war or a national emergency, are obliged to offer their services to the RNZAF.

In early 1940, Jim was mobilized with the RNZAF and began his training in New Zealand. He was commissioned as a pilot officer in August 1940, and in September he boarded a ship bound for the UK, where he arrived in November. After completing his pilot training in England, Jim was posted in March 1941 to 75 Squadron at Feltwell.

During his time with the squadron, Jim flew thirty-one operations over occupied Europe as well as searches over the Atlantic for German shipping. He was awarded the Distinguished Flying Cross for his courage during an incident on an operation to Düsseldorf in June 1941, when the aircraft he was flying was attacked several times from the ground and air, resulting in it catching fire. The crew managed to extinguish the fire, and Jim was able to fly the aircraft back to base safely.

After completing his first operational tour, Jim was posted to No. 20 OTU as an instructor. He was near the end of his posting when he died at the age of twenty-five. His body was recovered from the crash site in April 1942.

The second instructor on board Wellington R1646 that day was John "Jack" Riley, who came from Bentley, Yorkshire, in England. After leaving school, Jack had worked at Smiths Furniture Shop in Doncaster before volunteering for the RAF in April 1940.

In September 1940, Jack married Joyce Chapman at Askern Village Church in Yorkshire at a double wedding with Joyce's sister, Phyllis, who was also marrying an airman.

Jack trained as a wireless operator and air gunner and had completed the final stage of his training at No. 20 OTU at RAF Loss-iemouth in April of 1941, unaware that he would be returning later that year as an instructor rather than under training. His first post-ing to an operational squadron was in May, when he joined No. 218 Squadron at RAF Marham in Norfolk. Keen to get his first opera-tional trip over with and having had four trips cancelled for various reasons, Jack finally set off on an operation to bomb Düsseldorf on the night of Monday, June 2. On June 4, he wrote to his mother:

> Naturally it was quite thrilling being our first trip—the ack-ack was pretty fierce and quite a few bursts were pretty near. However, it was very comforting to have our Wing Commander Squadron Leader Price as a pilot, as he has done about forty trips altogether—strangely enough I wasn't in the least scared during the trip, only thrilled and excited naturally.
>
> Actually, this game is just a matter of luck; the majority of the blokes here have done over twenty trips. As you know, we have only thirty to do then we get grounded as instructors—I don't doubt for a second that I shan't come through this lot OK.

Tragically Jack would lose his life just six months after writing this, not on operations over Europe, but while instructing at an oper-ational training unit.

Jack flew thirty-one operations with 218 Squadron, the majority with Squadron Leader Price as captain. Most of these operations were over Germany, some to the Channel port of Brest in France, and one to Turin in Italy. These missions were not without incident. On the night of July 15, on an operation to Duisburg, the Wellington Jack was aboard was hit by flak in the port wing, engine, and several places along the fuselage. The rear turret was also rendered unserviceable by flak. No. 218 Squadron lost one Wellington on this operation, but Jack's landed safely back at base. Squadron Leader Herbert Lawrence Price was awarded the Distinguished Flying Cross for successfully bringing his aircraft and crew home.

In December 1941, after completing his tour of operations with No. 218 Squadron, Jack returned to the familiar grounds of No. 20 OTU at Lossiemouth.

Jack was buried in March 1942. His family, unfortunately, were not informed of his funeral until after the event had taken place, causing them great distress.

ROBERT "BOB" Jackson, born in the Birch Cliff neighbourhood of Scarborough, Ontario, was one of two trainee pilots aboard Wellington R1646. After leaving school, Bob worked first as a clerk in a grocery store before joining the staff of the Royal Bank of Canada.

In December 1940, Bob enlisted with the Royal Canadian Air Force and completed his primary pilot training in Canada. He arrived in England in September 1941 and received instructions to proceed to No. 20 OTU at Lossiemouth in Scotland.

The telegram bearing the dreadful news confirming Bob's death and funeral arrangements arrived at his mother Ella's home in Scarborough's Birch Cliff neighbourhood on April 17, the day his funeral took place at Dyce Old Churchyard. He was twenty-one years old.

In addition to his parents and two sisters in Canada, Bob left behind his sweetheart, Helen Garth. Bob and Helen had been seeing one another for three years but, like so many other young couples, had decided not to become engaged because of the war.

THE OTHER trainee pilot on board was Michael Kilburn, only child of Frank and Gladys Kilburn of Farnham, Surrey, in England. Michael was educated at Farnham Grammar School and was a member of the Cadet Corps. He was also a member of the Home Guard in Farnham.

After leaving school aged eighteen, Michael immediately joined the RAF Voluntary Reserve to train as a pilot. He was completing his last two weeks of training at No. 20 OTU when he died.

Initially Michael was buried at Dyce Old Churchyard alongside the other seven members of the crew of Wellington R1646. His family in Farnham, however, wanted him closer to home and on Saturday, January 23, 1943, one year and four days after his death, a funeral and reinternment took place at Green Lane Cemetery in Farnham.

Present at the funeral were his parents and immediate family, friends, colleagues, members of the Home Guard and the Farnham Grammar School Cadet Corps, as well as teachers from his former school. The coffin was draped with a Union Jack, and, at the close of the committal, the Last Post and Reveille were sounded on a cornet played by a member of Farnham Home Guard.

The floral tribute laid by his family indicated the enormous loss they had suffered of their only child. It read: "In proud and undying memory of our only and beloved child Michael Henry John. Resting at last near us."

HARRY "JOE" Kelley was born in Lackawanna, New York, USA, where his father worked in the steel industry. The Kelley family moved to Nova Scotia, Canada, when Joe was a small boy, and it was here that he grew up and had his early education.

At some point, the family moved to Westmount, Quebec. Joe attended Loyola College and studied commerce and science at McGill University, Montreal. During summer holidays, he worked as a chemist at the Dominion Steel and Coal Corp in Sydney, Nova Scotia; during the school year at both Loyola and McGill, he was a cadet in the Canadian Officers Training Corps (COTC).

In October 1940, Joe joined the Royal Canadian Air Force to train as a navigator. After completing his training with the BCATP, he was posted to Britain to complete the final stage at an OTU. He began his training at No. 11 OTU at RAF Bassingbourne, but on January 6, 1942, was transferred to No. 20 OTU at RAF Lossiemouth.

Joe was buried at Dyce Old Churchyard on March 2, 1942. In May 1942, Joe's father Harry accepted a posthumous Bachelor of Science degree on Joe's behalf from McGill University.

WILLIAM "BILL" Greenbank was born in Dent, Sedburgh, Yorkshire. Bill joined the Royal Air Force Volunteer Reserve (RAFVR) and trained as an air gunner. He was in the final stage of his training at No. 20 OTU when he lost his life.

Initially Bill was buried on March 2 alongside the other members from his crew at Dyce Old Churchyard. His family later applied for permission to have him buried in his local cemetery, and in November 1942, his remains were reinterred in St. Mary's Cemetery, Windermere, Westmoreland.

On January 9, 1942, ten days before he died, Bill wrote a letter to his parents that he would leave with his commanding officer for delivery only in the event of his death. In it he wrote:

> I have a feeling this will be my last letter to you both. I have always admired your amazing courage in the face of continual setbacks. My death would not mean that your struggle has been in vain. Far from it, it means that your sacrifice is as great as mine. I shall have lived and died an English-man, nothing else matters one jot.
>
> You must not grieve for me, I have no fear of death, and I am prepared to die with just one regret, and one only—that I could not devote myself to making your declining years more happy by being with you, but you will live in peace and freedom and I shall have directly contributed to that, so here again my life will not have been in vain.

The letter was signed "Your loving son Bill" and a PS was added to say, "I was hoping this letter was never to be sent."

TWO YOUNG Australians also perished on board Wellington R1646 on January 19. Beaumont Dickson and Alistair Milliken were allocated service numbers just two digits apart, indicating they joined the RAAF on the same day at the same time and place in October 1940.

Beaumont Churchill Dickson was born in Rockhampton, Queensland, Australia, and was educated there at Liechhardt Ward Boys School, where he was the senior swimming champion. On leaving school, he worked as a junior cerk at Australian Estates in Rockhampton and attended night school at the technical college to study typing, accounts, and bookkeeping.

Roy Alistair Milliken, known as Alistair by his family, was born in Mackay, Queensland, Australia. He began his education at school in Clermont, Queensland, before going on to the boys grammar school in Rockhampton and St. Joseph's College, Nudgee, near Brisbane. After leaving school, Alistair studied accountancy at the youth employment class at Rockhampton.

After enlisting that October, Beaumont and Alistair went on to attend the same basic training courses in Australia and sailed together to Canada to join the massive training effort of the BCATP. They studied at No. 2 Wireless Training School (2WTS) in Calgary, Alberta, and No. 2 Bombing and Gunnery School (2BAGS) at Mossbank, Saskatchewan, before sailing to Britain just days apart. That summer must have been an eventful one, for in addition to his intensive schedule of studies, Alistair found time to marry a local girl, Mary Donahoe, on June 24, 1941. Their time together was short as he was on his way to England a month later.

Once in England the two men's paths again joined at signals school in Yatesbury. They finally arrived for the last stages of their aircrew training at No. 20 OTU at RAF Lossiemouth in September 1941.

The two young Australians who had joined the RAAF on the same day and who had trained side by side in Australia, Canada, and finally in England, both lost their lives on that ill-fated flight in Scotland. They were buried together on March 2. Inscribed on Beaumont's headstone were the words: "Enshrined in noble memory for evermore." Alistair's epitaph read: "He served his country well."

THE LOSS of the eight young men was felt deeply by their families. The mothers of all eight corresponded with one another for several years afterwards, sharing their grief, exchanging photographs of their sons, and offering one another comfort and support.

Another person who was profoundly affected by the loss of these young men was Andy Brown from Braemar. He was the fifteen-year-old boy who had accompanied his father on the original search party that located the crashed Wellington. Their loss played on his mind over the years, and he always felt that something should be done to remember them.

In 1999, Andy applied for permission to recover some parts of the Wellington from the hillside in Glen Clunie, with a view to using them to create a memorial to the crew. The engines were recovered with the assistance of the Argyll and Sutherland Highlanders, who, appropriately, had been the regiment that guarded RAF Lossiemouth in 1942, and by the RAF Sea King helicopter that is based at RAF Lossiemouth.

Finally, in August 2003, after years of planning and months of preparation, a memorial to the crew of Wellington R1646 was unveiled by HRH Anne, Princess Royal, in the village of Braemar.

The memorial, consisting of one of the Pegasus engines from the Wellington standing on a granite plinth, is situated beside the Braemar War Memorial in the centre of the village, where it is visited by thousands of people every year. An information board with the history of the village nearby includes the story of Wellington R1646 and crew, so the memory of these young men and the record of their sacrifice will live on.

ABOVE, LEFT Flight Sergeant Harry Kelley, RCAF, air observer. KELLEY FAMLY ARCHIVES

ABOVE, RIGHT Sergeant Robert Jackson, RCAF, pilot. JACKSON FAMILY ARCHIVES

OPPOSITE Wellington R1646 Memorial in Braemar. LINZEE DRUCE

Chiselled into the walls of the cloisters at the Air Forces Memorial at Runnymede are the names of over 20,000 airmen and airwomen who were lost during the Second World War, fighting in Britain, northwestern and central Europe, and the eastern Atlantic. They have no known grave. Prominent on Cooper's Hill, overlooking the river Thames, stands the memorial's tower, featuring three stone figures depicting Justice, Victory, and Courage, looking inward, facing the central plinth's "Their Name Liveth for Evermore." At either edge of the memorial tower cloister, curved name-lined passages lead to name-lined lookouts, taking in views of Windsor and the endless air traffic at Heathrow. On the walls of the eastern look-out, panel 175 commemorates the name of 32-year-old Canadian Vernon William Byers, who lost his life on the night of May 16/17, 1943, piloting an Avro Lancaster of No. 617 Squadron RAF on the now famous Dambusters Raid, Operation Chastise.

2

ON THE ALTAR OF FREEDOM

STEVE DARLOW

VERNON BYERS was one of fifty-six men who did not return from the Dams Raid and one of fifty-three who lost their lives. Those who returned received the accolades they justly deserved, but what of those who had been killed or who became prisoners? Sir Arthur Harris made a recommendation of the wording that should appear in the records of personnel who took part in the raid and who failed to return. In accordance with this, Vernon's service records show: "On the night of 16/17.5.43 this airman (now officer) took part in the extremely hazardous and highly successful raid on the Möhne, Eder, Sorpe and Schwelm dams, from which he failed to return." A note from Harris in the official files also records: "I think it would be fitting if the Next-of-Kin Department would care to advise the next of kin of this notation." It went on:

> I would wish to point out, however, that the leader Wing Commander G. Gibson received the VC, and that most, if not all of those who returned from the raid on the Dams, received awards, and there is a possibility, therefore that next-of-kin might consider that such 'notation on the records of those who failed to return' is small measure when compared with the glory on those who did return, particularly as a number of those who did not return have paid the supreme sacrifice.

Born to Frank and Ruby Byers on September 24, 1919, in Star City, Saskatchewan, Vernon led a very active lifestyle as a young man. Sport was clearly a significant and important aspect of Vernon's life, and he took part in baseball, rugby, hockey, and swimming. When he left school, his work life was just as active. At the start of the war in Europe, Vernon was working on a farm in Pontrilas, Saskatchewan, and in October 1939, he took up duties in elevator construction with Harper Construction in Winnipeg. Then, early in 1940, Vernon began work as a miner with the Hudson Bay Mining and Smelting Company in the mining town of Flin Flon, Manitoba.

In March 1941, twenty-year-old Vernon William Byers put pen to an enrolment form for the Canadian Army and was taken on strength at No. 10 Clearing Depot, his papers recording "a healthy appearing young man, desirous of transferring for Active Service with the RCAF." Vernon took this desire to the next level on May 8, 1941, when he enlisted with the Royal Canadian Air Force in Winnipeg, indicating a preference for flying duties. His ultimate ambition was clear: Vernon wanted to be a pilot. He wanted to be at the controls. But first he had to negotiate the medical, and there were concerns over his eyesight. The examiner noted he had worn glasses when he was younger. He had a supernumerary nipple. His height was recorded as 5 feet, 8¼ inches, weight 156 pounds, complexion ruddy, with hazel eyes and dark brown hair. The medical report stated "Good development," and noted good hearing. His vision was noted as "right 20/30, left 20/40." The condition of his mouth and teeth were recorded as "satisfactory." In 1934, Vernon had fractured two ribs. The final remarks by the examining consultant recorded "Good type for pilot." The first hurdle was overcome. He was going to be in the Air Force "for the duration."

Initially Vernon was posted to No. 2 Manning Depot, Brandon, as AC2 (aircrew) pilot or observer. On May 24, 1941, he began training under the BCATP at No. 2 Bombing and Gunnery School, Mossbank, and on July 27, 1941, he arrived at No. 4 Initial Training School, Edmonton, his report recording: "Worked underground in Flin Flon Mines—sturdy—athletic type—keen to be pilot." From

September 25, Vernon's training continued at No. 5 Elementary Flying Training School, High River. He seemed to be adapting to the physical demands of training, his report recording he was a "very good, all around pilot," although his ground training remarks were not so glowing, specifying "below average, difficulty with signals," but going on to say he was a "sturdy type, slow to learn but reliable. Conduct excellent."

On November 23, 1941, Vernon arrived at No. 10 Service Flying Training School, Dauphin, Manitoba, where he steadily accumulated flying hours and experience. On January 12, 1942, however, a mistake led to a black mark on his record: "While piloting A/C #7885 at 1630 hrs., came in as if to land at No. 1 Relief Field with the wheels of the A/C in the retracted position, for which he received 14 days C.B."[15] But this was an isolated incident. On March 13, 1942, Vernon Byers received his wings, his final report concluding he was "a dependable average pilot in all phases of work" and "conscientious—[with] just average ability." Frank and Ruby Byers's son had partly fulfilled his ambition, but only partly. When considering his future service flying career, Vernon had indicated his desire to be a fighter pilot, but the recommendation on the final report was *bomber*. Vernon's role in the distant European war had been decided. He was going to become part of the escalating air offensive against Germany, one of nearly ten thousand Canadians who played this part and would not be returning.

Following a brief embarkation leave in March, Vernon crossed the Atlantic to the UK, arriving at No. 3 Personnel Reception Centre on May 13, 1942. Six weeks later, he was at No. 3 Pilots' Advanced Flying Unit, and on September 1, 1942, he arrived at No. 29 Operational Training Unit at RAF North Luffenham, to start the process of forming a crew. Then, on December 8, 1942, Vernon transferred to No. 1654 Conversion Unit, operating with Avro Manchesters and Lancasters at RAF Wigsley, to develop and familiarize himself with the workings and characteristics of flying these operational aircraft.

While carrying out the latter stages of his training, Vernon quite probably gained an indirect but first-hand appreciation of the escalation of the bomber offensive. The RAF Bomber Command attack on Cologne on the night of May 30/31, 1942, had proved a turning point in the strategic air offensive: it was the first thousand-bomber raid, with RAF bombers attacking, en masse, a specific target and overwhelming the German air and ground defences. Two further thousand-bomber raids were carried out in June. In each case, Bomber Command's commander-in-chief Sir Arthur Harris called upon the training units to bolster the numbers and maximize the attacks. Such a policy continued into the autumn of 1942. Vernon Byers would not have taken part in these operational sorties, but he witnessed colleagues at his respective training units join their main force colleagues in battle. On September 10, eleven aircraft from No. 29 OTU took part in a raid to Düsseldorf, and three nights later, eight aircraft would take off from North Luffenham for Bremen. On this night Pilot Officer John Leslie "Les" Munro RNZAF crashed his No. 29 OTU Wellington three minutes after takeoff owing to engine failure. There were no casualties, and Les would go on to take part in what would later become famous as the Dams Raid, Operation Chastise. On January 16/17, 1943, and January 17/18, 1943, No. 1654 Conversion Unit aircraft were detailed for raids to Berlin; two failed to return from the latter raid, with a total loss of life of fourteen airmen.

FOR THE final months of 1942 and into 1943, Bomber Command expanded its operational capacity in terms of both front-line strength and tactical innovation. Of note was the introduction of the Pathfinder Force—designated squadrons equipped with pyrotechnics to locate and mark targets for main force crews. In addition, many new squadrons were brought to operational readiness, including No. 467 (Australian) Squadron, within No. 5 Group, in November 1942, to which Vernon Byers was posted three months later.

By March 1943, Sir Arthur Harris felt his force was ready to embark upon a sustained attack against Germany, writing in his post-war memoir: "At long last we were ready and equipped." Harris would be focusing his force on the industrial spread of the

Ruhr, pitting his command's tactics and his crew's skill and bravery against the concentration and efficiency of the Ruhr ground defences and the enemy night fighter crews. As Bomber Command historians Martin Middlebrook and Chris Everitt commented, in respect of the forthcoming offensive: "The levels of death and destruction were about to mount dramatically." Operation Chastise, which Harris would describe as "one incident in the Battle of the Ruhr," would prove no exception.

ON THE night of March 9/10, 1943, Sergeant Byers carried out his first operational sortie in the Silverthorne area, *gardening*—code for mine-laying, a common approach to introducing new crews to operational flying in hostile skies. Landing at thirty-five minutes past midnight, following a seven-hour flight, the crew reported: "Mines laid on time and distance run from Arnholt at 2124 from 800 ft. Successful trip nothing to report."

Two nights later, the same crew (pilot, Sergeant Vernon Byers; navigator, Pilot Officer James Warner; bomb aimer, Sergeant Arthur Whitaker; flight engineer, Sergeant Alastair Taylor; wireless operator, Sergeant John Wilkinson; rear gunner, Sergeant James McDowell; mid-upper gunner, Sergeant Charles Jarvie) was sent to Stuttgart. Twenty miles from the target area, the rear turret lost power, McDowell being able to operate it only by hand. Byers was confronted with a stark choice—abort the sortie or carry on and risk, virtually defenceless, an enemy night fighter attack from the rear. The crew pressed on, dropping its bombs from 16,000 feet on two green Pathfinder target indicators. Landing at 02:39 hours, the crew reported: "Successful effort, one good fire seen going and fairly good concentration of fires." On March 22/23, the crew carried out what would prove to be its last operational sortie with No. 467 Squadron, to Saint-Nazaire, bombing from 12,000 feet in what they would record as a "very concentrated effort." A few days later, they became part of a new squadron, soon to be designated 617. The first crew nominated by 467 Squadron's CO declined to join the new venture, and Byers' crew was sent in their place, for unknown reasons.

A memo from Bomber Command Headquarters to the AOC No. 5 Group on March 17, 1943, recorded that the planned operations against the dams would not, "it is thought, prove particularly dangerous, but will undoubtedly require skilled crews. Volunteer crews will therefore have to be carefully selected from the Squadrons in your Group."

In such a context, it seems remarkable that, on March 24, 1943, Vernon Byers, who had to date carried out only two bombing operations from 12,000 and 16,000 feet and a mine-laying operation from a low-level 800 feet, was transferred to No. 617 Squadron. Most of Vernon's crew were similarly inexperienced, although Charles Jarvie and Arthur Whitaker had been with No. 467 Squadron since November 1942. At No. 617 Squadron, Byers and his novice colleagues would quickly have to reappraise their perceptions of what low-level operational flying could actually entail. As the month of March drew to a close, Sergeant Vernon Byers and his crew embarked upon a sustained period of intense training in order to attack a unique target with one of the most secret weapons developed in the war to date.

A further memo from Bomber Command Headquarters to No. 5 Group a month prior to the Dams Raid outlined future recruitment policy post-Operation Chastise, in which No. 617 Squadron's "duties will consist of performing operations that entail special training and/or the use of special equipment." It went on to note:

> The aircrew personnel for this Squadron should, as far as possible, be recruited from within the Group. [This was changed post-Chastise to all operational Groups.] As the work is not expected to be arduous, full use should be made of crews who have completed two operational tours and who apply to take part in further operations. It is not intended that crews at present in this Squadron should be moved, but the future policy should ensure that a high percentage of the aircrew personnel are time expired experienced crews that need a rest from normal operation, but one capable of performing in special tasks that may be allotted to this Squadron.

But such policy clearly had not been applied in the selection of the original No. 617 Squadron crews. Sergeant Byers was in the early stages of operational flying and certainly not experienced, and nowhere in his flying record is there a comment on any exceptional flying abilities. Nowhere is there evidence of the Byers crew being particularly skilled. Was this crew really appropriate for selection? It is very difficult not to question, in the light of the documentary evidence, the suitability of the Byers crew. However, as training continued it does appear that Byers was impressing CO Guy Gibson. On April 17, 1943, he was recommended for a commission, with Gibson recording, "a good type of NCO who is fully capable of holding down a commission. He keeps his crew in order, is punctual, and understands discipline. Recommended." A few days before the Dams Raid, Byers became a pilot officer.

BYERS'S LANCASTER (AJ-K) was the second Operation Chastise aircraft to take off, late on the evening of May 16, 1943, part of the five-aircraft first wave, which was detailed to fly a long northerly route to the Sorpe Dam. Barlow led the way, taking off at 21:28 hours, Byers at 21:30, Rice at 21:31, Munro at 21:39, and McCarthy at 22:01, delayed as a result of having to transfer to a reserve aircraft. The route to the target took the wave due east from Scampton and across the North Sea, toward the West Frisian Islands. Prior to reaching landfall at Vlieland, the wave was detailed to make a southeasterly turn, then pass the island of Texel to starboard and continue across the Ijsselmeer and on towards Rees and a dogleg to head east to the target area.

But McCarthy's crew would be the only ones to reach the target that night. Flak damage to Munro's aircraft resulted in a loss of communication and he aborted. Flying Officer Rice lost his Upkeep,[16] following contact with the sea, and he returned to Scampton. Barlow and Byers failed to return. Rice's crew reported seeing an aircraft shot down off Texel, and a post-raid summary recorded:

E [Barlow] or K [Byers] is thought to have been shot down from 300 feet off Texel by light flak at 22:57 hrs. If this aircraft was one of the second wave then; i) it was flying higher than detailed (possibly to obtain a pinpoint on the coast) or ii) it was either off track to the south of the leg from Base or had altered course from the D.R. position 5320—0454E too early so crossing the Texel area west of track.

It was well known, of course, that the West Frisians were a formidable defensive barrier, and timing and accuracy in penetrating these defences at low level were vital. Eventually it became clear that the aircraft shot down into the sea off Texel was indeed Byers's Lancaster. Could its loss be put down to a lack of operational experience? Or was it simply a case of tragic bad luck—an opportunistic lucky strike by a gunner who, it seems, had managed to lower, aim, and fire his weapon in what would have been a matter of seconds. Whatever the circumstances, a short while later Flight Lieutenant Barlow and his crew lost their lives when their aircraft struck an electricity pylon and crashed in flames.

VERNON BYERS had failed to return. As had happened thousands of times in the war, the awful news had to be conveyed to a next of kin, initially by telegram, followed by official and personal correspondence.

A letter to Frank Byers from Wing Commander Guy Gibson, commanding No. 617 Squadron, expressed deep regret and explained:

> Sergeant Byers encountered trouble on the way to the target and contact was lost with him, and nothing more was heard of the aircraft. If, as is possible, your son was able to abandon his aircraft and land safely in enemy territory, news would reach you direct from the International Red Cross Committee within the next six weeks. Please accept my sincere sympathy during this anxious period of waiting.

Although the Byers family received his meagre personal effects following his failure to return, they were given no closure in the short term. On January 11, 1944, Frank Byers finally received news from the RCAF casualties officer, that the International Red Cross had information concerning Sergeant McDowell—the Byers crew rear gunner—and that he had been killed and his body recovered on June 22, 1943. "I wish to point out that although the Air Ministry now proposes to presume your son's death, it is for official purposes only, and by such action the search being made for him will not be affected or diminished in any way."

The Royal Canadian Air Force's Certificate of Presumption of Death (No. 6853) was issued on January 31, 1944, recording:

> This is to Certify that J17474 Pilot Officer Vernon William Byers R.C.A.F. has been officially reported as missing since the 16th day of May 1943, and that, full inquiries having been made, no information has been received which would indicate that he may still [*sic*] alive. For official purposes therefore he is presumed to have died on or since the 17th Day of May, 1943.

Two and a half years after receiving his son's certificate of presumption of death, on August 15, 1946, Frank Byers received a package containing a letter.

> It is a privilege to have the opportunity of sending you the Operational Wings and Certificate in recognition of the gallant services rendered by your son Pilot Officer V.W. Byers. I realize there is little which may be said or done to lessen your sorrow but it is my hope that these 'Wings', indicative of operations against the enemy, will be a treasured memento of a young life offered on the altar of freedom in defence of his Home and Country.

A further two and half years passed before a final memorandum was added to Vernon's file, stating that the burial place of Flight Sergeant McDowell was recorded as Harlingen General Cemetery, along with the comment: "As the body of F/S McDowell was washed ashore off the Coast of Holland it is assumed that the aircraft was shot down over the sea. Classified. Lost at Sea. Case Closed."

ABOVE Air Forces Memorial, Runnymede, UK. Included among the names of the missing are P/O Vernon Byers, Sgt. Alastair Taylor, F/O James Warner, P/O Arthur Whitaker, Sgt. John Wilkinson, and Sgt. Charles Jarvie. STEVE DARLOW

OPPOSITE, TOP *Winnipeg Evening Tribune* coverage of Vernon Byers award of pilot's wings. WINNIPEG EVENING TRIBUNE VIA UNIVERSITY OF MANITOBA LIBRARY

OPPOSITE, MIDDLE, LEFT Vernon Byers, RCAF, during training. CVWM VIA OPERATION PICTURE ME

OPPOSITE, MIDDLE, RIGHT F/Sgt. James McDowell, RCAF, air gunner. CVWM VIA OPERATION PICTURE ME

OPPOSITE, BOTTOM Certificate of Presumption of Death for P/O Vernon Byers, dated January 31, 1944. NATIONAL ARCHIVES OF CANADA

Receive Pilot's Wings

Five Manitobans, four from Winnipeg, were among those receiving their pilot's wings from Wing Commander J. A. Kent, noted fighter pilot, in the graduation ceremony at No. 10 Service Flying Training school, Dauphin, on Thursday. They were, left to right: J. J. McGavock, J. L. Drysdale, W. S. Heaton, V. W. Byers (of Flin Flon) and A. R. McEwen.

R.C.A.F. G.64
H.Q. 885-G-64

Royal Canadian Air Force

COPIED
Archives
COPIE

CERTIFICATE OF PRESUMPTION OF DEATH   NO. 6953

This is to Certify that

J17474   PILOT OFFICER VERNON WILLIAM BYERS   R.C.A.F.
(Number)   (Rank)   (Name in Full)   (Unit)

has been officially reported as missing since the _____ 16TH _____ day

of _____ MAY _____ , 194 3 , and that, full inquiries having been

made, no information has been received which would indicate that he may be still alive.

For official purposes, therefore, he is presumed to have died on or since the above

mentioned date: 17TH DAY OF MAY, 1943.

Dated at Ottawa, Canada, this 31st day of JANUARY 194 4

(T.K. McDougall)
Group Captain,
R.C.A.F. Records Officer.

One hundred and thirty-three airmen were on the nineteen aircraft that participated in the extraordinary Dams Raid of May 16/17, 1943. Thirty of these were RCAF flyers, of whom only half would return. Fourteen Canadians would be killed; Vernon Byers was one. One other, John Fraser, would be one of three men who failed to return—but survived the raid. Two of these survivors were from the same crew: the crew of Lancaster M-Mother. They both lived, even though the odds stacked against their survival were overwhelming. And they both lived thanks to the outstanding bravery of their skipper, who performed an act of courage that might have earned higher reward.

3

MOTHER'S LOVE

SEAN FEAST

OF ALL THE personalities who took part in the Dams Raid, Tony Burcher is undoubtedly one of the most colourful and controversial. He was also one of the most complex.

Born on March 15, 1922, in Vaucluse, an eastern suburb of Sydney, New South Wales, Australia, Tony was the fifth of no fewer than twelve children of Harvey and Estelle, described in the quaint language of the time as being Australians of pure European descent. A steady if unspectacular school career was punctuated by greater success on the sports field and on water, as Tony captained the local rugby league team and won various local swimming and sailing championships.

Since his father had been a grazier, it was perhaps not surprising that Tony followed him into the world of sheep and cattle and earned a place as a student at Wagga Experimental Farm, where he was studying when war was declared. Farm certificate in hand, Tony took a variety of jobs as a grazier and wool sorter. By February 1940, with the age of majority in sight, he volunteered to join the Royal Australian Air Force (RAAF). Indeed, Tony was so impatient to train as aircrew that he wrote to the authorities the following month to ask if his application had been lost!

It was not until July that Tony was finally enrolled in the reserve at the No. 2 Recruiting Centre at Woolloomooloo. Passing the

necessary test to serve as aircrew and having satisfied the authorities that he had no police record and was not a member of the
Communist Party, he was placed on a list to await his turn in the
BCATP training system. Although he was physically fit, the eighteen-
year-old's personality was described as "not very impressive." While
his first choice for service was as a pilot—like almost every youngster
at that time—the interview board recommended he train as a wireless telegraphist/air gunner (abbreviated on the official paperwork
to W/T AG).

Tony formally enlisted on December 11, 1940, "for the duration of the war and a period of 12 months thereafter." After initial
training at Bradfield Park, he embarked for No. 3 Wireless School
in Winnipeg to train as a wireless operator (W/Op). Four months
later, after crossing the Pacific and spending the depths of winter in
Winnipeg, he moved to No. 1 Bombing and Air Gunnery School in
Jarvis, Ontario, to complete an air gunnery course. It was in October
1941 that he finally arrived in the UK for a wireless refresher course
at No. 2 Signals School, Yatesbury, before moving to No. 14 Operational Training Unit (OTU) in Cottersmore. He was five months at
OTU before eventually receiving his first operational posting: 106
Squadron, RAF Coningsby.

WHILE TONY Burcher was arriving in England to start the second half
of his training, Canadian John Fraser was on his way to Edmonton
to start his observers' course at No. 2 Air Observers' School (2AOS).

John was seven months younger than Tony, born on September 22, 1922, in Nanaimo, British Columbia. His father, William,
had served in the trenches as an officer in the Canadian Army and
was considerably older than his mother. It was not a surprise, therefore, that William died before John had reached his teenage years,
leaving the young boy as the man of the house with his mother and
four sisters. He took odd jobs around the neighbourhood to make
ends meet. Passionate about sports and the outdoor life, he also
excelled in the classroom, particularly in math, with his headmaster
describing him as "the cleverest boy he'd ever taught."

A desire to go to university was thwarted by lack of money rather than ability, and instead John found a job at a sawmill in Port Alberni. As the war increased in intensity, he enlisted on May 20, 1941, having been suitably attested and recommended for pilot training. From No. 2 Manning Depot (2MD) in Brandon, he moved straight to No. 4 Service Flying Training School (4SFTS) in Saskatoon for basic pilot training but was soon after remustered as an observer. Exactly what happened is not clear, for it appears John got partway through his pilot training (he had at least fifteen hours to his name) before a medical examination suggested his eyesight was not quite up to the mark. Although he had 20/20 vision, the muscular action of the two eyes lacked coordination. Notwithstanding the excitement and occasional dangers of flying, it was a setback to pursuing a discipline that he was clearly enjoying. His letters home reflected his keen disappointment. One, dated June 30, 1941, is typical of many:

> I have been up for six and a half hours now—nothing to it—just like riding in an empty truck—lots of fun when they do loops and rolls—stomach feels as if it is in the bottom of the seat—pilots are not supposed to do aerobatics in these planes but they do them.
>
> Saturday night when we came back from Varsery (an auxiliary field) we hedgehopped all the way back—about 150 ft. from the ground—scared all the cows and horses on the farms. Friday, another fellow, Hubbert and I went down to Osler (another auxiliary field) to guard a crash there—one engine was laying about 40 ft. from the plane—landing gear was smashed—the tail wheel was off and half of one wing—the plane was considered a total wreck, but nobody was hurt. There were three other crashes that day—nobody hurt though.

Switching to his new career, John was posted to No. 4 Initial Training School (4ITS) in Edmonton for ten weeks of intensive study in math, map reading, and Air Force law as well as a host of other related subjects. He obtained ninety-eight percent in his mathematics exam and finished ninth overall out of a class of 146. Described as "NCO material" by his commanding officer, LAC Fraser passed on to No. 2 Air Observer School (2AOS), where he spent three months and finished sixth out of twenty. He was not yet deemed suitable for a commission, the chief instructor describing him as "moody."

A further two months were passed at No. 8 Bombing and Gunnery School (8B&GS) in Lethbridge, learning the range of skills then expected to earn him his observer brevet (the role was later separated into dedicated *navigator* and *air bomber* categories).

His navigation skills, specifically, were honed still further at No. 1 Air Navigation School (1ANS) at RCAF Station Rivers, Manitoba, where he learned the art of celestial navigation, using the stars and moon for guidance. Although he was assessed as average, John nonetheless finished fifth in his class of twenty. Proudly sporting the "Flying Arsehole" single wing observer's brevet on his tunic, he finally embarked from Halifax for the long and potentially treacherous voyage across the Atlantic to the UK. He arrived in April 1942, about the same time that Tony Burcher was reporting for duty at RAF Coningsby.

NO. 106 SQUADRON, to which Tony arrived in the late spring of 1942, was rapidly gaining a reputation as one of the crack units in No. 5 Group and the whole of Bomber Command. This was perhaps not surprising, given that the squadron had recently received a new officer commanding—Wing Commander Guy Gibson. Its flight commanders were no less impressive: Squadron Leader John "Dim" Wooldridge, DFC, DFM, was a former sergeant pilot of considerable experience who would go on to add a bar to his earlier DFC and command 105 Squadron; and Squadron Leader Francis Robertson, DFC, a southern Rhodesian, was also an experienced operator and one of Gibson's inner circle.

Their OC (officer commanding), meanwhile, polarized opinions: to some, he was little short of a god; to others, a fanatic who would drive both men and machines beyond their physical endurance. Not for nothing was he quickly nicknamed "the boy emperor" by the ground crews—an accolade not meant as a compliment.

The squadron had only recently exchanged its outdated Handley Page Hampdens for the rather disappointing twin-engined Avro Manchester. This brief flirtation did not last long, however, and soon after the crews began converting to the Manchester's rather more illustrious successor, the Avro Lancaster. They never looked back.

Tony was allowed some time to settle in before being listed on the battle order for his first operation, which turned out to be an historic one. The squadron put up some fifteen Lancaster and Manchester aircraft to take part in an attack on Essen on the night of June 1/2, 1942—one of the first of the Bomber Command Commander-in-Chief's showpiece thousand-bomber raids. The Captain of Tony's Lancaster was an experienced senior NCO, Warrant Officer Peter Merralls, DFM (later DFC, DFM). Merralls had won the Distinguished Flying Medal for a tour of operations with 49 Squadron, and would later become somewhat of a celebrity, appearing in *Life* magazine in an article headlined "Captain Pete bombs Cologne."

On the night of June 25/26, Tony was again selected for operations and another thousand-bomber trip. This time he was going to Bremen with a novice pilot, someone with whom he would go on to complete his first tour and who would himself become a distinguished Pathfinder: Sergeant James Cassels. "Jock" Cassels had arrived at 106 Squadron about the same time as Tony and flown a handful of second-dickey trips (trips in which a rookie pilot observed more experienced crews) in May. He was now considered ready to captain his own aircraft. The author of the squadron's *Operations Record Book* was in no doubt as to the success of that night's operation: "For the Squadron, the raid cannot be classed as anything but outstanding."

Towards the end of July, Tony was the mid-upper gunner in Jock's aircraft when they were chased by a night fighter over Duisburg but managed to escape. Less than a week later, and they were again intercepted, this time with rather more conclusive results. The combat report tells its own dramatic story:

On the night of 29/30th July a Lancaster 'M' was attacked at 0052 while flying at 10,000 feet by a single-engined aircraft, at position 5140 N 0230 E. The enemy aircraft came in from the starboard quarter at the same height firing cannon from 500 yards. The Lancaster took evasive action losing height to 5,000 feet. The enemy aircraft was lost and our own aircraft did not return fire.

At 0117 hours at 10,000 feet 15 miles SE of Lille, Lancaster 'M' was attacked by an unidentified aircraft. The enemy aircraft came in from starboard beam, tracer passed ahead of the aircraft, rear gunner and mid-upper gunner returned the fire. The enemy aircraft was then seen to pass from starboard to port a few feet below the Lancaster; the enemy aircraft was then lost.

Five minutes after leaving the target approximately 20 miles west of Saarbrücken at 0220 hours at 5,500 feet a single-engined enemy aircraft was sighted by the rear gunner of the Lancaster dead astern at approximately 400 yards. It passed from astern to port quarter and opened fire with cannon at about 200 yards. The rear gunner returned the fire and the fighter passed then from port to starboard; as he did so tracer was seen to enter the enemy aircraft's fuselage. The enemy aircraft then passed to the starboard beam to make another attack. The mid-upper gunner gave instructions to the pilot to turn to starboard into the attack; as the pilot did so the enemy aircraft closed in on the starboard beam to 150 yards and the mid-upper gunner opened fire and tracer was seen to enter the engine and fuselage.

The enemy aircraft then broke [sic] into flames and dived to the ground. It was seen to crash by the observer, mid-upper and rear gunners. The pilot also saw it burning on the ground.

The enemy aircraft was claimed as definitely destroyed. At 0225 hours near Soulay while flying at 7,500 feet the Lancaster was shadowed for ten minutes by two unidentified aircraft. One on the starboard beam that did not open fire and one astern that opened fire from 600 yards. The pilot then took evasive action and both aircraft were lost.

The crew returned safely.

FURTHER OPERATIONS followed, including trips to Mainz (August 12), Düsseldorf (August 15), and Kassel (August 27), when they were forced north off track by strong defences. Four trips in September were interrupted by the squadron's move from Coningsby to Syerston, followed by an operation on October 1 that proved very nearly their last. Ordered to attack Wismar, their aircraft was coned by searchlights and immediately hit by flak. Jock pushed the aircraft's nose down to escape, losing more than 10,000 feet before finally pulling out at 2,500 feet and jettisoning his bombs.

Perhaps the highlight of Tony's tour at 106 Squadron was a showpiece daylight attack that had the officer commanding, Guy Gibson, leading the squadron. Nearly one hundred bombers flew to the target—the Schneider factory at Le Creusot—in formation at treetop level, only breaking formation for their bombing run. A contemporary of Tony's, Pilot Officer R.A. Wellington, described the operation as "both successful and enjoyable." The Cassel crew reported seeing direct hits on the factory.

By the end of November, Tony's first operational tour was coming to an end, and his abilities as an air gunner were recognized in three different ways: the award of the Distinguished Flying Medal; a posting to Central Gunnery School (CGS) to complete a gunnery leader's course; and a commission. His joy, however, was tempered by some terrible news from home, reporting the death of his brother Stephen while fighting the Japanese in Papua New Guinea.

Like all aircrew having completed his tour, Tony was entitled to six months' rest. With the dangers facing his own native land, however, and the poignancy of his brother's death, there was a suggestion that he might be able to return home. A considerably higher authority decided this was not to be, and Tony found himself posted to 1654 Conversion Unit (CU) at Wigsley as an instructor. But his posting did not last. Within two months he was on his way to Scampton and a very special squadron.

AS TONY Burcher was coming to the end of his first operational tour, twenty-five miles further north at Skellingthorpe, home to No. 50

Squadron, John Fraser was just starting out on his. As part of No. 5 Group, No. 50 Squadron had also recently replaced its Manchesters with Lancasters and was also gaining a proud reputation for "pressing on." The example was being set by its officer commanding, Wing Commander William Russell, DFC (later Bar), a Canadian who had won his first DFC with the same squadron two years earlier. (Russell would later be killed in action with No. 138 Squadron in May 1944.) He exemplified the spirit of the squadron motto: "Thus we keep faith."

John reported to the squadron from No. 9 Conversion Flight (Waddington) on November 9, 1942. Unlike Tony, however, John arrived as part of a whole crew that had earlier met and trained at No. 25 OTU (RAF Finningley) under the command of a fellow Canadian, Sergeant Norman Schofield. John was the air bomber.

Schofield, affectionately known as "Pop" on account of his age (he was then twenty-eight), was almost immediately on the battle order, flying a second-dickey trip to Genoa, unsuccessfully as it turned out, on the night of November 13/14. Ten days later, John found himself on the battle order as part of the crew of Flying Officer E.N. Goldsmith. He wrote of the experience to his family on November 23, 1942:

> Last night I did go on 'ops'—not with my own crew, but as a fill-in bomb aimer on another crew. Last night was a good success as far as our crew was concerned—we got the aiming point in the centre of the photograph of where the bombs burst. Quite lucky I am that on my first trip on the squadron I got such good results. I'm not shooting a line either—just plain honest to God facts.

John's regular crew flew its first operation together on December 6/7, a comparatively easy gardening (mine-laying) trip, followed by two operations to Turin. John wrote (somewhat poetically) of the experience a little later:

For the last two nights I've been to Italy—as you most probably saw in the papers—we gave them hell both nights—I would not care to live in Turin now or what there is left of it. The Alps are beautiful at night—covered with snow—when I went to Italy 10-days ago the moon was just past full moon, but it did light up the mountains wonderfully.

In a short space of time, John was beginning to make his mark on the squadron, earning the nickname "Fearless Fraser." He was also fitting into squadron life, comforted by the occasional food parcel to remind him of home. On December 10, he wrote:

Thanks for the parcel. I was getting short of shirts and it arrived just in time for our next leave in approximately two weeks' time. You know where the nuts, cookies, cheese, peanut butter, gum, [and] chocolate bars went—right into my stomach—the parcel travelled well and everything was swell. I had about ½ tin of Nescafe left from a former parcel—sure makes a warm drink in the evening before crawling into bed. We'll make some soup one of these nights too and the pineapple juice—I haven't tasted anything like it for so long I could hardly believe it.

While John and the crew enjoyed a comparatively "soft" introduction to operations, there was nothing easy about the target to be attacked on the night of January 16/17—Berlin. A dangerous trip at any stage of the war, it nearly proved the crew's undoing. Heading home, some sixty-five miles to the northwest of the city, their Lancaster—which had already been damaged by flak—suddenly came under attack from a Junkers Ju 88 night fighter. Cannon and machine-gun fire smashed home, shattering the rear turret and severely injuring the rear gunner, Sergeant "Johnnie" Bell. Only when the Junkers came in to attack the second time did the mid-upper gunner (Sergeant Baker) manage to fire off a long burst at very short range, seeing his tracer enter the belly of the machine, which broke off trailing smoke from its port engine. Schofield, meanwhile, had put the Lancaster into a steep dive, losing more than 8,000 feet before levelling out and heading for home. The drama was far from over and is brought into sharp relief by another of John's letters home:

> We really bombed Berlin as they did London... 'Pop' deserves a medal for bringing us back. Our rear gunner is in hospital with a cannon shell through his right arm and another through his ankle. The kite was a mess of holes: a flak hole in the bomb doors that you could put your head and shoulders through, controls to the elevator shot away. Pop and I held the nose of the plane down with a haywire scheme with the trailing aerial wire for 600 miles, while the flight engineer joined the wires to the controls in the back. The navigator did a bang-up job, while the wireless operator gave Johnnie hot coffee and oxygen. The compressed air tanks were punctured and Pop could not blow down the landing carriage but he jarred one wheel down and bounced the plane... we had no brakes, so we taxied along on an angle until we buried ourselves in a mud-hole. The trip looks better in my log book than it did then.

A week later, the crew very nearly came to grief again. This time they were on their way back from Düsseldorf and ten miles south of Utrecht when Sergeant F.C. Basham, in the mid-upper turret, spotted an aircraft some eight hundred yards away on a reciprocal course. Three minutes later, the replacement rear gunner (Sergeant Brian Jagger) identified a Messerschmitt Bf 110 coming in from the port quarter down and called for the pilot to turn to port and dive, presenting him with a decent shot. Both gunners opened up just as the night fighter also started shooting. The rear turret was again hit and an electric circuit damaged, causing an inspection lamp to flick on unexpectedly, temporarily robbing the gunner of his night vision. The mid-upper gunner was also hit and wounded in the right arm. Despite this, as the Messerschmitt passed again to the rear, the gunners filled its belly with tracer, seeing it roll over, seemingly out of control, and confident enough to claim it as probably destroyed.

The regular navigator, Canadian Pilot Officer Ken "George" Earnshaw, wrote about this raid soon after, and how close they came to disaster:

> We just saw him in time, but even at that he got in quite a burst at us. Our mid upper gunner was hit and our plane was riddled with bullet holes. We managed, however, to get home okay and the wounded gunner is doing fine too. It could have been a lot worse. Well, I guess as long as one is around to tell of these things they really aren't that bad, are they? Ha! Ha!

After the excitement of the previous fortnight, the crew settled into a routine of operations, at some considerable pace, flying no fewer than eight in February and nine in March, including three further trips to Berlin—happily without incident. Two attacks on Duisburg on consecutive nights at the beginning of April brought John's tour to a conclusion. By this time, he had chalked up thirty-one operations (including the first one while still at OTU) and with a further two operations noted in his logbook as DNCO—duty not carried out.

John now had a choice: he was entitled to six months' rest—perhaps at an OTU imparting his experience to others—or he could request to continue operations. Should he complete a further twenty trips (the criteria for a second tour), he could return home and be out of the war for good. There was also another influence: while at Finningly, he had met Doris Wilkinson, a young secretary. As the months had gone by their affection had turned to love, and they were shortly to be married.

It proved to be a busy and eventful month: an interview for a commission; a wedding with his sweetheart; and a posting to a new squadron to begin his second tour.

IN THE weeks prior to John's arrival at Scampton, 617 Squadron had been fully occupied with hour upon hour of cross-country and low-level training flights, both during the day and at night. Wing

Commander Gibson, the man handpicked to lead this special unit, had chosen his pilots with great care, and both Tony Burcher and John Fraser found themselves in the crew of Flight Lieutenant John Hopgood.

Hopgood was an Englishman raised in the village of Shere on the outskirts of Guildford, Surrey. Gentle yet determined, he had accumulated a commendable operational record with both 50 and 106 Squadrons—certainly enough to earn him two awards for gallantry. Gibson himself described Hopgood as "probably the best pilot on the squadron."

On April 23, John wrote to Doris, briefly outlining the men in his new crew:

> There is one Australian P/O DFM in the crew called Tony, one Scot P/O DFM called Jack, a sergeant wireless op called Minchie, a navigator P/O called Ossie, engineer sergeant called Charlie (a Canadian who came over here seven years ago and settled in Leeds, an attempt to colonize this country), the pilot called 'Hoppy' (F/L DFC and Bar), and me. I feel a bit strange after flying with Pop, but everything should work out OK.

The original navigator reported sick at the beginning of May and was shortly after replaced by George Earnshaw, no doubt much to John's delight. The bomb aimer and navigator often worked closely together, and that was much easier when a bond of trust and friendship had already been established. They also fit in well with their new crew, the skipper describing them as "grand chaps."

The intensity of training increased, John getting to grips with the Dann bombsight, a somewhat jury-rigged affair that had been knocked together in the station workshops and that would enable the bomb aimer to drop his secret weapon at the correct distance from the target. At last, the day of the operation arrived, and the targets were revealed. The reason behind the need for extremely accurate low-level flying over water at night had now become clear.

THE CREWS were divided into three groups. Hopgood was selected to fly with Gibson and seven other crews in the first group, whose target was the Möhne and Eder Dams. Takeoff was an impressive affair, the first three aircraft of the group (Gibson, Hopgood, and "Mickey" Martin) thundering down the runway in vic (V-shaped) formation and lifting off together at 21:39 hours.

In Hopgood's aircraft, M-Mother, the crew busied themselves with their duties. Aircrew would often speak of sometimes being too busy to be scared, and perhaps this was one of those occasions. The enemy coast came and went quickly by with the formation finding itself a little off track, having underestimated the winds. The Lancasters eased themselves lower to the ground but were soon picked up by searchlights and on the receiving end of some light flak. Hopgood took evasive action, taking the aircraft so low that he actually flew underneath some high-tension cables, frightening himself and his crew.

It began to go wrong over Dulmen; flak, which they had so far seen but avoided, this time caught up with them and inflicted serious damage. Tony smelled the unmistakable aroma of cordite in the aircraft and noted that the port outer engine had been hit and was on fire. He had also been hit himself, sustaining slight injuries to his stomach and groin. Others had not been so lucky: John Minchin, the wireless operator, had been more seriously hurt and could not move his legs; the skipper was hit and bleeding from a head wound; and there was no response to his captain's calls from George Gregory in the front turret.

With one of his crew possibly dead, one seriously wounded, and one other with minor injuries, Hopgood would have had every justification in abandoning their mission. But he did not. In the best traditions of the RAF and the desire to "press on regardless," Hopgood remained steadfast to his task.

M-Mother arrived at the Möhne, and the three aircraft in the first flight—Gibson, Hopgood, and Martin—began orbiting the target. There were no balloons or searchlights to contend with, but every crew was mindful of the flak guns positioned on the dam and in the immediate vicinity. Gibson flew a dummy run before committing to the attack, reminding Hopgood to be ready to assume command should something happen. Then he went in and had the great satisfaction of seeing his bomb skip across the water toward the dam, followed by a terrific explosion and a great spurt of water leaping into the air. But the dam held. Hopgood had an anxious wait before his attack. The water needed to settle and the spray to clear. M-Mother held off for a further five minutes before Gibson finally gave his deputy the order to attack, reassuring Hopgood that it was "a piece of cake." It was to prove anything but.

Gibson had the advantage of catching the German flak batteries off guard. By the time Hopgood came in to attack, however, they were more than ready for him, and an almost predictable tragedy unfolded. Tony and John were at exact opposite ends of their aircraft. Tony was at the rear and could see nothing, save for the vicious streaks of tracer passing close by his turret; he prepared to shoot at the flak gunners once they were over the dam. John, on the other hand, had arguably the best seat in the house, but as he held the bombsight in front of him, and waited for the release point, the aircraft was hit and almost immediately burst into flames. The bomb was seen to release but a fraction too late, and instead of hitting the dam it skipped over the wall and exploded in a power station a little way beyond.

A red Very flare (named after its inventor Edward Very) was fired from the aircraft, in accordance with instructions, to indicate that the bomb had been dropped, but by now one wing was almost enveloped in flames, and the aircraft appeared all but doomed. Hopgood desperately tried to gain height to give his crew a chance to bail out, and with only two engines still functioning managed to struggle up to around five hundred feet before the aircraft exploded and plunged burning to the ground.

In the thirty or so seconds from the time that the aircraft cleared the dam to the moment it exploded, the activity within the aircraft had been frantic. Both pilot and flight engineer had tried desperately and against overwhelming odds to extinguish the flames, before Hopgood gave in to the inevitable and shouted for the crew to bail out.

John, in the nose, needed no second bidding and opened the escape hatch to see the tops of the trees uncomfortably close. Ignoring what he had been taught, he clipped on his parachute and pulled his ripcord inside the cockpit, letting the parachute billow out in front of him and pull him out after it.

At the rear, Tony was faced with a similar dilemma. With the loss of hydraulics, and therefore power, he had been obliged to crank his turret round by hand in double quick time to get back into the fuselage and retrieve his parachute. With his usual escape route blocked, he too was obliged to ignore the manual and jump from the rear door. But as he was planning to leave the aircraft, he was suddenly halted by the sight of the badly injured John Minchin edging his way down the fuselage towards him. Tony took the only decision he could, and pushed Minchin out of the aircraft, pulling his D-ring as he went and hoping for the best. He then prepared to jump himself, also pulling his ripcord inside of the aircraft and gathering the silk in his arms at the very moment that the aircraft exploded. Tony was blasted out through the entrance and suddenly and painfully understood why using the crew entrance door was discouraged as his back struck the Lancaster's tail fin.

As he tumbled out of the front hatch, John distinctly remembered seeing the tail wheel whizzing past his ear and then within less than two or three seconds hitting the ground. What happened next is difficult to determine with a hundred percent certainty, and stories have undoubtedly become confused over time. According to official records, including his German prisoner of war *Personalkarte*, John was captured on the same day that he was shot down. In the section marked *Gefangennahme* [taken prisoner] its reads, "Soest. 17.5.43." This appears to be confirmed in another record held by the Canadian archive reporting: INFORMATION RECEIVED FROM GENEVA 24 JUNE STATES BERLIN CABLES FOLLOWING CAPTURED R73769 SERGEANT ALLAN K T 17/4 R106546 FLIGHT SERGEANT FRASER J W 17/5. There is also no mention of John evading capture in his "Questionnaire for returned evaders, escapers and prisoner of war."

Documents, therefore, point to John being captured on May 17. John's family, however, have a different and very definite memory of what happened. According to them, John managed to make his escape from the immediate area and evaded for ten days, living off the land, before finally being captured, exhausted, near the Dutch border. Whether captured immediately or some time after, John finished his war in a POW camp, first in Stalag Luft VI and later (once his commission had been confirmed) at the officers' camp at Stalag Luft III, the scene of the Great Escape.

What happened to Tony is equally obscure. The injuries to his back sustained upon hitting the tail fin left him in no position to make good his escape. Landing in a recently ploughed field undoubtedly helped cushion his landing, but his back was seriously damaged and possibly even broken. He also had a broken kneecap. Despite being in considerable pain, Tony managed to crawl towards a culvert, where he hid for almost three days before finally surrendering to a young Hitler Youth. His memory of those days, and what happened immediately afterwards, were confused by delirium brought on by his injuries and lack of food and water, save for a few Horlicks tablets his mother had sent him and that he had had the foresight to take with him that night. In letters and interviews many years after the war, Tony claims to have been interrogated by a German with an Australian accent, and doggedly revealed only his name rank and number. He credits the treatment given to him by the German doctor who tended to his injuries as being the reason he was still able to walk. That may or may not have been true, but what we do know for certain, and the records confirm it, is that Tony ended his war as a prisoner in Stalag Luft III.

John and Tony met again in the camp, but perhaps surprisingly never reunited after the war. John took his young wife with him back to Canada, where they had two sons and a daughter: the boys were named John and Guy, and the daughter, Shere, after the village in which "Hoppy" Hopgood had lived. It was their tribute to the man that John said saved his life. John Sr. achieved his ambition to fly, and became president of the Nanaimo Flying Club. Sadly, he did not long survive the war: in June 1962, while on an aerial survey flight of log booms near Saltery Bay, his aircraft crashed and he was killed.

Tony's fortunes were rather more mixed. Although he determined to remain in the air force after the war, he never settled. He married Joan, an English WAAF he had met at Coningsby, in June 1945, and returned to Australia, but she struggled with being so far from home and her family. In early 1950, he applied for and was granted a posting to serve in the UK, but a succession of commanding officers expressed dismay at his attitude and behaviour, the more generous describing him as "unsatisfactory." It is interesting to note that in many of his records his peers cite his exceptional war record in mitigation, but such sympathy could not last. His honesty and sense of propriety were called into question more than once, and tales of financial irregularities were never far away. It was perhaps a relief when he resigned his commission and left the Service in February 1952.

Sadly, Tony's peers appear to have been good judges of character, for some years later, in 1963, the former Dam Buster was jailed for two years for fraud. Even after this incident and his release, his name was frequently attached to a succession of dubious business ventures. Tony had always lived life on the edge but was inclined too often to step beyond it. He died in Tasmania in 1995, his reputation sadly tarnished by his post-war peccadilloes.

It is difficult for us to imagine what it must have been like for these men, serving their countries so far from home. It is difficult also to imagine the extremes of excitement and terror that must have accompanied them throughout their respective operational tours. Given their magnificent war record, it seems a pity that both men were cheated out of the happy ending they so richly deserved. What will always be remembered, however, is their bravery and the bravery of their skipper, "Hoppy" Hopgood.

To Mrs. John William Fraser

I have learned with deep regret
Flight Sergeant Air Observer
that John William Fraser, D.C.A.F.
has been reported missing.

The Government and people of Canada join
me in expressing the hope, that more favourable news
will be forthcoming in the near future.

Charles G. Power
Minister of National Defence for Air

FLT LT HOPGOOD'S AIRCRAFT WAS HIT BY FLAK ON THE WAY TO THE
TARGET, INJURING FOUR CREW INCLUDING HOPGOOD. DESPITE
THIS, THEY CONTINUED AND WERE SECOND TO ATTACK THE
MÖHNE DAM. UNFORTUNATELY, THE ALERTED FLAK DEFENCES
SCORED MANY HITS ON THE ALREADY DAMAGED LANCASTER.
AJ-M WAS SEEN TO STREAM FLAMES FROM THE PORT WING AS
IT RELEASED THE WEAPON FRACTIONALLY LATE. THE MINE
BOUNCED OVER THE DAM AND HIT THE POWER STATION BELOW.
HOPGOOD DESPERATELY TRIED TO GAIN HEIGHT TO ALLOW HIS
CREW TO BALE OUT, BUT ONLY THREE, FRASER, BURCHER AND
MINCHIN, GOT OUT. THE REST OF THE CREW DIED AS THE
AIRCRAFT CRASHED AT THIS LOCATION. MINCHIN WAS BADLY
WOUNDED AND DIED SHORTLY AFTERWARDS.

OPPOSITE, TOP, LEFT Tony Burcher wearing the ribbon of the DFM under his air gunner's brevet. SHERE LOWE

OPPOSITE, TOP, RIGHT John (front row, far left) with his first skipper, "Pop" Schofield (front row, fourth from left), and crew. SHERE LOWE

OPPOSITE, BOTTOM John Fraser proudly displaying the single wing brevet of the "Flying Arsehole." SHERE LOWE

ABOVE, LEFT Official letter of condolence to the Fraser family. SHERE LOWE

ABOVE, RIGHT Plaque marking F/L Hopgood's crash site. STEVE DARLOW

Accurate navigation was a vital element of the Dams Raid, Operation Chastise. Flying that night in ED937, AJ-Z, with the "B" Flight commander, Squadron Leader Henry Maudslay, was the flight's navigation officer, Flying Officer Robert Urquhart. Urquhart hailed from Moose Jaw, Saskatchewan, where, by coincidence, his pilot had completed his advanced flying training. Almost one-third of the navigators involved that night were members of the Royal Canadian Air Force, no mean achievement when navigation over the intense landscape of Western Europe was a far cry from the wide open prairie of their native land.

4

"I THINK SO, STAND BY"

ROBERT OWEN

BORN ON AUGUST 2, 1919, Urquhart was the eldest of two sons of Canadian Pacific Railway accountant Alexander James Urquhart and his wife Susie Grace. Two daughters rounded out the family. After attending the King George Public School, Robert transferred to the Moose Jaw Collegiate Institute at the age of fourteen for a year before completing a four-year drafting course at Moose Jaw Technical High School. He was a diligent student and participated in a range of sports including baseball, rugby, hockey, and track events.

In 1937, his father secured him his first job as a crew call boy for Canadian Pacific Railway. Within six months, he had found himself a more creative outlet in an engraving apprenticeship with Eiler's Jewellery Store, Moose Jaw. Despite showing promise, in 1939 he switched jobs again, moving to Vancouver as a buyer and stock controller for the Aristocratic Hamburger Company.

With the outbreak of war, like many Canadians of eligible age, Robert was drawn to military service. In October 1940, while waiting for a decision on his written application to the RCAF, he completed a month's training as a private and acting lance corporal in the 2nd Battalion Seaforth Highlanders of Canada. His RCAF application was finally accepted, and on January 8, 1941, at the

Vancouver Recruiting Centre, he passed his medical exam as fit for training as a pilot or observer and applied for a commission. The following day, he reported as an AC2 to No. 2 Manning Depot, Brandon. On April 11, he was posted as a member of 23 Course at No. 2 Initial Training School, housed in Regina College and Regina Normal School, Regina, Saskatchewan, for evaluation as a member of aircrew. He came 55 out of 232, rated as above average, steady, alert, and with quick reactions. Promoted to LAC and having acquired the sobriquet "Turk"—earned who knows how—on May 28, 1941, he arrived for pilot training on No. 29 Course at No. 2 Elementary Flying Training School, formerly Thunder Bay Air Training School, in Fort William, Ontario.

Robert made his first flight, lasting forty-five minutes, on June 1, but any initial euphoria, and the allocation of flying pay, was short lived. It soon became clear that he lacked the coordination required by a competent pilot. By the time he had completed just over ten hours of flying, his instructor decreed that he should be scrubbed as a pilot. While his groundwork was "average" and behaviour "satisfactory," his ability to control the Tiger Moth was lacking. On takeoff he would move the stick to one side and then hard back, instigating a swing and making no attempt to correct. His flying was extremely poor and inaccurate, completely lacking air sense or any idea of manœuvre. Landing, he ignored a conventional approach, simply flying to within a few feet of the ground before pulling the stick hard back, stalling the aircraft onto the ground. "He shows no promise of getting the hang of flying." There was no question of sending him solo.

Robert was dispatched to Trenton on June 15, 1941, "for disposal." Here, the composite school was responsible for assessing and reallocating scrubbed RCAF, RAF, RAAF, and RNZAF pilots under training in Canada. A fortnight later he was recategorized as an air observer, reporting to No. 6 Air Observers' School at Prince Albert, Saskatchewan, on August 2. He was to spend two months on No. 30 Course, learning the craft of navigation in the unit's drafty

Ansons. It turned out that he had finally found his niche, being assessed as "above average in nearly all subjects. A very good man, responsible and cool headed . . . suitable as an instructor."

His training continued at No. 5 Bombing and Gunnery School at Dafoe, where he practised the duties of both bomb aimer and gunner, flying Fairey Battles (single-engine bombers deemed obsolete by the Second World War), and surviving a forced landing because of an oil leak. Scoring "above average" for the former and "average" as the latter—"he should make a good air observer"—Robert was awarded his air observer's brevet on December 6 and promoted to temporary sergeant. Two days later saw the start of the final stage of his training, celestial navigation, on No. 30 Course at No. 1 Air Navigation School, Rivers, Manitoba. However, although he had a better grasp of astronomical navigation than his results would suggest, he was inclined to make careless errors at times. His anticipated instructor's posting would not be forthcoming.

Robert received his commission on January 4, 1942, along with a train ticket to Y Depot at Halifax, prior to posting overseas. After a period of holding and ten days' embarkation leave, he returned to the depot to board the troop ship that would bring him to the UK. A month after arriving on March 24 at No. 3 Personnel Reception Centre at Bournemouth, he was posted to No. 2 (Observer) Advanced Flying Unit in Millom, Cumbria. Reacquainted with the familiar Anson, he would now be required to orient himself to the different scale and visual appearance of the European landscape and the variable weather and to learn the difficulties of navigation over a blacked-out countryside.

A future assignment to Bomber Command was confirmed with a posting to No. 14 Operational Training Unit, Cottesmore, on May 19, 1942. With a little more experience, Robert might have been among the unit's students who were selected to participate in the three "Millennium" attacks—thousand-bomber raids—against Cologne, Bremen, and Essen, but it was not to be. However, instead of the more usual "nickel" run, dropping leaflets over occupied territory,

Robert's first operation was to be on the night of July 31/August 1 against Düsseldorf, in a Hampden flown by Pilot Officer P.D. McGee. By the time the crew arrived the target was alight, aiding navigation, and their four 500-pounders were released from 11,000 feet over the centre of the town. Engine problems and shortage of fuel forced them to land at Wattisham on the return journey.

Also passing through the OTU while Robert was completing his training were two others who would later participate with distinction on Operation Chastise: Sergeant Les Knight and Pilot Officer Joe McCarthy. As the course came to an end and they prepared for posting to an operational squadron, Robert was reassured to find his navigational skills assessed as "above average."

Ten days later, on August 24, he arrived at RAF Swinderby, home to No. 50 Squadron, to join the crew of "A" Flight commander Squadron Leader Philip Moore. The squadron operated Lancasters, and, under the recently introduced Pilot, Navigator, Bomb Aimer (PNB) scheme, Robert would relinquish his bomb-aiming role to concentrate on navigation. Within four days of his arrival, his crew was one of twelve from the squadron detailed to join a 159-aircraft force bound for Nuremberg. At this period No. 50 Squadron was perfecting its accuracy by making medium-level attacks. The crew had to run into the target at only 9,000 feet after pinpointing a river and canal in bright moonlight. On this night, however, they didn't have the opportunity to assess their results; almost immediately after bomb release the aircraft was caught in searchlights, giving a few tense moments until they were shaken off.

Karlsruhe was the target on the night of September 2/3. There was only moderate opposition that night, and the target was well illuminated by marker flares, with the dock basins clearly identified. The crew added its bombs to the conflagration below from 8,000 feet. The following night, the Atlas shipyards at Bremen were the target. Again, from 9,500 feet the river and docks were clearly identified, facilitating an accurate attack. This precision was not to be repeated on September 8/9, when, unsure of their position, the Pathfinders scattered flares over a wide area, resulting in the bulk of loads falling on Russelsheim instead of the intended target of Frankfurt. Thinking that they recognized the target by the shape of the river, Robert and his crew released their bombs from 10,000 feet, only to realize their error after bombing, as they passed over Frankfurt before turning for home. Two nights later, the searchlights and flak were very active over Düsseldorf as they released a 4,000-pounder and 30-pound incendiaries from 10,500 feet, seeing buildings disintegrating in the bomb bursts.

On September 12, Robert was posted "non-effective/sick" and was hospitalized at RAF Halton with a minor infection. He returned to the squadron on the September 23, and a week later was promoted to Flying Officer.

Poor weather made navigation difficult for an attack on Aachen on October 5/6. The aircraft "spent a lot of time wandering around France, avoiding defended areas," arriving late on target, where bombs were released on dead reckoning but no results were seen. Bad weather the following night made it difficult to find Osnabrück. After circling a couple of times, guided by PFF flares, the bomb aimer spotted a built-up area, assumed to be the target, and bombs were released after a timed run from a nearby lake. A week later, Robert's skills were put to the test when operating against Kiel. The Gee (a key electronic navigation aid) set went unserviceable, and navigation was dependent on dead reckoning and loop bearings. Once again, a timed run from a nearby lake saved the day, and Robert was complimented in the squadron's *Operations Record Book*: "This trip was notable for outstanding navigation."

Participation in the unopposed daylight formation attack on Le Creusot of October 17 presented no navigational difficulties. But the weather proved trying again on October 22/23; the crew pinpointed Northampton, but then cloud hid the ground until Robert's accurate navigation brought them over the Alps to Genoa, where the harbour outline was seen. Two days later, another transalpine trip brought them to a cloud-covered Milan, where they descended to

4,000 feet to bomb the already burning town. Further trips to Genoa were made on the nights of November 6 and 7. On the second of these, immediately after bombing and leaving the target with bomb doors still open, the Lancaster shuddered as it was hit by flak. As they climbed to 16,000 feet, the port inner engine burst into flame. The fire was extinguished and the propeller feathered, but the port outer engine now also indicated rising temperature and required constant monitoring for the return journey. Maintaining safety height to clear the Alps, they returned without further incident. A week later the crew was once more over Genoa, again sustaining minor flak damage and forced to land at Waddington on return.

At this point, Squadron Leader Moore completed his tour and Robert found himself as an experienced, but "spare bod," seeking a new crew. On December 17/18, he joined the crew of Squadron Leader Peter Birch when the squadron dispatched five aircraft as part of a small twenty-seven-aircraft attack against the marshalling yards at Soltau. Although it was a bright moonlit night, three of the squadron's aircraft had great difficulty in locating the target. However, Robert, aided by other crew members, had no difficulty in identifying the River Weser and then following the Nienburg–Soltau road to the target just southeast of the town. Despite lively light flak, they bombed from only 1,500 feet. A large building alongside the yards was seen to catch fire, with a substantial blue explosion being seen five minutes later. There was no sign of any other attacks. On the return, they were attacked and damaged by fighters. During the action, Robert sustained a minor injury, but Birch brought the Lancaster safely back to base. Two of the squadron's aircraft were not so fortunate and failed to return.

In the New Year, Robert teamed up with a new captain, Flight Lieutenant Henry Maudslay, DFC, who was commencing his second tour after a period as instructor at No. 1654 Conversion Unit. Their first trip to Essen on January 21/22 was inauspicious. Thick haze made identification of ground detail impossible, and no PFF flares were seen. After loitering for thirty minutes, the crew bombed what they believed to be a genuine fire in the Ruhr area, but not before significant flak had damaged the port wing and tailplane. The same aircraft suffered minor damage to both wings six nights later over Düsseldorf, while the crew searched for a break in the cloud that enabled them to bomb the final green marker. Accurate flashless flak was also experienced over Cologne on February 2/3, but their fortunes improved two nights later when they went to Turin. Operations continued until the middle of the month, with attacks on Wilhelmshaven, Lorient, and Milan. March saw a resumption of German targets: Hamburg on 3/4, Munich on 9/10, and Essen on 12/13, before attention was turned again to the U-boat offensive with an attack on Saint-Nazaire on 22/23 March 22/23.

The crew were now well into their tour and becoming key members of the squadron. However, in the third week of March, as with selected crews from other No. 5 Group units, they were abruptly posted to Scampton for the formation of a new squadron under the command of Wing Commander Guy Gibson, formerly Officer Commanding No. 106 Squadron. The move was accompanied with a promotion for Maudslay, who became squadron leader and was appointed "B" Flight Commander of the new unit. In recognition of his expertise and exemplary record, Robert was appointed the flight's navigation officer.

No. 617 Squadron, as it was to become, soon began training for its yet unspecified task. Robert reported to the squadron navigation officer, Flight Lieutenant Jack Leggo, and as flight navigation officer was responsible for overseeing ten navigators, reviewing their logs, and addressing any difficulties. Several set routes were established for the crews to follow, facilitating the work of the Observer Corps, and hopefully reducing the number of complaints about low flying. Henry Maudslay and his crew carried out their first daylight cross-country on March 31 in a borrowed No. 9 Squadron Lancaster, followed by a second exercise on April 3.

Owing to the navigator's restricted view, visual navigation would be performed by the bomb aimer, using large-scale roller maps produced in conjunction with the navigators. These maps would be carefully studied before flight and key pinpoints marked: water features, or bridges over rivers, would be most prominent at night. The navigator calculated the timing between each landmark and notified the bomb aimer of the next point's ETA, providing the pilot with course adjustments, based upon drift and speed. The navigator would be fully occupied performing these calculations, checking the aircraft's track and position. Drift was calculated using forecast winds, checked by drift sightings taken by the gunners and updated at turning points. To assist him, the navigator had Gee—assuming that it was working and not jammed—and also the new Air Position Indicator, an analogue computer taking inputs of speed and course to calculate the aircraft's present position, then displaying it as latitude and longitude on an odometer-style read-out. Although this new unit was in short supply, the squadron was given priority. The device was not perfect and required occasional manual resetting, the navigator using reports of observed landmarks and his own expertise to update the position. It was realized that it would be imprudent to rely too heavily on these aids, so more training was carried out using dead reckoning and pinpointing with drift sighting, using flame floats over the sea.

Robert was also the first squadron navigator to get experience with the spotlight altimeter. The device had been resurrected by Royal Aircraft Establishment technicians, and on April 4, Maudslay flew a standard Lancaster to Farnborough, returning to Scampton four days later with the lights installed to demonstrate the equipment's accuracy.[17]

The crew then began training in earnest. A four-and-a-half-hour cross-country on April 11 was followed by a two-hour-fifteen-minute daylight run on the April 13, followed by a five-hour night flight. Strangely, after a four-and-a-half-hour flight to the north of Scotland on April 15, the crew did not fly during the period of the full moon, possibly to allow less-experienced crews an opportunity to practise. By April 16, intensive practice was paying dividends, and most pinpoints were now being found exactly on ETA. Flying experience was supplemented by ground training. Navigators and bomb aimers attended the screening of a film emphasizing the importance of teamwork for low-level navigation, and a training room was established to refine use of the Gee set.

By the beginning of May, the training was rationalized. In addition to using the synthetic two-stage amber,[18] crews were now undertaking short cross-countries at dusk to simulate moonlight flying. From May 5, training exercises were instigated over Eyebrook Reservoir, near Uppingham, sometimes also taking in Abberton Reservoir near Colchester, to practise operational tactics. On May 8, the crew first flew a Type 464 Lancaster, modified to carry the purpose-designed Upkeep bomb. The aircraft was taken up to test the prototype VHF radio installation that would enable Wing Commander Gibson to direct the crews while over the target.

With the deadline for the operation approaching, and with the crews still ignorant of the nature of their target, the squadron now began to practise dropping inert Upkeeps. Maudslay's opportunity came on May 12, when he flew down to Reculver. Because it was daylight, the spotlight altimeter could not be used, and the aircraft was too low on release. The rising plume of spray from the weapon's initial impact with the water struck the aircraft, tearing off a panel and distorting others. The aircraft was damaged, but still flyable, and Maudslay nursed it back to Scampton, where it was deemed too badly damaged to participate in the operation. The following day, the crew reverted to a standard aircraft, for a bombing and tactics exercise. A replacement Type 464 aircraft was delivered on May 14. After an air test and bombing detail, the crew flew it that night on what transpired to be their final exercise before Operation Chastise.

The morning of May 16 would have been one of intense activity as Robert was briefed on the planned route for the operation, prepared his flight plan, and checked those of others in his flight. By 17:00, briefing was over, and crews were heading for their respective messes for the pre-flight meal. Then, there was an opportunity

for freshening up, writing a quick letter, or generally getting organized before it was time for crews to don flying clothing and wait for
the buses to take them out to the aircraft. The Maudslay crew was
detailed with Flight Lieutenant Astell and Pilot Officer Knight as
the third section of the main formation heading for the Möhne Dam.

The three aircraft took off without incident at 21:59, forming
into a loose vic with Maudslay in the lead (although each navigator
kept his own plot), and headed southeast to Southwold. Crossing
the North Sea, they entered Holland over the Scheldt Estuary. All
appears to have gone according to plan until the formation reached
a T-shaped canal junction at Beek, east of Eindhoven, when Flight
Lieutenant Astell fell behind in the turn. East of the next pinpoint at
Rees, on the Rhine, the aircraft ran into light flak, further fragment-
ing the formation. From then on each proceeded independently.
Only Maudslay and Knight would reach the Möhne.

Entering a holding pattern to the south and east of the target,
out of range of the defences, the crew listened over the VHF to the
progress of the attack, no doubt joining in the brief elation as the
dam collapsed. But there was work to do. Robert gave his captain
the prepared course for the Eder Dam, and ED937 turned southeast. As ETA approached, Pilot Officer Michael Fuller, the bomb
aimer, peered anxiously for a sign of the target. The rolling terrain surrounding the Möhne Dam had transformed into steeper,
twisting valleys that were now beginning to fill with mist, making
identification of the reservoir difficult. With tension mounting, the
crew would have seen the red Very light fired by Wing Commander
Gibson, who had located the target. Along with Young, who was acting as Deputy Leader, Flight Lieutenant Shannon and Pilot Officer
Knight, Maudslay's crew homed in on the Eder Dam to familiarize
themselves with its topography. The briefing model had not been
completed in time, and the crew had seen only photographs and
maps, but already appreciated the difficulty of the task ahead. There
was no flak but protruding spurs of high land prevented a straight
and level approach to the target. Attacking aircraft would have to

approach from behind the promontory upon which was perched the village of Waldeck with its distinctive castle, dive steeply for a spit projecting into the lake and then turn sharply to port before levelling out to attain the release parameters of 60 feet and 230 miles per hour within the remaining half mile before reaching the release point 425 yards from the dam. At release, full power would be required to enable the aircraft to execute a climbing turn to starboard and avoid the steep 300-foot hillside rising less than a mile ahead. There were only three Upkeeps available to be dropped, but given the difficulties of approach, would these be sufficient?

Unsurprisingly, given the circumstances of this attack, official records and personal recollections conflict. There is no dispute as to the fact that both Maudslay and Shannon made a number of abortive attempts, both finding it exceedingly difficult to achieve the release criteria. As time passed, Gibson's frustration began to manifest itself, and his radio communication acquired an impatient edge. It appears that Shannon may have finally made a successful attack, his Upkeep detonating to the right of the dam's centre—not surprising considering the line of attack. At about 01:45, Maudslay was called in again. There is a record that something was seen hanging beneath the aircraft, which suggests that it may have been hit and damaged on the way out. Whether or not this had any influence on the events that followed is debatable. The Lancaster levelled out over the lake, having probably gained speed in the dive. There can have been little time for Robert to assess the spots and for Maudslay to respond to any instructions before Pilot Officer Fuller released their Upkeep. Whether it struck the water and bounced, or fell directly onto the target, cannot be ascertained, but those watching saw a gigantic flash on the parapet marginally behind and beneath the Lancaster, which was seen banking steeply away, its exit manœuvre possibly exaggerated by the force of the explosion, before being lost to sight against the black hillside. Unsure of what had happened, Gibson called several times over the VHF, asking Maudslay if he was all right. Eventually a faint reply was received:

"I think so, standby." The aircraft was still flying, although its condition and that of its crew must remain to speculation. At Grantham, a message was received "Goner 28B"—"mine released, overshot, no apparent breach"—although, frustratingly, the time of its receipt is corrupt.

As the Lancaster had crossed the dam, its crew, especially Robert, standing in the cockpit behind Sergeant John Marriott, the flight engineer, would have braced themselves for the steep climbing turn. This may have indirectly prepared them for the jolt as the blast from Upkeep struck the aircraft. This unexpected event can only have tested Maudslay's airmanship to the limit as he struggled to maintain control of the aircraft. After assessing their condition, the crew appear to have continued to fly their briefed route home—almost the reciprocal of their outward route as far as the Rhine, although their timings to reach this point suggest either a slower airspeed, or that they gave a wider berth to the defences; it is also possible that damage may have made it difficult to maintain course. No more is known of the aircraft's return flight until shortly before 02:30, when flak gunners defending the port of Emmerich heard the engines of a large aircraft approaching low from the east. For whatever reason the aircraft was marginally off track and heading towards the town. As it came within range, 20-mm light flak around the port area opened fire at minimum elevation, shells scything the tops off tall poplars as the gunners brought their sights to bear. The Lancaster turned to starboard to avoid their fire, but it was too late. There was a flash, and the aircraft caught fire, disappearing to the north, followed by the sound of an explosion as it fell to earth adjacent to a brickworks near to the small settlement of Netterden.

The following morning, German officials inspected the wreckage, finding the remains of its seven crew, all of whom must have died instantly. All were recovered and taken to the Nord Friedhof in Düsseldorf, where they were laid to rest on May 19, although such was their condition that only Sergeant Marriott and Sergeant Cottam could be positively identified. There they would remain, in the company of many other comrades from Bomber Command whose lives had ended prematurely in the skies over the Ruhr, until 1948, when representatives of the Imperial War Graves Commission began the sad task of exhumation prior to concentration and reinterment in the newly created War Cemetery at Reichswald, southwest of Kleve.

There was one final act. At the end of his service with No. 50 Squadron, on March 20, 1943, Wing Commander William Russell had signed a recommendation for a non-immediate award of the Distinguished Flying Cross for Flying Officer Urquhart, who had completed twenty-eight operations. The recommendation had been approved by Air Vice-Marshal Cochrane on May 4, but had then been lost in official channels. It surfaced in 1945, and since it had been submitted prior to the recommended officer's death, it was approved and promulgated in the *London Gazette* on July 29, 1945. Writing to Robert's parents the following day, Colin Gibson, Canadian Minister for National Defence and Air, explained the delay rather confusingly: "there were times when recollections of the most important incidents were deferred by the exigencies of the conflict." The administrative process would continue to grind slowly, and it would be another four years before they would receive the actual award. There would be no formal investiture nor official presentation, the medal having been unceremoniously dispatched by registered mail on November 7, 1949.

TOP Inscription on the headstone of S/L Henry Maudslay. STEVE DARLOW

BOTTOM F/O Robert Urquhart, DFC, RCAF, in happier times. CVWM VIA OPERATION PICTURE ME

OPPOSITE Upkeep test drop: The aircraft, possibly flown by S/L Maudslay, is struck by the plume from its mine being released too low. DR. ROBERT OWEN COLLECTION

During the winter of 1943/44, with Berlin featured on the battle order, many aircrews understandably felt trepidation and fear. They knew they would be fighting for their lives on the long flight to the target and back again. Canadian Bruce Sutherland had become a "spare" navigator when his pilot, assigned to another crew on a second-dickey trip to Berlin seven days earlier, failed to return. Now it was Bruce's turn to face a baptism of fire with an unknown crew. Tragedy struck, with five crew members killed in action and two taken prisoners of war.

5

FATE INTERVENES

HOWARD SANDALL

IN SUFFOLK, the last of the day's winter sun cast shadows from the natural foliage and buildings across the expansive airfield at RAF Mildenhall. The shadows stretched widely from the Avro Lancaster bombers of Nos. 15 and 622 Squadrons resting at their dispersal points, as if reaching into the night prematurely, searching for signs of impending doom or lucky survival.

For many, the approaching night brought peace and quiet behind closed doors. For the men of Bomber Command, the night was the start of another fearful adventure.

By dusk, Flight Sergeant Earnest "Bruce" Sutherland felt his stomach tighten at thoughts of the coming operation deep into enemy territory. The hour before briefing was particularly unnerving as the target was unknown, although the amount of fuel that had been pumped into each Lancaster was an early indicator of the potential length of the trip. Full tanks meant an operation deep into Germany; less fuel might mean a trip into occupied France and reduced time in the air to be targeted. On this particular evening, the fuel tanks were full to brimming, signifying a deep-penetration mission. After briefing was over, the airfield was a hive of activity and a distraction. Once on board and in crew position, it was down to work for Bruce.

EARNEST "BRUCE" Sutherland was born on December 28, 1920, in Beachville, Ontario. He attended Woodstock College, achieving a high standard of education before working briefly in a munitions factory in Ingersoll, Ontario. Bruce enlisted in the Royal Canadian Air Force on July 8, 1941, in London, Ontario. His initial aptitude tests revealed his ability in mathematics, and he was classified for training as a navigator.

Like so many of his fellow volunteers, Bruce began his basic training at No. 1 Manning Depot in Toronto. This was followed by a posting to the city's No. 6 Initial Training School for six weeks of theoretical tuition in air navigation, then a transfer to No. 12 Elementary Flying Training School (EFTS) at Goderich in Ontario. Elementary training took approximately eight weeks and included at least fifty hours of flying in the de Havilland Tiger Moth or the Fairchild Cornell. Navigation students then began to pursue their specialized trade in the classroom, learning how to read and use the astral compass and how to plot a course using landmarks. Next, they were trained in the ground simulation trainer, and finally tested in day and night navigational flights.

From Goderich, Bruce moved the short distance to No. 1 Service Flying Training School (SFTS) at nearby Camp Borden for eight weeks of intensive instruction in an intermediate training squadron followed by six weeks in an advanced training squadron. A final two weeks were undertaken at a bombing and gunnery school.

At No. 9 Air Observer School (AOS) in Saint-Jean, Quebec, Bruce was given more exposure to basic navigation techniques of dead reckoning and visual pilotage through an additional sixty to seventy hours of practical airtime experience. Flying in a twin-engined Anson, Bruce learned to use the range of tools of the navigator's trade: aeronautical charts, magnetic compass, watch, trip log, Douglas protractor, and the Dalton navigational computer. By December 1942, he had successfully passed his training and was classed as "above average." He was awarded his navigator's wing, which he proudly sewed on his tunic.

Overseas posting papers in hand, Bruce departed from Halifax, Nova Scotia, for the two-week voyage to England. He arrived at No. 3 Personnel Reception Centre in Bournemouth for processing in the spring of 1943, before being sent to No. 10 (Observer) Advanced Flying Unit in Dumfries, Scotland. Here, he was given practical navigation experience over the very different terrain of the British Isles.

His next and final navigation training location was No. 12 Operational Training Unit at RAF Chipping Warden in Oxfordshire. It was at Chipping Warden OTU that Bruce and his colleagues crewed up with Pilot Officer Stanley Earnest James, an Australian from Camberwell, Victoria. Subsequent postings to the Heavy Conversion Unit at RAF Woolfox Lodge and Lancaster Finishing School (LFS) at RAF Feltwell completed the crew's training.

Instruction complete, the James crew finally arrived in early December 1943 at RAF Mildenhall in Suffolk to join No. 622 Squadron, part of No. 3 Group Bomber Command. The squadron was formed as part of the expansion of Bomber Command in August 1943, operating the Short Stirling bomber. The crew's arrival at Mildenhall coincided with the squadron converting from the Stirling to the Avro Lancaster. It was a return to the training routine, starting with crucial lectures on survival, particularly escape and evasion techniques. Familiarisation flights in the Lancaster were frequent and mainly "circuits and bumps."[19] Night exercises were included when weather permitted.

During the early stages of the Battle of Berlin, the squadron had suffered many losses flying their Short Stirling bombers. The Stirling operated for the last time against a major target (Berlin) on November 22 and was withdrawn due to high attrition rates. The Stirling could not reach the altitude required to be afforded the protection of the "bomber stream" and was therefore more vulnerable to German flak and fighters. The loss rate was considered unsustainable in terms of aircraft and aircrew, hence the welcome conversion to the Lancaster.

It was customary for newly arriving pilots to undertake one operation as a so-called second dickey to experience battle conditions. On January 20, 1944, Pilot Officer James was assigned to the crew of Flight Lieutenant D.A. Claydon, RCAF, for a mission to attack Berlin. It turned out to be a bad night for the squadron. Shortly after bombing the target Claydon's aircraft was shot down by a night fighter, killing all eight crew members on board. All the airmen rest in Berlin War Cemetery. Pilot Officer R.A. Deacon and his crew were also lost. He too was carrying a second pilot who lost his life along with five other crew members. Two of the team were fortunate to survive, both taken as prisoners of war.

Bruce Sutherland now found himself without a crew and was designated a "spare" navigator. This situation was far from ideal. Aircrew were superstitious about being assigned a different crew member for operations as it was considered extremely bad luck. Bruce was briefed on two occasions for operations with different crews, but for unknown reasons didn't fly these missions. The squadron navigation leader, Flight Lieutenant McKay, considered Bruce a jinx and ordered him to fly when next on the battle order— or be grounded.

On January 27, 1944, Bruce found himself on the battle order flying with Flight Sergeant Hugh Howie Graig, a Scotsman from Ayrshire. The target was the "Big City," Berlin. Aircrews knew that the route there and back would be fraught with danger. Berlin was the most heavily defended target of any city, with a flak belt stretching for forty miles and a searchlight belt some sixty miles across. The flak defences comprised the very effective 88 mm-type artillery guns strategically placed around the city with three massive flak towers. Each contained eight 128-mm heavy guns. The eight guns could fire a salvo every ninety seconds up to a height of 45,000 feet. The exploding shells would send out a shower of molten shrapnel covering a diameter of 260 yards. This was a particularly unsuccessful period for Bomber Command and the German night fighter force reaped revenge on the bomber crews, inflicting seriously heavy losses.

Hugh Craig had joined the squadron in October 1943 and completed two second-dickey trips in the Short Stirling towards the end of November under the command of Squadron Leader J. Martin, DFC. He then completed two minor operations with his crew before the squadron was stood down in the early part of December 1943 for conversion to the Avro Lancaster. Severe winter weather restricted the number of operations the squadron could mount in January until that fateful night of January 27, Craig's first operational trip in a Lancaster. The other members of the crew who had arrived at Mildenhall included:

Sergeant J. MacFarlane (Navigator)

Flying Officer Godfrey G. Sproule, RCAF, from Ottawa, Canada (Bomb aimer)

Flight Sergeant Bertrand Patrick Dineen (Wireless operator)

Sergeant Frank William Flower (Mid-upper gunner)

Sergeant Frank George Aldred from Beccles, Suffolk (Rear gunner)

Sergeant Denis Dart from Shapwick, Dorset (Flight engineer)

That January night, with the operational briefing over and parachutes collected, Bruce and his assigned crew were transported in vans to the dispersal point for G-George. Once aboard, there quickly followed the pre-flight inspection and intercom check. Bruce spread his navigational charts across his table and extracted his Dalton computer, sextant, and numerous pencils from his canvas bag. Flight Sergeant Craig lined up the Lancaster at the end of the runway awaiting his turn to take off. Final checks were made, and the brakes applied, while the four Merlin engines were run up to maximum power, the aircraft straining against the brakes. Finally Craig released the brakes and ED624 surged down the runway gathering speed until the tail wheel came up and the heavily laden bomber lifted off the runway. Bruce Sutherland noted the time of takeoff as

17:45 hours in his navigational log and gave his skipper a course to steer to the rendezvous point over Cromer in Norfolk.

ED624 had seen considerable service since April 1943 at a Conversion Unit, and its engines were worn and ready for an overhaul. Craig struggled to gain the required height, opening the throttles further to increase power. Slowly, they began to fall behind the rest of the bomber stream, well aware they could become vulnerable to the German defence's night fighter force. Despite the risks, the consensus of the crew was to continue to the target.

The route to the target was fraught with danger. Fighter flares were dropped by the enemy and the crew witnessed other aircraft catch fire and tumble to earth. As the aircraft droned on its set course, Hugh Craig instructed his gunners to look out for fighters. The tension was palpable, everyone on high alert for an impending attack. Then, on the final approach to Berlin, rear turret gunner Sergeant Frank Aldred was suddenly blinded by lines of tracer from an unseen attacker. With his night vision compromised he screamed into the intercom "Corkscrew port!" Hugh Craig pushed the nose forward and forcibly manoeuvred from the lines of tracer, which narrowly missed the top of the rear turret. The Lancaster creaked and groaned under the severe and vigorous action. Pulling out of the last dive, Craig levelled out and asked the crew for an update on any battle damage. No one had been injured and the bullets had missed their target, but it was with severely rattled nerves that they continued towards their objective, fear and trepidation at their very souls.

There were no further incidents as they arrived at the target. Green and red flares floated down as target markers were dropped by the Pathfinder Force. White flares released by the enemy were intermingled with the Pathfinder's flares, causing confusion; nonetheless, guided by Flying Officer Sproule in the bomb aimer's position, Hugh Craig started the bomb run. Sproule's instructions over the intercom were clear: "Left, left, steady, right steady—bombs gone!" The silhouettes of other aircraft could be seen above them as bombs fell from their cavernous bomb bays. The chances of being hit by falling bombs or a mid-air collision were extremely high. They flew straight and level for what was only a matter of seconds but felt like an eternity to the crew. This allowed the photo flash and bombing photograph to be taken. Bruce Sutherland gave the skipper a course to steer. Gradually the crew left the fire and flak behind. They felt relief to be homeward bound, but they could not relax or let their guard down for an instant.

THE GERMAN night fighters had grown into an efficient and formidable force. The Germans utilised new radar systems such as the ground radar Himmelbett method, which controlled a series of imaginary boxes of space in the sky, and night fighters were vectored into position with the radar box sections. The mainstays of the *Nachtjagd* (night fighters) were the Me 110 and Ju 88 twin-engined fighters, equipped with the Lichtenstein and SN-2 airborne radar devices. Their armaments were formidable: the destruction of many bombers was attributed to the introduction of the *Schräge Musik* (literally "slanted music," which was German colloquial for Jazz) upward-firing 20-mm cannon assembly. The night fighter would approach a bomber from slightly below its crew's vision, using radar detection aides. Once in position, unseen, the fighter would fire into the bomber's fuel tanks situated in the wings, causing almost certain fire and destruction. The bomber's gunners were at a complete disadvantage looking down into the dark night sky, unaware of the *Schräge Musik* directly below.

Oberleutnant Wilhelm Johnen was a proficient and accomplished night-fighter pilot. He knew the dangers he faced from a bomber's gunners only too well. In 1942, he had attacked a Vickers Wellington, striking home his cannon shells in a deadly crescendo that reverberated through his aircraft. As he started to turn away, he was hit by return fire, wounding him in the leg and killing his *Bordfunker* (radio operator), Gefreiter Risop. Johnen bailed out and spent time in hospital to treat his burns and a wounded leg. Once recovered, he returned to the fray with *Nachtjäger* unit 5 (NJG5).

On this fateful, night Wilhelm Johnen was directed by a radar controller to the southwest side of Berlin to look for prey. At around 20:50 hours, his *Bordfunker* picked up blips on the cathode ray tubes. They felt it could only be bombers! Johnen was given a course to steer and crept slowly up on the Lancaster of Flight Sergeant Craig. Manoeuvring his Messerschmitt Bf 110G night fighter stealthily underneath his quarry, he noticed the lack of evasive action. The gunners had not seen his approach. In position, hidden beneath the lumbering bomber, Johnen unleashed his *Schräge Musik* and the 20-mm cannon shells slammed into the bomber's starboard engine and fuselage. The wing was instantly a mass of flames. Satisfied the bomber was badly damaged, Johnen pulled away into the darkness to observe from a safe distance.

In the stricken Lancaster, Hugh Craig fought with the controls, knowing that the bomber was doomed to go down. The wing fire became a beacon in the dark. With no alternative he ordered the crew to bail out. Wilhelm Johnen claimed ED624 as one of his three victories that night within forty-five minutes of each other, bringing his victory tally to thirteen.

Bruce Sutherland recalled the attack:

The aircraft was not able to climb to operational height and we fell far behind of the stream, making us vulnerable to the German fighter forces. We had turned for home over Germany when we were suddenly hit hard by a fighter. The pilot was trying to evade with a corkscrew manoeuvre and he went into a dive, I found myself suspended from the ceiling. By the time I got back on the floor the fighter had gone and I heard the skipper telling us to put our 'chutes on.

I had clipped mine on when we were hit again and the front turret was blown off. The aircraft was spinning and the only way I could move was to crawl along the floor. I was heading towards the escape hatch when I think the aircraft exploded as shells hit the bomb bay I assume. At this point I passed out. I came to swinging backwards and forwards beneath my opened parachute. I managed to stabilise the swinging, then I tried to put my gloves on because I felt cold and wet. The next thing I remember I was in a wood on the ground.

I got rid of my 'chute, checked my escape kit and started walking generally westward. I walked all that night and throughout the next day. The following evening I came across a group of large buildings. I was pretty tired and I stepped inside one. I found myself at the head of a large corridor with many doors. The rooms appeared to be the female living quarters of some sort of industrial complex. Someone got hold of me and took me to the factory canteen, but I was unable to communicate with anyone. Eventually a Nazi Party official came along and identified me as shot-down aircrew and took me into custody and I was taken under guard to Dulag Luft at Frankfurt.

Godfrey Sproule's experience was similar. On his arrival back in England, he wrote to the family of the crew's flight engineer, Denis Dart, and described what happened:

All the way to the target and all the way out of the target there was a continual stream of fighter flares along our path. We evaded them as much as possible. Before we reached the target we had a fighter attack but managed to get away. We bombed and were on our homeward journey when we received an underneath attack. The tracer entered our starboard inner engine. The rear gunner reported the attack and I heard Denis say that the starboard engine was losing revs. Then there was the second attack. Cannon shells exploded in the front of the aircraft and I was stunned and knocked out. When I came to my senses the aircraft was in a dive, the front of the aircraft was badly smashed. I managed to work my way to the pilot Hughie Craig who gestured to me to abandon the aircraft. At the time I saw Denis and the other members getting ready to abandon. I forced my way down the nose of the aircraft, removed the safety hatch and jettisoned it, found my 'chute and jumped. The last I saw of the aircraft it was still in a dive.

I was captured in Germany the following night. I had been travelling in a south-easterly direction toward France and hoping at the same time to meet up with the rest of the crew. Later I met the navigator Bruce Sutherland. He had no news of the other members. Sometime later I made enquires of the German authorities. They reported the other members were killed and the bodies of Sergeant Dinnen and Sergeant Dart were the only two identified. I was sure till then that the other members would get out. As you probably know there is a definitive sequence to the abandoning of the aircraft. The rear and mid-upper gunner go out the escape hatch rear, the five in the front go out the escape hatch in the nose. He had practised this procedure often so that no time would be lost. It was my duty as air bomber to open and jettison the hatch and get out first. The others were to follow, the last being the pilot. I have no idea what happened after I left the aircraft, there are any number of things that might have occurred. I am sure something went wrong because they had a reasonable time to get out.

Five of the crew were ceremonially removed from the wreckage and buried in Stifts Cemetery in Chemnitz, a district of Ebersdorf, Saxony, at the time. They were later reinterned in Berlin War Cemetery, the same resting place of Flying Officer James, Bruce's first pilot.

AT RAF Mildenhall, the committee of adjustment officer wrote the words *Failed to Return* in red ink in every logbook. The crew's personal possessions were cleared from their rooms and lockers. Detailed inventories were made and presented to the squadron adjutant for onward presentation to the families. Among the personal possessions received by Denis Dart's mother was a small RAF diary that Denis had started to complete from January 1, 1944. The last entry on January 27 reads "ops to Berlin." Flicking through the pages to February 8, 1944, reveals an entry in pencil that reads "leave due." Denis was not destined to take that leave, or ever to be with his family again.

The official telegram and squadron commander letters were drafted and sent to the families informing them that their loved ones were missing in action. They were advised to wait for official confirmation as to whether they were prisoners of war and to remain hopeful. Waiting to hear if their loved ones were alive was always a heart-wrenching experience for families. For the parents of Bruce Sutherland and Godfrey Sproule, the news was worth the wait; five other families received the notification of death confirmation from the Red Cross Society. Sadly, they endured months of heartache and hope before discovering the reality.

BRUCE SUTHERLAND and Godfrey Sproule were eventually incarcerated at Stalag Luft VI at Heydekrug, near the edge of the Baltic Sea in what is now Lithuania. On the morning of July 14, 1944, all prisoners were made aware that the camp was to be evacuated. The Russian Army had made significant inroads into the German defences, and the camp was in danger of being surrounded and cut off. With very little warning, the prisoners packed their meagre possessions and were given two Red Cross parcels for the coming journey. Bruce and Godfrey marched out of the camp gates with 250 to 300 other prisoners. They passed through Heydekrug, where local people lined the road. Some threw stones and shouted obscenities at the prisoners.

At the railway station, Bruce, Godfrey, and their fellow prisoners were herded into filthy cattle trucks that were crammed so full they were unable to sit down. The conditions were deplorable. Men had to urinate and defecate where they stood. They travelled for thirty-six hours in these conditions until they reached Stalag 20A at Thorn, north of Warsaw in Poland. The camp was mostly inhabited by Army prisoners of war and already severely overcrowded. Food was a constant preoccupation. Bruce and Godfrey were continually hungry. All prisoners lost weight on the meagre and inadequate

German rations. The occasional Red Cross food parcels that arrived were a most welcome addition.

The POWs could hear artillery fire approaching as the Russian Army continued to capture ground and closed in on their camp. On August 9, 1944, the prisoners found themselves on the move once more. Again, Bruce and his fellow prisoners were crammed into cattle trucks for a forty-eight-hour train journey before arriving at Stalag 357 at Fallingbostel. This camp was built on a hill adjacent to the small village of Oerbke, around thirty miles from Hanover. Bruce and Godfrey spent Christmas in the camp. As before, food was in short supply, and the unusually cold winter weather made conditions very depressing.

In March 1945, Bruce and Godfrey again vacated their camp, setting out on a forced march that would become infamous for its cruelty and needless loss of life. The men marched in groups of 250 to 300, with inappropriate clothing for the cold weather. The hardship endured was unimaginable and the lack of humanity beyond belief. The German guards pushed the men to march for twenty to forty miles each day. They often rested in churches or barns and sometimes slept out in the cold by the side of the road. Bruce and his fellow prisoners were in poor physical health—dysentery was common, and disease was rife among prisoners. On April 19, Bruce witnessed an event that he would remember all his life. A column of marching prisoners was attacked by RAF Typhoon fighters. The pilots had mistaken the men for retreating German troops. Many prisoners were killed in four strafing attacks. Bruce managed to throw himself into a ditch at the side of the road, which saved his life. A few days later, Bruce and his group of prisoners were liberated by a band of British soldiers. They quickly summoned trucks and food supplies. The hot food, drink, and safe shelter were a dream come true for the starved and weary prisoners.

Bruce Sutherland passed away in April 2016 at the age of ninety-six. He led a full life, raising a family and becoming a successful businessman—freedoms denied to so many of his compatriots in

Bomber Command. Bruce lost six companions from two different crews, but fate intervened, and his own life was spared.

Denis Dart's mother was asked to provide the words for an inscription on her son's headstone when his body was moved from its original burial place to the Berlin War Cemetery. Her response was emotional and poignant, and representative of so many who had made that final sacrifice: "For your tomorrow we gave our today."

TOP Earnest "Bruce" Sutherland, RCAF, navigator. HOWARD SANDALL COLLECTION

BOTTOM The crew of P/O S.E. James, RAAF, that arrived at RAF Mildenhall in December 1943. Left to right: Sutherland, Berkley, Stringer, James, unknown, Notley. Missing is flight engineer Woolston. HOWARD SANDALL COLLECTION

OPPOSITE, TOP No. 12 OTU Chipping Warden. Bruce Sutherland is in the middle row, fourth from right. Next to him toward the right are fellow crew members James, Berkley, and Notley. Stringer is fourth from right in the back row. HOWARD SANDALL COLLECTION

OPPOSITE, BOTTOM Full 622 Squadron photo taken October 1943, before converting to Lancasters in January 1944. F/S Craig's crew are identified with arrows—left to right, Craig, MacFarlane, Sproule, Dart, Aldred, Flower, Dinneen. HOWARD SANDALL COLLECTION

BACK ROW:—SGTs MORROW   LAWRENCE   WELLS   SHEPHERD   EATON   STRINGER   DAVEY   RODRIQUE   MERRITT
                                                                                                        BISHOP

SECOND ROW:—SGTs MARTIN   GRANT   MASTERS   NATHANSON   TAYLOR   SYMMONS   SUTHERLAND   JAMES   BERKLEY
                                                                                                        NOTLEY

FRONT ROW:—SGTs CLOUGH   IRVING   GAGE   P/O WARREN   P/O DENHAM   P/O FREEMAN   P/O DOWNING
                                                    SGTs FARQUHARSON   STEAN   CLAUSON

SECTIONS 1 and 2

Left to Right :- Hugh Craig - John MacFarlane - Godfrey Sproule
Sgt Denis Dart - Frank Aldred - Frank Flower - Bert Dinneen

RAF Bomber Command's contribution to the success of the 1944 D-Day landings has been mostly overlooked. In recent years, there have been significant commemorations of the Normandy beach landings. Media have focused on the army's primary role but have failed to acknowledge the achievements and, equally important, the cost of Bomber Command's efforts in support of Operation Overlord, the Allied re-entry into German-occupied Western Europe. Aircrews, ground crews, and Bomber Command station and headquarters personnel had, in fact, put up an immense effort. They had operated directly in support of the landing for the three months prior to D-Day, June 6, 1944, carrying out a strategic campaign of bombing against the rail network that led to Normandy and through which the Germans would have to move reinforcements and supplies. Closer to D-Day, bombing raids on major defensive emplacements were aimed at facilitating the actual landings. And following the actual Normandy D-Day beach assault, bomber crews continued with the attacks on the railyards, frustrating German deployments. At the time, the airmen involved received little recognition. Unfortunately, little has changed since. But thousands of Bomber Command aircrew lost their lives ensuring the success of the invasion—a sacrifice that deserved recognition then and certainly now.

6

OVERLORD SACRIFICE

STEVE DARLOW

THE RAIL COMMUNICATIONS bombing attacks opened on the night of March 6/7, 1944, with a raid on the Trappes rail facilities. History is now clear in showing that the attacks on the French and Belgian rail targets through the spring of 1944 and into the summer significantly hampered Germany's ability to respond to the invasion. But this came at a cost. In village and town cemeteries across Normandy, the Somme, Picardy, and the Pas de Calais, Commonwealth war graves headstones mark where Bomber Command airmen now rest, having died in Overlord support operations. This sacrifice was overlooked in recent commemorative events; it was also overlooked in 1944. At the time, Air Chief Marshal Sir Arthur Harris had voiced his concerns to Chief of the Air Staff Sir Charles Portal (on July 1), stating in a letter: "I think you should be aware of the full depth of feeling that is being aroused by the lack of adequate or even reasonable credit to the RAF in particular, and the Air Forces as a whole, for their efforts in the Invasion." Harris went on to quote some statistics:

> Up to June 28th in this battle (which is regarded both officially and publicly as mainly a land battle), the British Army has lost some 2,500 killed; the U.S. Army approximately 5,000. In April, May and June which are the three months in which my Command had

been engaged almost entirely on invasion work (including the
Rocket and Flying Bomb work which must be regarded as part of
the invasion war although the casualties on those targets are negli-
gible) my Command alone lost 6,038 killed, wounded and missing.
Of those, 5,804 are missing. Of the missing we know from experience only about 20% survive. Therefore my Command alone in
this invasion war has suffered nearly 2½ times the number killed
as the whole of the British Army and more than the U.S. Army...

Yet when it comes to official communiqués and the balanc-
ing of publicity the country as a whole and world at large is quite
entitled to think that this is almost entirely a land war with the
Air Forces doing what they can to assist; whereas in fact they are
bearing the brunt.

Harris concluded the letter: "There are 10,500 aircrew in my
operational squadrons. In three months we have lost over half that
number. They have a right that their story should be adequately told,
and it is a military necessity that it should be."

Bomber Command recorded the accounts of airmen who had
initially failed to return from an operation and yet later made their
way home, in a "K" report (Report on Loss of Aircraft on Operations). These records, while matter of fact, provide an invaluable
insight into the extraordinary experiences of aircrew and the difficulties and dangers they faced while flying through hostile airspace,
under attack, and while trying to get out of a severely damaged aircraft. What follows are three such accounts of Bomber Command
airmen "bearing the brunt."

ON THE night of April 18/19, 1944, Bomber Command set a new
record, aircrew flying a total of 1,125 sorties. The majority were carried out against French rail targets. Almost 1,250 airmen manned
the 112 Halifaxes, 61 Lancasters, and 8 Mosquitoes that flew to
attack the rail marshalling yards at Noisy-le-Sec. Four Halifaxes
would not be returning. There was a total loss of life on three of the
aircraft, but on one RCAF No. 432 Squadron Halifax one man would

eventually be able to tell the tragic circumstances in which some of his Bomber Command colleagues died.

REPORT ON LOSS OF AIRCRAFT ON OPERATIONS

Aircraft	Halifax III No. LW. 643 'E' of No. 432 Squadron
Date of Loss	18/19 April 1944
Target	Noisy-le-Sec M/Y
Cause of Loss	Collision
Position of Loss	Target area
Information from	Sgt. Shaughnessy G.J. Mid Under Gunner on 14th operation
Captain & Pilot	P/O Mercer A.C.G. This crew had completed about 20 operations. All, except the informant are believed to be killed.
Navigator	P/O Bell J.B.
W/Operator	Sgt. Pett S.D.
Ft/Engineer	P/O Kent W.H.
Bomb Aimer	F/O Redman A.H.
M/U/Gunner	Sgt. McCluskie A.
R/Gunner	P/O McGregor A.M.
Briefed Route	Base—Newbury—Selsey Bill—4918N 0010W—4820N 0210E—Target—4855N 0230E—4955N 0055E—Reading—Base.
Narrative	The informant who was a spare gunner in his squadron had not flown with this crew before. He manned the mid under gun on this occasion. The Halifax took off from East Moor at 2058 hours, crossed the French coast at 13,000 ft. and continued to climb to 15,500 ft. before reaching the target. The night was clear, there being little cloud and visibility was good. The outward flight was uneventful. The Rear Gunner once reported that they were being followed by a twin-engined fighter, but the Pilot executed a corkscrew and no attack developed.
	On the approach to the target a fire was observed to port probably coming from Juvisy which was also attacked that night. In the target area there was a small amount of flak and many aircraft were seen below the Halifax.
	The Halifax made a good bombing run at 15,500 ft. and as far as is known on the briefed heading. The bombs were dropped on T.I.'s. The Bomb Aimer had just called out 'Bombs

gone' and the Pilot had not yet made any alteration of course, when there was a terrific crash and informant, who was in the mid lower gun position keeping a look out below was thrown violently about. He was considerably bruised and winded, but not seriously hurt. Sgt. Shaughnessy is convinced that the violence of the crash could only be due to a collision with another aircraft, but he never saw the aircraft or heard any warning from any other member of the crew to suggest that a collision was imminent. From the direction of the sound and the damage subsequently observed he believes that the collision must have taken place head on.

The Halifax immediately appeared to turn completely over several times and then went into a steep spiral dive. When Sgt. Shaughnessy recovered his faculties he left his turret intending to put on his parachute. He found that this had been opened and torn in the collision and was unserviceable. With considerable difficulty he made his was forward as far as the front main spar. Passing under the mid upper turret he looked up and noticed that the top of the turret had been broken off. The Gunner appeared to be dead. The Flight Engineer was lying across the main spar unconscious, the Pilot was slumped forward over the controls and the Wireless Operator also appeared to be dead or unconscious. Sgt. Shaughnessy decided that there was nothing he could do to assist them as the whole front part of the aircraft was completely wrecked. There was no sign of fire. Sgt. Shaughnessy then returned to the rear exit and attempted to open it. He managed to get it about three quarters open, but then it jammed. He then sought the spare parachute which was kept close by. The side of the fuselage was considerably buckled and the parachute container was badly dented. He was quite unable to extract the parachute and realised that he could not leave the aircraft.

He therefore crouched down on the floor close to the entrance door awaiting the crash.

The next thing that Sgt. Shaughnessy remembers is being half dragged and half carried along the ground by two German soldiers. They were still within the precincts of the marshalling yard and he noticed two crashed bombers burning nearby. Later he was told that a third had crashed at the other end of

	the yard. The raid was still in progress and after a few minutes a stick of bombs fell fairly close. The Germans immediately made for safety as fast as they could leaving Sgt. Shaughnessy who escaped in the opposite direction.
O.R.S. Comment	Several reports were received of a collison in the Noisy-le-Sec area on this night.

Canadian Sergeant Shaughnessy would go on to evade capture. One other member of the crew, Sergeant Pett, also survived and was captured. Canadians Flying Officer Angus Cameron Graeme Mercer[20] (from Vancouver), Pilot Officer James Bond Bell (from Coleman, Alberta), and Pilot Officer Alexander Mor Van McGregor (from Regina) all rest in Clichy New Communal Cemetery, together with RAF airmen Pilot Officer Kent, Flying Officer Redman and Sergeant McCluskie.

ON THE night of May 6/7, 1944, Bomber Command sent 149 aircraft and crews to attack the rail facilities at Mantes-La-Jolie (recorded in the Bomber Command records as Mantes-Gassicourt). Three aircraft failed to return, resulting in the loss of ten lives, with seven men evading capture and four men caught.

REPORT ON LOSS OF AIRCRAFT ON OPERATIONS

Aircraft	Lancaster III No. MD449 'M' of 156 Squadron	
Date of Loss	6/7 May 1944	
Target	Mantes-Gassicourt	
Cause of Loss	Fighter	
Position of Loss	Conches area	
Information from	F/Sgt. Meer G.M.G. Flight Engineer on his 31st operation, F/O Jones P.V. Bomb Aimer on his 38th operation.	
Captain & Pilot	F/Lt Churchill H.D.	On his 35th operation Fate unknown
Navigator	F/O Foster J.D.	About 35 operations completed Fate unknown

Wireless Operator	Sgt. Marle R.	About 35 operations completed Bel. evading
Mid Upper Gunner	Sgt. Hayward D.D.	About 35 operations completed Wounded but bel. evading
Rear Gunner	F/O Warren D.F.	About 10 operations completed Fate unknown
Narrative		The Lancaster took off from Upwood at 0048 on 7th May, set course at 2,000 feet and climbed on track to cross the enemy coast at 10,000 feet. Visibility was excellent and the moon was nearly full.

The crew had been briefed to bomb towards the end of the attack and as the target was approached, the Pilot reported that fighters seemed to be busy over the target area. Bombs were released at the briefed time of 0221 and then, in view of the signs of fighter activity, the Pilot asked the Flight Engineer to come up beside him to keep a look-out.

The route involved a turn to starboard after bombing and holding the new course for about 35 miles before making a 90° turn on to the homeward route. This 90° turn had just been made and the aircraft was flying straight and level at about 9,000 feet when the Rear Gunner reported sighting a suspicious aircraft on the starboard quarter down. He asked the Mid Upper Gunner to watch on the port side and warned the Pilot to prepare for combat. The route involved a turn to starboard after bombing and holding the new course for about 35 miles before making a 90° turn on to the home- ward route. This 90° turn had just been made and the aircraft was flying straight and level at about 9,000 feet when the Rear Gunner reported sighting a suspicious aircraft on the starboard quarter down. He asked the Mid Upper Gunner to watch on the port side and warned the Pilot to prepare for combat. (The Wireless Operator had not reported any suspi- cious indication on FISHPOND). The Flight Engineer directed his search in the direction indicated by the Gunner and saw a twin-engined aircraft, probably a Ju 88, at a range which he estimated as over 1,000 yards.

The Rear Gunner began to speak again, advising a dive to starboard, but as he spoke, the fighter opened fire and scored hits on the bomber. The Flight Engineer is confident that the range of firing was exceptionally great and estimates it as nearly 1,000 yards.

The details of the damage sustained in this attack are not known precisely but the effect was that GEE and H2S immediately became unserviceable, the Mid Upper Gunner was wounded and the Rear Gunner reported his "guns had gone," but that he was not wounded. The informants believe that cannon fire was responsible as bursts were heard inside the aircraft.

The dive, initiated on the Gunner's warning as the attack began, was carried through steeply and about 4,000 feet of altitude was lost. No sooner was the aircraft levelled out at about 6,000 feet than the Rear Gunner gave warning that the fighter was coming in again from the port quarter. A further dive to 2,000 feet was carried out. The fighter scored no hits in this attack and was engaged by the Mid Upper Gunner

The Pilot began to gain some height but almost immediately the fighter was reported by the Rear Gunner to be coming in again and he decided that, with only the Mid Upper turret available for defence, his best chance of escape lay in going low enough to prevent the fighter from having room to manoeuvre beneath the Lancaster. He therefore dived again and flew on at about 800 feet. The fighter however, attacked repeatedly, usually coming in from the port, i.e. from out of the moon. The only defensive manoeuvre which the Lancaster was able to make was a steep bank and although the fighter did not score hits in every attack, the bomber received some additional damage. The fighter made seven or eight attacks in all. They were made in such rapid succession that informants think it possible that they were assailed by more than one aircraft. Throughout, the Rear Gunner continued to give directions clearly and steadily.

The Bomb Aimer was sent aft to inspect damage and to ascertain the condition of the Rear Gunner. He found that all the visible damage was at the rear of the aircraft and that the Gunner was unhurt.

After the last attack the Pilot reported that he had no rudder control and that the crew should prepare to abandon the aircraft. He added immediately that the aircraft was uncontrollable and told the crew to bail out quickly. The height of the aircraft was then about 700 feet.

The Flight Engineer left first from the front hatch and was followed immediately by the Bomb Aimer. Both pulled their rip cords as they left the aircraft and they both made good descents. They landed rather heavily but unhurt within 50 yards of one another in an open field surrounded by trees. They saw no other parachutes although the Navigator was right behind them as they baled out. The aircraft flew on for about 4 minutes after they left and then hit the ground and burst into flames. A preliminary report received by the informants was that three bodies were found, but the number was later corrected to two.

The place of landing was Le Fidelaire about 30 miles N.W. of Conches.

RAF Flight Lieutenant Churchill, who had been awarded the Distinguished Flying Cross and Bar, lost his life and is buried in Fidelaire Communal Cemetery along with RAF Flying Officer Foster, DFC. Canadian Flying Officer Earle F. Warren, DFM, is buried in the Bretteville-sur-Laize Canadian War Cemetery. The other four men survived to evade capture.

ON THE night of June 12/13, 1944, Bomber Command sent 671 aircraft to attack communications targets in France, including the railyards at Cambrai. A total of seventeen Halifaxes and six Lancasters failed to return, including the RCAF No. 408 Squadron Lancaster flown by RCAF Squadron Leader W.B. Stewart.

REPORT ON LOSS OF AIRCRAFT ON OPERATIONS	
Aircraft	Lancaster II No. DS.726 'Y' of 408 Squadron
Date of Loss	12/13 June 1944
Target	Cambrai Railway Junction
Cause of Loss	Fighter attack followed by fire
Position of Loss	Target area

Information from	P/O B.J. La Pierre Gaston Jean Mid Under Gunner on 31st operation	
Captain & Pilot	S/Ldr. Stewart W.B.	All but two believed killed
Navigator	F/O Mallory G.E.	
Wireless Operator	P/O Bray G.	
F/engineer	Sgt. Varley H.	
Air Bomber	F/O Burns W.C.	
Mid Upper Gunner	P/O Ochsner R.D..	
Rear Gunner	W/O Murphy H.F.	
Route	Base—Flamborough—Docking—Sheerness—Dungeness—4955N 0113E—4953N 0205E—Target—5012N 0322E—5036N 0252E—5108N 0240E—Orfordness.	
Narrative	The Lancaster took off from Linton-on-Ouse at about 2200 hours. The French coast was crossed at about 5,000 ft. and the sortie was normal as far as the target area. The weather was fairly clear with starlight but no moon.	

The target was reached at 2355 hours, and the Lancaster made a run across the target, but the Air Bomber missed the T.I. markers. During this run the Mid Under Gunner saw an Me.110 pass below from astern to ahead. The Pilot turned to begin a second run, for which the Air Bomber was giving him directions. The Mid Under Gunner was throwing out WINDOW when he suddenly heard the Rear Gunner firing. Looking round he saw an Me.110, about 300 yards, below and astern, at which the Rear Gunner was firing. The Mid Under Gunner turned his gun round and saw his tracer strike the cockpit of the enemy aircraft which he believed was shot down.

The Lancaster was hit about the nose, in front of the bombbay and near the root of the port wing. Informant stated the strikes were M/G fire, not cannon. The port inner tank caught fire at once and the flames streaming back, enveloped the Mid Under Gunner's turret. The aircraft was now diving steeply and the Pilot gave the order to bale out. The Mid Under Gunner helped the Mid Upper Gunner to get out of his turret which was rendered difficult by the aircraft's acceleration. Flames were now entering the fuselage and the Mid Under Gunner baled out from his turret (pushing the M/Gs aside). His parachute worked normally and he made a good landing at midnight at Riemilly, south of Cambrai. He noticed one other 'chute descending.

Information was told afterwards that the aircraft had crashed on a German airfield nearby and that there were five bodies on board; also that one German fighter had been shot down.

On the Cambrai raid, nine aircraft were lost: forty-two men lost their lives, eleven men were captured, and fourteen men evaded capture. Canadian Squadron Leader William Benjamin Stewart (New Richmond Station, Quebec) was one of those who lost his life, along with fellow Canadians Flying Officer Gordon Mallory (Vancouver), Pilot Officer Robert Ochsner (Bittern Lake, Alberta) and Warrant Officer Harry Murphy (Kirkland Lake, Ontario). RAF airmen Sergeant Varley and Pilot Officer Bray similarly did not survive. The six airmen who died now rest in Seranvillers-Forenville Military Cemetery. Canadian Flying Officer Burns was captured, and Canadian Pilot Officer La Pierre evaded capture and was able to provide the information from which the "K" report was produced.

GERMAN AIR MINISTRY REPORT, 13 JUNE 1944,
DESCRIBING THE EFFECT OF THE ALLIED BOMBING
ATTACKS ON RAIL COMMUNICATIONS.

The raids carried out in recent weeks have caused the breakdown of all main lines; the coastal defences have been cut off from the supply bases in the interior, thus producing a situation which threatens to have serious consequences. Although even the transportation of essential supplies for the civilian population have been completely stopped for the time being and only the most vital military traffic is moved, large scale strategic movement of German troops by rail is practically impossible at the present time and must remain so while attacks are maintained at their present intensity.

TOP, LEFT Headstones of the Stewart crew: S/L Stewart, P/O Varley, W/O Murphy, P/O Ochsner, P/O Bray, F/O Mallory. STEVE DARLOW

TOP, RIGHT Rear gunner Alex Morvan McGregor, RCAF. McGregor was a pilot officer when he was shot down. CVWM VIA OPERATION PICTURE ME

BOTTOM, LEFT Enlistment ID card of W/O Harold Frederick Murphy, Stewart crew rear gunner. CVWM VIA OPERATION PICTURE ME

BOTTOM, RIGHT P/O Robert Duncan Ochsner, RCAF, mid-upper gunner. CVWM VIA OPERATION PICTURE ME

ABOVE, CLOCKWISE FROM TOP, LEFT F/O Earle Freeman Warren, RCAF, rear gunner; F/O Gordon Ewert Mallory, RCAF, navigator; P/O James Bond Bell, RCAF, during navigator training, Alberta, 1941–42 ; and P/O Angus Cameron Graham Mercer, RCAF. CVWM VIA OPERATION PICTURE ME

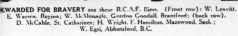

EWARDED FOR BRAVERY are these R.C.A.F. fliers. (Front row): W. Leavitt, E. Warren, Regina; W. McMonagle, Gordon Goodall, Brantford; (back row), D. McCable, St. Catharines; H. Wright, F. Hamilton, Mazewood, Sask.; W. Egri, Abbotsford, B.C.

ABOVE, LEFT *Toronto Star* coverage of DFM award to Earle Warren, 1943. CVWM VIA OPERATION PICTURE ME

ABOVE, RIGHT S/L William Benjamin Stewart, RCAF. CVWM VIA OPERATION PICTURE ME

The outstanding graduates of BCATP training often found themselves where they didn't want to be—training others who would go on to operational postings while they stayed behind as instructors. Edward "Teddy" Blenkinsop's professionalism, courage, and outstanding airmanship skills brought him this dubious reward for the first couple of years after graduating near the top of his class as a multi-engine pilot. When he finally made it to operations in the North African theatre, the same skills and self-discipline helped him and his crew survive a first tour. Starting his second tour with RCAF 405 Pathfinder Squadron, Teddy quickly rose to the role of deputy master bomber. On one of the leadup raids to D-Day against the rail yards at Montzen, however, a *Luftwaffe* night fighter ended their run. Teddy's luck held for a while longer, only to run out so close to war's end.

7

PATHFINDER LOST
AND ON THE RUN

KEITH C. OGILVIE

A S HER DUE date approached, Edward "Teddy" Blenkinsop's mother Winsome realized her isolated home in the Chilcotin region of British Columbia's interior might not be the best place to have her first child. Somewhat reluctantly, she made the decision to stay with her parents in Victoria where Teddy was welcomed into the world on October 8, 1920. A few months later, mother and child were back on their Bell Ranch homestead in Big Creek where Teddy spent his early years in what was perhaps a child's ideal growing environment: outside on his own, doing what he wanted in the fresh air.

Faced with putting Teddy into school, Winsome returned to Victoria in 1926, followed the next year by her husband. Teddy thrived in the Victoria school system, excelling in academics and athletics, particularly swimming. At sixteen, however, he developed back problems that required him to wear a body corset and, eventually, a body cast to support his spine. This personal challenge, his traditional Anglican upbringing, and the example of his strongly self-reliant parents no doubt provided the solid foundation of character and strong leadership that would win him respect for the rest of his life.

His cast made it impossible for Teddy to take a job that summer. He was soon brilliantly compensated, however, by an invitation from the Jukes family (four daughters and a son, school friends) to spend the vacation at their rented cottage on the ocean near Victoria. Son Arthur Jukes was at militia camp, and other contemporaries were working, so for five days every week, Teddy had the company of the girls to himself. He made a powerful impression on them all when he demonstrated his ingenuity in dealing with a leaking boat overloaded with teenagers when they foolishly tried to cross the open water of Haro Strait to the US islands. He beached the boat on an island, filled the cracks with pine resin heated over a fire and made it home safely with his passengers.

At the end of his memorable summer of leisure, Teddy moved to Vancouver to train as an apprentice accountant. He turned his attention and self-discipline to long days of work and making a home and friends in the city. His back was healing with regular exercise, and for the next two years, Teddy continued to advance through the learning stages in his prospective career.

MEANWHILE, THE drums of war were beating overseas. Teddy was unhappy with the loss of his first girlfriend, one of the Jukes sisters from his sixteenth summer, to an older rival. Three days after war was declared by Great Britain and a week before Canada made the same commitment, Teddy wrote to tell his parents that after careful thought he was considering joining the Royal Canadian Air Force. He was discouraged by family—he was only one of two men of his generation and the other was already serving. However, his sense of civic duty, a long-time interest in the experiences and sacrifices of family members in the trenches and Flying Corps during the First World War, and, no doubt, the loss of his girlfriend were the backdrop to his decision. He sent in his application and turned his attention back to his accounting studies, filling in the waiting days by spending his spare time watching the activity at what was then Sea Island Airport and talking to the local engineers about aircraft.

On March 8, 1940, the RCAF informed him that the previous enlistment conditions had changed and that he would have to resubmit his application. After further consideration—and more efforts to discourage him on the part of his family—he simply went to the Vancouver recruiting office on June 3 and enlisted. This time, the follow-up was quick. The next day he was signed in and put on a train to Toronto's No. 1 Manning Depot, absorbed as another small cog in the rapidly expanding BCATP machine. Two weeks of marching, polishing, and the usual humiliations to which recruits were traditionally subjected followed, then it was on to the Eglington Hunt Club (living in the horse stables, not the clubhouse) and No. 1 Initial Training School. Teddy and the other successful graduates were awarded the coveted propeller badges for their sleeves and issued flying suits, a helmet, and goggles. Excited at what lay ahead, Teddy returned whence he came, to Sea Island near Vancouver to join the first group through No. 8 Elementary Flying Training School's basic flight training course. He excelled in his ground school studies and did well in the air, especially on instrument flying. The next step—choosing between further training as a fighter or a bomber pilot—was a tough one for Teddy. Unusually, he opted for multi-engine training. His clear and honest understanding of his own strengths was reflected in a letter home:

> So many want to be fighter pilots and only a few will be so I thought I might as well apply for the big planes before they stuck me on them. You see I'm good on aerobatics but far better on instruments. Besides these fighter plans are too damned uncomfortable and anyway I black out easily.[21]

His choice was accepted. The Canadian prairie near Saskatoon was his next stop, building time on the Avro Anson, still a relatively straightforward aircraft but miles more complex than the simple Tiger Moths on which he had started. Again, Teddy did well on both ground and aerial elements but found a particular passion for navigation—perhaps his head for figures, honed through his accountancy apprenticeship. In any case, he demonstrated enough proficiency that the instructor began to use him as an assistant, casting the die for subsequent assignments. The head of the training unit noted him to be "an unusual man for his age. Has the greatest interest in Navigation . . . an excellent instructor with initiative . . ."

By the end of December 1940, Teddy had won his wings, standing near the front of his class. His performance also won him an officer's commission and, perhaps less rewarding in light of his anxiousness to get overseas, an eventual posting as an instructor. But first he was off to Rivers, Manitoba, for an advanced navigation course in the coldest place in Canada. Station records for January 24, 1941, state, "Coldest day. 41.7° below zero. Flying all day and night." Weather notwithstanding, Teddy again excelled, this time at the very top of his class.

A short break the following March allowed him time to travel home for the first time since his training began. He took advantage of the time not only to see his family and friends, but to build the start of a serious relationship with Helen Woodcroft. It was a short and intense visit with a lot of ground covered in ten days by the time he got on the train for the next phase of his career as an instructor back at Rivers.

The days were long and demanding, but Teddy made every effort to maintain his own flying proficiency as well as supporting other instructors as a check pilot. The class photos in which Teddy appears show a serious face among the smiles of his graduating students—but his off-duty photos suggest the ability to enjoy life when the opportunity arose.

At the end of August 1941, he left for the east coast to help set up an astronavigation school at Pennfield, New Brunswick. His performance as an instructor was again assessed as "outstanding." This, along with his unusual qualifications as both a trained pilot and a skilled navigator, led to a promotion to flight lieutenant and a unique appointment, in April 1942, to help the Royal New Zealand Air Force improve its own training performance record. This was a major responsibility indeed for a junior officer, and a reflection of Teddy's developing leadership capabilities as well as his technical skills.

Teddy and several colleagues left almost immediately from Montreal on the small arms carrier *Port Huon* for another type of adventure altogether—his first exposure to the shooting war. While off the American coast, his ship's convoy was attacked, and he witnessed several ships sunk. Two of the victims were Mexican ships, the result of which was that Mexico declared war on Germany.

On reaching the Caribbean, the convoy broke up, and Teddy's ship made its way through the tropical heat for Panama. This too was a new challenge, and more than enough for Teddy. He confessed to his parents that he would "sooner be at Rivers at 40 below."[22] The ship's supply of reading material was quickly exhausted, but Teddy was grateful for the forced rest. The trip provided some professional interest for him and his companions as well, as they were able to observe the impressive astronavigation skills of the ship's crew. Finally, two months after departing Montreal, they arrived at their destination in Wellington, New Zealand.

The original two-month assignment stretched into six months; by then Teddy was anxious to move on to an operational position. Avoiding a last-minute attempt to further delay his departure with a temporary attachment to the US Army Air Force in New Zealand, he left for Canada with several BCATP-bound RNZAF trainees on November 1, 1942. A short reunion with his family (and Helen) was followed by a brief assignment in Ottawa at RCAF headquarters, where he made clear his frustration with a life of instructing. Apparently, the message reached the right ears, for his long-sought posting overseas was confirmed not long after. He left for Britain to join active operations shortly after the turn of the year.

LIKE ALL the other new arrivals into the European theatre, and despite his now comparatively extensive flying experience, Teddy was put through the same introductory routines his students had encountered. As he waited for his advanced flying unit attachment, Teddy managed to get in touch with his uncle Max and spent some happy hours at the family home, a manor house in Royal Leamington Spa. This and subsequent breaks with the extended family made him feel quite at home and to some extent succeeded in keeping his mind off the delays in his further training. Finally, in the middle of February, Teddy was off to No. 3 AFU at Long Newnton in Wiltshire. He was grateful to be back in the air, honing his skills in night flying, blind flying, and navigation, now over unfamiliar territory.

Two months later, with a rare rating as an "above average pilot," Teddy reported to the Operational Training Unit at Wellesbourne Mountford, just southeast of Birmingham. On his first day, the chief navigation officer, an Australian with a DFC ribbon, greeted Teddy with the reminder that he had been one of Teddy's star students at Rivers... and was now in charge of the final stages of Teddy's own training.

The aircraft they would fly were Wellingtons, with a five-man crew. In this critical last stage before getting onto actual operations, the new crew would learn to work together while receiving an intensive introduction to the aircraft they would fly on operations. Teddy was determined that at least his navigator would be the best he could find. After a few days of careful observation in the classroom, Teddy approached Theodor "Ted" Howlett, a Canadian former math teacher from Nova Scotia. He probably used his network to hand pick the other members of the crew: John Miskae, from Winnipeg, as bomb aimer; Dennis "Ren" Renvoizé, an RAF volunteer, as wireless operator; and John "Jack" Nash as rear gunner. The Blenkinsop crew went through an increasingly challenging training regimen, starting with familiarization flights to get accustomed to the aircraft and moving on to complex navigation, practice bombing and night flying missions.

Under Teddy's leadership, the crew pulled together and on June 5, 1943, flew their "graduation" mission, an operation dropping leaflets on Vichy, south of Paris. There were the inevitable challenges—real or imagined sightings of enemy night fighters that made accurate navigation almost impossible and difficulties getting the leaflets out the correct hatch. The leaflets came back in as fast as the crew pushed them out, with the result that the inside of the aircraft, according to Ren, "soon resembled a newspaper office." The mission was finally accomplished, but with some doubt among the crew about who might have received the propaganda. Nonetheless, it was their first real mission, and they returned tired but satisfied.

A MONTH later, Teddy said his goodbyes to Uncle Max and family and departed from RAF Portreath in the southwestern corner of England for the sandstorms, heat, and flies of the Tunisian desert home of RCAF 424 Squadron. They spent eight and a half hours getting to Ras El Ma, only to meet a rocky start to their first operational posting. Teddy's crew arrived with no personal equipment suited to the environment, inappropriate clothing for the desert, and met an apparent lack of interest on the part of the receiving squadron officials—although their new aircraft immediately disappeared into another crew's hands.

A short stay was enough. Teddy quickly took matters in hand and a transfer to 425 "Alouette" Squadron followed. This time they were warmly welcomed. After a familiarization flight with another experienced aircrew, Teddy and his men were immediately thrown into the campaign against Italy. By early August, he had been tapped as deputy flight commander in addition to his flying responsibilities. On operations, Teddy was demanding, but his skills were openly acknowledged by his crew and their record of precision and successful missions, including assignments acting as "illuminator"—a kind of pathfinder role—spoke for itself. The powers that be acknowledged this record as well, awarding Teddy the rank of acting squadron leader at the beginning of October. Shortly thereafter, with thirty missions and an assortment of adventures under their belts, Teddy and the rest of the wing were ordered to return to Britain.

After two weeks of leave, Teddy returned to the squadron having determined to volunteer for a second tour of operations, preferably in a pathfinder role. Although they highly respected Teddy's leadership, his now well experienced crew members declined to join him, each preferring for individual personal reasons to be assigned to a safer instructor role. Teddy proceeded on his own to a conversion course for the four-engined Halifax III. On a brief leave in late January 1944, he was able to meet his friend Helen, now RCAF LAC Woodcroft, at a training base in York. Helen made a very cheerful report to Teddy's mother, Winsome, on the time they spent together: short, but enough for the two to agree on more serious plans for the future, once the risks of war had passed.

With something to look forward to, Teddy returned to 425 Squadron and its new aircraft. In wartime things rarely develop as expected. Teddy soon found himself in temporary command of the squadron when the CO was admitted to hospital on February 11. It wasn't to last, however; just over two weeks later, he was transferred to RCAF 405 (PFF)[23] Squadron to fly under the highly respected Wing Commander "Reg" Lane. Teddy's record shows 425 Squadron held him in high regard and were sorry to lose him: "This officer was an extremely capable leader of men and was respected by all. An excellent officer in all respects."

Joining 405, Teddy would have another chance to demonstrate these leadership skills in putting together a new crew. He invited two men he knew to have outstanding records and who had also applied for a second tour to join him in the Pathfinders. RCAF Flight Lieutenants Lawrence "Larry" Allen and David Ramsay, respectively the former navigation leader and bombing leader for 420 Squadron, both knew Teddy and immediately accepted. The nucleus of the new crew was in place.

Larry Allen was a first generation Canadian raised in Windsor, Ontario, by immigrant Jewish parents from Lithuania and Poland. He was also a university graduate whose intended career of journalism was interrupted by the war. Like Teddy, he was planning a more settled life after the conflict with his teenaged sweetheart, June Handley, but felt strongly he wanted to contribute to the Allied cause. His vision was poor enough to eliminate him from his first choice of pilot training, but he graduated from No. 1 Air Observers School as an "above average" navigator. Also like Teddy, he had completed his first tour with 420 Squadron in North Africa with an "exceptional" rating by his commanding officer, having served as squadron navigation leader.

David Ramsay was the son of immigrants who had settled from Scotland in Dysart, Saskatchewan, but who were forced to move when farming conditions on the prairies became disastrous during the 1920s drought years. They found a home in Port Alberni on Vancouver Island, where David pursued a successful career in banking. He joined the RCAF in 1941 and entered the training whirl, becoming one of the last graduates of the "long course" at No. 1 Air Navigation School at Rivers, Teddy's alma mater. David also served with 420 Squadron in North Africa, where his record of success and leadership earned him the Distinguished Flying Cross, appointment as squadron bombing leader, and high accolades from his commanders. On returning to England at the end of his first tour, David was initially assigned to an instructor role but managed to have this rescinded in favour of a transfer to 405 Squadron where Teddy invited him to join his growing crew as navigator/radar operator.

Another alumnus of 420 Squadron known to Larry and David was chosen as the crew's wireless operator. Flight Sergeant James "Sonny" Bradley was a Royal Air Force volunteer serving with the RCAF squadron. Trained in England, starting at 7 Initial Training Wing at Newquay in Cornwall, he had joined 420 Squadron with his crew and also served in North Africa, returning with the squadron to England. His crew was sent for conversion training on the four-engined Halifax, but in January of 1944, an engine failure and crash left two of his colleagues dead and the pilot seriously injured. Now on his own, James applied for a second tour, ending up in the company of familiar faces as the only non-Canadian member of the crew.

The new flight engineer, Pilot Officer Robert "Bob" Booth, had completed his first tour flying over Europe on some of Bomber Command's most dangerous missions, including Hamburg, Peenemünde, and Berlin, mostly with RCAF 419 Squadron. Bob was another prairie boy, born in Carberry, Manitoba, and raised in Winnipeg. He was working as a vehicle mechanic when he enlisted and initially served as a technical sergeant with RCAF 404 "Buffalo" Squadron in Sussex. In March 1943, after remustering to aircrew, he began his first tour as a flight engineer. He was commissioned in December 1943 to pilot officer before being invited to join Teddy's crew.

The two gunners were also Canadians. Pilot Officer Leslie Foster was a family man originally from Medicine Hat, Alberta. In late January 1943, after completing training at No. 3 Bombing and Gunnery School at MacDonald, Manitoba, he left his wife Florence and two daughters for an advanced gunnery course in England. He completed a harrowing first tour with RAF 77 Squadron and moved on to an instructional posting, all the time desperately missing his family. Rather than going home for a month and then having to return to operational duty, Leslie applied for a second tour and was assigned to 405 Squadron. He settled into the position of mid-upper gunner with the intention of heading home permanently at the end of his tour.

Nicholas Hugh Clifford, another family man, was the rear gunner and the oldest member of the crew. He had met Leslie during training at MacDonald and been posted to RCAF 432 Squadron as rear gunner on Wellingtons and Lancasters. Eschewing the inevitable instructional posting, he too applied immediately for a second tour of operations and was transferred to 405 Squadron ten days before his promotion to pilot officer. Hugh was all of thirty-five when he joined Teddy's crew, immediately earning him the honorific "grandpa."

ON MARCH 10, 1944, Teddy and his new crew returned from specialized pathfinder training to a squadron desperate for replacements. During the six weeks between mid-December 1943 and the end of January alone, eighty-seven pathfinder crews had crashed or gone missing.²⁴ After some additional training that included a flight for Teddy as second dickey on a mission to Stuttgart, the crew were put on the roster for a deep penetration raid to Nuremberg. It turned out to be a trial by fire, one of the costliest missions of the war. One hundred and five aircraft and crews were lost on that raid—with more airmen than were lost in the Battle of Britain—out of nearly eight hundred bombers assigned to the target, almost all destroyed by German night fighters or downed by flak. Teddy and his crew returned unscathed, but so many others had not been as lucky.

Bomber Command was now turning its attention to the buildup to D-Day and changing tactics accordingly. Greater attention was paid to key targets in Belgium and France: the railway system that might be used to reinforce German defences; coastal fortifications; radar stations and similar installations. Teddy's crew flew several of these missions, building their proficiency and performance record. In April, Teddy was notified that he had been awarded the Distinguished Flying Cross (DFC) in recognition of his successful operations against the enemy. The Blenkinsop crew's record and Teddy's exemplary leadership were further recognized with a singular honour when late that same month the Squadron Commander, Wing Commander Reg Lane, appointed Teddy the deputy master bomber—essentially Lane's designated successor as 405 Squadron's commanding officer.

This assignment carried with it the requirement to add another crew member, an experienced visual bomb aimer to support the pilot and navigator in ensuring the greatest accuracy possible in setting target markers for the incoming bomber stream. David Ramsay was the ideal choice for this position, but his move meant finding another radar set operator. F/L George Smith had been raised on a Saskatchewan farm and initially applied as a pilot but finished his training and served his first tour as a bomb aimer with RCAF 432 Squadron. He had also volunteered for an immediate second tour in the hopes of getting back to his new wife, Audrey, in Canada as quickly as possible. It was his old friend from 432 Squadron, Hugh Clifford, who introduced him to Teddy and the rest of the crew.

AS THEY arrived for lunch on April 27, 1944, the Blenkinsop crew were informed that Larry Allen had been awarded the DFC, the third in the crew. They also discovered they were on the duty roster for that night in their customary aircraft, "S-for-Sugar," leading a secondary raid over Montzen as backup to W/C Reg Lane, the designated master bomber. For Teddy and most of his crewmates, it was their fortieth operation over enemy territory. Teddy and his crew took off from Granston Lodge one minute after midnight. With W/C Lane, they made it to the target unmolested and began to set out the visual bombing markers. The main force bomber stream arrived shortly after, heavily harassed by enemy night fighters, flak and the ever-probing searchlights. Lane continued to provide direction to ensure the needed accuracy, resulting in significant damage to the Montzen rail yards. As the attack ended around 01:45, Lane directed Teddy and his crew to return to base, mission accomplished, and Lane's crew turned to follow shortly thereafter.

At the end of the returning bomber stream, Lane witnessed several aircraft shot out of the sky by the marauding night fighters, most employing the deadly *Schräge Musik* upward-firing cannon that allowed the attackers to close in below their victims without being seen. About twenty minutes after turning away from the target, he saw a massive explosion some ten miles ahead, with coloured pyrotechnic markers filling the sky. "I knew immediately that it was Teddy Blenkinsop's aircraft," Lane said, "as we were the only two bombers carrying those specific colours . . . judging from the size of the explosion, [I reported that] there was absolutely no chance of any survivors."[25] Pending formal confirmation of this assessment, Teddy and his crew were listed as missing.

AS THE first shells pounded through the aircraft from below and the bomber's remaining payload began to ignite, Teddy put the nose down and tried to keep his doomed aircraft stable. At about 300 feet, "S-for-Sugar" finally exploded and disintegrated. Only three of the crew seem to have been able to leave the blazing wreck at low altitude. The first of the crew recovered had jumped without a parachute, with the inevitable result. The second came down very close to the final point of impact and was later reported by local witnesses to have survived the low-level exit with serious injuries, only to be shot by his captors. The third was George Smith, who was picked up, also seriously injured, by the local Blackshirts—the Nazi collaborator organization—and taken to a German hospital in nearby Diest. An RCAF War Crimes Investigation Unit later determined that he had been "locked in a room, denied medical attention, food and drink for three days" and subsequently died from his injuries.[26]

The bulk of the wreckage and the balance of the crew, with the exception of Teddy, came down just west of the town of Webbe-kom in Belgium. The locals, those who were not associated with the Blackshirts, were respectful and sympathetic in dealing with the fallen airmen. The casualties were laid in state in the parish hall and later buried in the town churchyard.

UNAWARE OF the circumstances of the rest of his crew, Teddy regained consciousness on the ground near his open parachute. Miraculously, he had been blown clear as the Lancaster's fuselage came apart in the final explosion. His parachute somehow had opened in time to break his fall to earth. His whole body hurt, and he had lost his boots, but he found himself more or less intact. The commotion of enemy search parties and dogs soon motivated him to distance himself from the burning remains of his aircraft. He almost immediately ran into a sympathetic couple who gave him some water, farmer's clothes, and a pair of clogs, then led him to a nearby wood. Determined not to be caught, Teddy decided to strike out on his own, heading south until exhaustion overcame him. Hungry, cold, and in need of medical help for a painful shoulder injury, he fell asleep in a haystack. There he was discovered by another sympathetic farmer who gave him food and water, then contacted local members of the resistance.

By now, his parachute had been discovered and the local forces knew there was an airman on the run. On enemy soil, Teddy now had to rely on the skills and daring of others. Playing cat and mouse with the searchers, the resistance took Teddy to the farm of a partisan family in the remote village of Struik where he was cleaned up and finally had his shoulder—dislocated in the crash—attended to. But with the search for the missing airman intensifying around Webbekom, it was obvious Teddy had to move quickly to a more secure location.

On the evening of May 1, he was relocated to the home of a family in the town of Waanrode, about eight kilometres southeast of Webbekom. Teddy and his hosts became good friends during the two weeks he stayed with them, but that was the longest the resistance felt comfortable leaving their charges in the same place. He moved in for a little over a week with another family in Meensel, then billeted with a farmer named Schotsman in somewhat austere and isolated conditions in the neighbouring woods.

The amalgamated towns of Meensel and Kiezegem were a hotbed for the resistance movement but were also the home of a couple of notorious and committed families of Nazi sympathizers who were active in the local Blackshirts. For the most part the two sides lived in a kind of balance, knowing they could do each other severe harm, but the presence of different factions within the resistance meant that balance was not always respected. At some point while he was at the Schotsman farm, Teddy was convinced to accompany members of one of these factions on a nighttime mission to destroy the home of a well-known collaborator. The plan went awry, but Teddy, unarmed and having only been an observer to the action, returned unharmed . . . little knowing how this experience would ultimately determine his fate.

Teddy's stay at the Schotsman farm ended in the most innocent of circumstances when the younger brother of the person who regularly brought Teddy food bragged about the arrangement to school friends. After a couple of further moves, Teddy arrived at the farm of the Pypen family on the outskirts of Meensel. To prevent a repeat of the previous leak, he was presented to the family as the French boyfriend of the eighteen-year-old daughter, Paula. The arrangement worked until an incident on July 30, 1944, brought tragedy to the towns.

That day, a team of partisans from nearby Leuven killed the twenty-four-year-old son of one of the leading collaborator families. The SS responded in force. Despite attempts to get Teddy out of the area, he was captured on the early morning of August 11 as he fled the Pypen farm. A local man, under torture, identified him as having participated in resistance actions despite his only having observed that single event. Together with more than seventy locals—members of the local resistance and several other uninvolved townsfolk who were picked up in the Gestapo's sweep because of personal grudges—he was taken to the notorious St. Gilles prison in Brussels.

Teddy repeatedly asserted his status as an Allied airman and his entitlement to the norms for treatment of prisoners of war, but his civilian attire and lack of identification—and in particular his alleged association with the active resistance—worked against him. At one point in his incarceration, he found himself across a cell wall from an American prisoner of war. Talking through the pipes after lights out, Teddy was able to recount his incredible escape from the Lancaster and subsequent evasion, now ended with a death sentence. The American passed the story on in the prison shower to Stuart Leslie, another RCAF prisoner and—like Teddy—the sole survivor of his own bomber crew's being shot down.[27] The American had stated that Teddy "sounded desperate; wanted people to know what was happening to him." Leslie never met Teddy but was able to pass on his story months later to a debriefing officer in London, putting his situation on the formal record.

In late August, as the Allies closed in on Brussels, Teddy was loaded along with a first group of Meensel prisoners onto a train bound for Germany. A second trainload of prisoners, with Stuart Leslie aboard, never left the station in Brussels, thanks to what Leslie described as "the heroic efforts of the local resistance generally, and one particularly determined train engineer." As the second so-called Ghost Train waited to depart, fully loaded with its human cargo, the railcar doors were thrown open and the prisoners jumped to freedom as their captors disappeared. The train was commandeered for a more urgent priority: to transport retreating German troops.

Teddy had just missed by hours his last opportunity for escape. For him and his companions, conditions on the train were frightful, but not as frightful as those in their destination: Neuengamme concentration camp. Despite his ongoing protestations, Teddy continued to be held as a political prisoner and was put into forced labour at the Hamburg shipyards. Severe malnutrition, constant heavy physical work, and lack of proper clothing took the inevitable toll and Teddy contracted tuberculosis as the winter set in. Sometime early in the New Year, he was transferred to the notorious Bergen-Belsen, where he died on January 23, 1945, according to German records from "heart failure"—usually the consequence of a lethal injection. His body was cremated.

EVERY YEAR at the end of April, the people of Webbekom commemorate with fresh flowers and a Sunday mass the sacrifice of the seven members of the "S-for-Sugar" crew who are buried in the churchyard. Only seven of the locals detained by the SS in the August 1944 raid came home. Like the others who were taken that fateful day and failed to return, Teddy has no known grave. He is instead commemorated with thousands of other lost airmen at the Air Forces Memorial in Runnymede, England. He is also honoured on a headstone in the memorial park erected in Meensel-Kiezegem to keep alive the memory of all the victims of the tragic events of that summer. An annual service at the beginning of August commemorates their collective contribution to their town, Teddy among them.

TOP, LEFT Newly commissioned Pilot Officer Edward "Teddy" Blenkinsop in front of an Avro Anson at No. 4 SFTS. BLENKINSOP FAMILY, VIA JOHN NEROUTSOS AND PETER CELIS

TOP, RIGHT Robert Booth, RCAF, flight engineer. HARRY BOOTH VIA PETER CELIS/ GRUB STREET

BOTTOM, LEFT David Ramsay, RCAF, H2S set operator and visual bomb aimer. PETER RAMSAY VIA PETER CELIS/GRUB STREET

BOTTOM, RIGHT George Smith, RCAF, H2S set operator. HERMAN SMITH VIA PETER CELIS/GRUB STREET

TOP, LEFT James "Sonny" Bradley, RAF, wireless operator. MICHAEL PARKER VIA PETER CELIS/GRUB STREET

TOP, RIGHT Larry Allen, RCAF, navigator. JUNE HANDLEY VIA PETER CELIS/GRUB STREET

BOTTOM, LEFT Leslie Foster, RCAF, mid-upper gunner. LESLIE W. FOSTER VIA PETER CELIS/GRUB STREET

BOTTOM, RIGHT Nicholas Clifford, RCAF, rear gunner. ROBERT C. DICKSON VIA PETER CELIS/GRUB STREET

TOP, LEFT A painting by John Rutherford of action over Montzen. The aircraft in foreground is Lancaster "S-for-Sugar" being followed by a Ju 88 night fighter. The Lancaster in background is LQ-V, piloted by W/C Reg Lane. COURTESY BOMBER COMMAND MUSEUM OF CANADA

BOTTOM, LEFT Elementary flying training at No. 8 EFTS, Sea Island, BC. Ed Fleishman, Ed Burton, Jim Grant, and Teddy Blenkinsop returning from August 1940 training flights in Tiger Moths. CAF PL1532 VIA PETER CELIS

RIGHT Teddy Blenkinsop with Hilaire Gemeux, May 1, 1944. Hilaire was a resistance fighter whose family were among the first to hide Teddy. LEA GEMOETS VIA PETER CELIS

In the early hours of Friday, April 28, 1944, the familiar droning sound of heavy bombers could be heard by those far below. RAF Bomber Command was sending hundreds of Lancasters and Halifaxes, laden with thousands of gallons of fuel and thousands of pounds of bombs, into the dark sky, heading east. Numerous targets had been designated, including the rail yards at Montzen, detailed as part of the air plan to support the forthcoming D-Day landings. For one of the crews chosen to attack the target that night, made up of seven Canadians and one Briton, it was to be their final flight. They, like Teddy Blenkinsop and his crew, would not be returning home.

8

ST. TROND,
A CHANCE MEETING

MARC HALL

THE MAIN TARGET for the night of April 27/28, 1944, was the military factories at Friedrichshafen, but other smaller raids were detailed in an attempt to keep the night fighters from the main bombing force. These smaller attacks included targets at Montzen in Belgium and Aulnoye in France, together with another diversionary raid by operational training unit aircraft over the North Sea towards Jutland.

At 23:23 hours Canadian Bomber Command pilot John Gilson pushed the throttles fully forward and the four Hercules motors roared under the strain. Slowly the heavily laden bomber lumbered down the runway, gathering speed, leaving British soil for the last time. With a belly full of high explosives and wings full of fuel, Halifax MZ536 slowly gained height. On board the vibrations from the four power plants ran through the fuselage as the motors steadied into a constant drone and the crew settled to their tasks. The target for this particular crew was the busy marshalling and railway yards at Montzen, located in Eastern Belgium and a short distance from the German border.

H-hour was planned for 01:30 hours, the raid consisting of three separate waves of aircraft, the second and third of which were to suffer the heaviest losses. It appears that there were delays with the assembly of the enemy night fighters, and most of the first wave managed to evade their attention. The night fighter controllers were confronted with four separate bomber streams, and it took some time before they could coordinate an adequate response against the intruders. Once the possible route of the bombers was established, several night fighters were sent at speed towards Aachen, to the northeast of the marshalling yards. But most arrived too late, and by 01:44 hours the raid was over, with the stream already heading for home and the target in flames. However, as the main bomber force withdrew, the German night fighters began to mount a ferocious and effective response against the bomber stream. Several of the interceptors were being flown by *Nachtjagdgeschwader* 1 aces who had taken off as the raiders flew past St. Trond. A meeting was being held nearby which several high-ranking night fighter aces and commanders were attending, and when the alarm was sounded, they responded. Many Bomber Command airmen would lose their lives at the hands of these experienced pilots, some of whom pursued their foe out across the North Sea. The night fighters managed to shoot down fifteen of the heavy bombers: fourteen Halifaxes and a Lancaster failed to return that night. One of these was Halifax MZ536, destroyed with the loss of all the crew.

As the Halifax neared the target, Dale Loewen, bomb aimer on MZ536, had issued directions to the pilot, with the bomb doors open. Bombs released, target photograph taken, and bomb doors closed, the crew now had one objective: to set course for home and get there as quickly and safely as possible. Approximately forty minutes after H-hour, however, the bomber came into the sights of a stalking Messerschmitt Bf 110 G4 interceptor captained by Oberleutnant Georg-Hermann Greiner of II/NGJ1. From below and behind, most likely unseen under the cover of darkness, the Bf 110's guns opened up and riddled the aircraft. The fate of the crew and bomber was sealed. The second victory of the night for the night fighter ace Greiner—his twenty-third claim.

It is likely that the unsuspecting crew never knew what hit them. There was an instant fire in one of the wings, the fuel was ablaze, the surrounding night sky illuminated. Even if the night fighter had been seen, it appears it had been too late for anything to be done about it. With the Halifax, then at approximately 4,200 metres, engulfed in flames the aircraft immediately began falling. One can only surmise that those inside stood little prospect of escape. The aircraft was witnessed plummeting from the sky at 02:12 hours—a large red fireball plunging earthwards, hitting the ground and exploding with great force, completely destroying it, and scattering wreckage. The place of the crash was one kilometre to the northwest of a small village named Trognée, Belgium. Sometime afterwards the remains of the crew and wreckage was cleared from the site and the airmen were buried two days later on the April 30, 1944, in the Fort Borsbeek Antwerpen-Deurne cemetery. (There was another cemetery at St. Trond near Trognée, but the salvage team came from another base in Belgium. This may explain the distance between the crash site and the burial location.) The Germans were unable to correctly identify all the crew and the *Totenlist* (death list) number 219 recorded: Sergeant Greig (also shown as *Grnid*), grave 129; Sergeant Wilson, grave 130; Airman Vorsith (also shown as *Forsith*), grave 131; Airman Holloway, grave 132; Flying Officer Loewen, grave 133; Sergeant Hanson, grave 134; two unknown airmen, graves 135 and 136.

THE INFORMATION was relayed back to the Air Ministry via an International Red Cross telegram quoting German Information. As there was no Airman Holloway in this crew and this name was not identified as a casualty anywhere within the Air Ministry's files, he was assumed to be another unknown until he could be identified and the case of the missing crew could be cleared up by the Missing Research and Enquiry Service. When the investigation was carried out, taking into account that five airmen were identified and that the Halifax had a crew of eight, these three unknown men were assumed to be part of that crew. The bodies were eventually exhumed from their original graves and reburied in December 1945 in the Antwerp Schoonselhof cemetery, Wilrijk, a suburb of Antwerp, Belgium.

THE RAID proved to be only partly successful. Just the eastern parts of the railway yards were hit, with destruction and damage to railway tracks, sheds, storage depots, a good number of locomotives and wagons. Even so, it appears the rail yards were up and running again within two weeks.

THE EIGHT-MAN crew of MZ536 had been with No. 431 Squadron since the March 13, 1944. The bomb aimer was Flying Officer Dale Howard Loewen, born on October 30, 1920, in the small town of Scott, Saskatchewan, to John and Catherine Loewen. Dale was their youngest son, one of six siblings. Dale worked as a labourer after leaving school in 1937 but had his sights set on aviation and found his opportunity to study aeronautics at a technical school in Saskatoon with the Royal Canadian Air Force. He enlisted as ground crew and qualified as an air frame mechanic, a profession he continued with until late 1942, when he volunteered for aircrew. His assessments in June 1942 described him as "alert" and of "good material," so Dale started training with No. 7 Air Observer School in Portage la Prairie, Manitoba. He received his commission on June 25, 1943. Although he scored well in the exams, he was found unsuitable for the role of navigator and so transferred to the bomb aimers course, his assessors recording, "Good type lad. Above average intelligence. A bit torn down after flunking out at the Air Observers School but should equal to the task of air bomber if he gets down to work." He was subsequently found to be above average, and at the end of July 1943, he was boarding a ship in Halifax, bound for the UK. After the usual welcome and familiarization training, he was sent to No. 82 Operational Training Unit, prior to a transfer to RCAF 431 Squadron.

PILOT OFFICER Richard William Pratt was the aircraft's wireless operator. Born on June 1, 1911, in Quebec, Richard was one of the older members of the crew. He had four sisters and two brothers at home. His father had passed away in 1935, and he had lost a younger brother in 1924. Following school, Richard worked with the International Paper and Pulp Company as a logger. In his spare time, he played soft ball, baseball, and hockey, and seemed to enjoy outdoor life. He had applied to the RCAF on December 5, 1939, and was told to wait, but he reapplied and was enlisted on June 11, 1940, for ground duties as an equipment assistant. Not content, Richard requested to be trained for aircrew, as a gunner, stating he was not accustomed to working indoors. Following several failed applications, he was finally successful.

Richard trained at No. 2 Wireless School in Calgary from December 8, 1941, through to June 22, 1942, and came forty-two out of seventy-three in the class with a score of 74.3 percent—"average ability." He was sent on a gunnery course in July 1942, coming fourth in the class, earning comments from his instructors including "dependable" and "ground training very satisfactory." Leaving Canada for the United Kingdom in January 1943, he finally arrived at No. 103 Squadron, but eleven days later was sent to No. 487 Squadron where he remained until October 1943. His next posting was to No. 82 Operational Training Unit prior to arrival at No. 431 Squadron.

THE REAR gunner, the loneliest job in the crew, was Pilot Officer John Wilson, a Scottish national born on July 19, 1923, in Possilpark, Glasgow. He was one of four children to John and Margaret Wilson. Six years after his birth the family emigrated to Canada and settled in Toronto. When he left school, John took a job as a busboy at the Royal York Hotel, where he stayed until April 1941, leaving to work for the Dunlop Rubber Company. A month later he volunteered for the RCAF as an air gunner. Following training in which he scored 74 percent on his final exam, he left Canada and arrived in the UK on September 19, 1943, to undertake further training with the No. 82 Operational Training Unit. Flying mainly on Wellingtons, and building up a total of 82.25 flying hours, John impressed his instructors, his senior armament officer remarking: "Quite good results. Willing to work hard, a very good type." John had only taken part in six operations with the squadron, including the raid to Montzen. His mother appeared to be unaware that her son was actively flying on operations. Perhaps John had not wished to burden her with the reality of war. A handwritten letter below from John's mother to the RCAF, dated May 25, 1944, stated:

Dear Sirs

In reference to file number 198432b (No. 4) will you please give me a little further information regarding my son who is missing after air operations overseas. I did not know that he was flying, he held it back from me to keep me from worrying. Could you please let me know how many operations he had taken part in.

PILOT OFFICER Gordon Templeton Greig occupied the mid-upper gun turret aboard the Halifax. Born in Saskatoon on the June 3, 1922, to James and Jessie Greig, Gordon was one of six children, with two brothers and three sisters. He left Fort Frances High school in 1940 to study business at Brantford Business College, then started work with the Slingsby Manufacturing Company. Gordon enlisted for flying with the RCAF on November 5, 1942, and it seems he was certainly keen, his interviewing officer commenting "Neat, clean cut type, fond of sports, wants aircrew in any capacity." Having been accepted as an air gunner, Gordon started his gunnery course on the July 12, 1943, completing it on August 20, 1943. His commanding officer commented: "good student, no difficulty in understanding but routine worker, not much initiative. Dependable, takes the lead occasionally." He shipped out for the UK on September 13, 1943. At No. 82 Operational Training Unit, he completed further training on the Wellington, obtaining comments such as "good crew member, good gunner" from his seniors.

THE MID under gunner was Flight Sergeant George Quist Hansen of Standard, a remote village surrounded by miles of open farmland in Alberta. Born on April 6, 1919, George was the son of Hilda and James Hansen, both Canadian citizens but originally from Sweden and Denmark respectively. George was one of six children, three of his brothers also serving in the Armed Forces. He completed his education locally and left school in 1933 at the age of fourteen. He helped his father in their family store until 1938 before becoming a miner. He left in 1939 to take up driving positions with two different companies until 1940, finishing as a clerk with a grocery business in 1942. When he enlisted for the RCAF the medical officer's report mentioned "considerable flying experience as pilot." George expressed an interest to serve as a pilot or air gunner but was assessed as medically unfit for the role of pilot owing to poor eye muscles. He was sent on a wireless operator's course, but it seems he struggled, finding Morse code difficult to grasp and having missed part of the course when briefly hospitalised. Brought back for reselection in January 1943, George expressed a desire to be an air gunner, and eventually undertook a gunnery course, faring much better and qualifying on June 23, 1943. His instructor noted: "Displays good gunnery sense in the air, obliging, co-operative and should make a capable Air Gunner." George was posted overseas in July 1943. He left behind a wife, whom he had married on August 27, 1942, and a one-year-old son.

FLYING OFFICER Thomas Rex Forsyth was the aircraft's navigator. Born October 22, 1912, in Magrath, Alberta, he was one of the older members of the crew. Following his basic education and a period of general work on a farm, Thomas went on to study philosophy and English at university prior to enlisting with the RCAF on April 8, 1942, in Calgary, Alberta. Thomas's hobbies included skating, swimming, and softball, and particularly photography as an amateur and a professional developer. He scored well on his assessment; his interviewing officers rated him highly and recording that "his life on the farm has trained him to be constantly on the alert and he can be depended on for clear thinking and prompt decisive action in the event of serious emergencies." Other comments from his interviewing officer included "resolute, straight forward and above average air crew."

Thomas had enlisted with the RCAF because he saw it as an alternative to the army draft and one that offered better learning opportunities. Although he claimed a long-standing interest in flying, he did mention to his assessors that he felt insecure in the air but could get used to it. He wanted to be an observer, feeling that he was not particularly well equipped to be a pilot. Thomas soon began navigator training and seemed at home with both the theory and practical work. Having qualified as a navigator on March 19, 1943, rated as "above average," he was commissioned as a pilot officer and posted overseas in April 1943. He was promoted to flying officer on September 19, 1943, and continued his training at No. 6 Advanced Flying Unit and No. 82 Operational Training Unit before being taken on strength with No. 431 Squadron on March 13, 1944. His wife would become a widow a few short weeks later.

SERGEANT ROBERT WALLACE of the Royal Air Force Volunteer Reserve was the flight engineer on the crew. Unfortunately, little is known regarding this particular airman.

THE CREW'S PILOT, Pilot Officer John "Jack" Gilson was born on June 20, 1921, in Traynor, Saskatchewan, the only son of Thomas and Elizabeth Gilson. At an early age, John moved with his parents and two sisters the short distance from the town of Scott, where he struck up a friendship with the boy who would years later become the bomb aimer on his crew, Dale Loewen. They would follow different paths to their ultimate positions: while Dale was learning to become an airframe mechanic, John enlisted with the RCAF on October 29, 1940, for ground duties. He clearly saw a chance to aim higher, for in early 1941 he applied to re-muster for aircrew and started the path to becoming a pilot. On completion of his elementary flying training in April 1942, John was deemed of "average ability" with a weakness in aerobatics, though it was mentioned that he should do well if pushed. John qualified as a sergeant pilot, received his wings on August 28, 1942, and was posted overseas to the UK. Intensive training followed at No. 6 Advanced Flying Unit, from November 17, 1942, until February 6, 1943—night flying, instrument flying, and general-purpose flying. His commanding officer reported him as "a tough but dependable type who has coped well with the course on the whole, should make a good operational pilot." John quickly progressed with two further promotions. He was to receive his commission on April 26, 1944, just two days before he was killed.

In 1942, when he first arrived in the UK, John had contacted some of his relatives. During a break in training in early 1944, they all met up at his Aunt Nell's home in Staffordshire for some "home cooking." As John was leaving his Aunt asked him to "come back soon,'" John had turned to her and said, "Somehow, I don't think I will be." Whether this was a thoughtful response or an off-the-cuff remark, John's prescience was sadly accurate. He and his boyhood friend Dale would be lost together in only a few short months.

TOP, LEFT Childhood friends Dale Loewen and John Gilson on leave in Edinburgh. RUSS AND FRED BUGLAS

TOP, MIDDLE Thomas Forsyth, RCAF, navigator. CVWM VIA OPERATION PICTURE ME

TOP, RIGHT George Hansen, RCAF, mid-under gunner. NATIONAL ARCHIVES OF CANADA VIA MARC HALL

BOTTOM, LEFT Gordon Greig, RCAF, mid-upper gunner. NATIONAL ARCHIVES OF CANADA VIA MARC HALL

BOTTOM, MIDDLE Richard Pratt, RCAF, wireless operator. THOMAS AND RICHARD MACLEOD

BOTTOM, RIGHT John Wilson, RCAF, rear gunner. CVWM VIA OPERATION PICTURE ME

TOP The Halifax crew. Dale Loewen is in the back row, far right, and John Gilson,
second from right. RUSS AND FRED BUGLAS

BOTTOM *Saskatchewan Star Phoenix* coverage of the loss of boyhood friends
Gilson and Loewen. CVWM VIA OPERATION PICTURE ME

The Canadian-built Lancaster KB713 of RCAF No. 419 Squadron failed to return to RAF Middleton Saint George on the night of May 12/13, 1944, following a raid to the rail yards and junctions at Louven (Louvain), a small town in Belgium. A previous strike on the evening of May 11 had produced disappointing results, so a large force of heavy bombers was sent two nights later to smash a target deemed essential in the run-up to the forthcoming invasion. The entire seven-man crew of Pilot Officer Burdel Edward's Lancaster, all graduates of the BCATP, would perish that night. Each now rests in a Belgian cemetery, his life and stories prematurely ended.

9

UNBEKANNT FLIEGERS

MARC HALL

PATHFINDERS ILLUMINATED THE target at Louvain at approximately 00:26 hours. The main force arrived a few minutes later. The full attack opened at 00:30 hours and was over within fifteen minutes. This time the results appeared to be considerably better than those of the previous night's raid, with plenty of damage to the rail network and sheds. But there had been losses. Five heavy bombers failed to return, with many lives on the ground sacrificed. Lancaster KB713 did not make it to the target, shot down not far from the French coast with the loss of all its crew.

Sometime before 22:00 hours, seven crewmen had boarded the aircraft and settled into their positions. The pilot and flight engineer carried out their pre-startup checks under the dim lights in the cockpit. The first of the four Rolls-Royce engines turned over, then slowly popped and spluttered into life, the three others following until all were smoothly running in rhythm. Permission was given to taxi to the runway and join the queue of waiting aircraft.

A quick flash of a green Aldis lamp gave the all-clear, and KB713 lined up on the runway for the last time. Flying Officer Edwards pushed the throttles forward, easily countered the swing and the Lancaster left the ground, climbing into the dark night sky and slowly gaining altitude. Flight time was estimated at four hours forty minutes with the crew due back at 02:40 hours the following morning.

As they crossed the French coast the crew ran into trouble, receiving the unwanted attention of a prowling twin-engine Ju 88 night fighter that opened fire on the lumbering bomber, still heavily laden with fuel and bombs. KB713, almost certainly set ablaze, reddening the night sky, was believed to have fallen quickly to the guns of Unteroffizier Martin Siegel from II/NJG 2, between 00:45 and 01:00 hours near Dunkirk at a height of 2,400 metres. The burning Lancaster slammed into the soft ground of a farmer's field close to the Yser canal and exploded in a large fireball with the larger parts of the aircraft burying themselves deep into the ground. The impact left a large crater twelve metres deep. The entire crew were killed, unable to escape the falling aircraft.

Following the end of the Second World War the loss was investigated by No. 7 section of the No. 2 section Missing Research and Enquiry Service, led by Squadron Leader P.E. Laughton-Bramley. The crash site was located at Reninge, Belgium. It was established from eyewitness reports and local villagers that the aircraft still had its full bomb load on board when it hit the ground, causing an almighty explosion. When the investigating officer visited the town on February 28, 1946, four eyewitnesses were interrogated, including the former pro-German burgomaster, the former pro-German secretary of the town hall and cemetery wardens. All declared that on the night in question a four-engined bomber had come down at Hameau De Knokke, Reninge, from the direction of the coast. The witnesses thought that an anti-aircraft battery had shot the aircraft down; however, captured German documents showed the aircraft had been claimed by a night fighter at 01:00 hours. An extract from the German records stated: "Lancaster shot down by a night fighter on 13-05-44 at 01:00 hours at Reninge, 10 km South West of Dixmuden. The aircraft crashed and exploded with the bomb load, 100% destroyed. Only parts of bodies were found, all crew probably dead."

What remained of the crew had been collected by the villagers on the same day as the crash and buried in three small wooden coffins in grave No. 16 in the British plot at Reninge Military cemetery.

Two days later the upper body of a deceased airman was found with an identification disc inscribed "R.118580 SMITH, R.S, RCAF." The body was taken by the Germans and buried separately on May 16 in the military cemetery at Coxyde, located in West-Vlaanderen, in a single grave at the end of a row of British soldiers killed in 1940. An exhumation at this cemetery confirmed that this was the remains of Flight Sergeant Smith. The aircrew buried at Reninge in three coffins were located in the corner of the cemetery, a small gap being cut from the boundary hedge to make room for the grave. A small wooden cross with a union jack painted on it read "*Unbekannt Fliegers 13 mai 1944*" (Unknown Airmen, May 13, 1944). Several items were recovered including parts of the navigator's bag, engine number plates, and clothing.

In July 1947, Reverend Harvey Campbell and his wife Grace Campbell (a well known and respected Canadian author), the parents of twins Robert and Alexander Campbell, travelled from Canada to the continent via London to visit the graves of their two sons. Flying Officer Robert Roy Campbell and Pilot Officer Alexander Campbell were killed in action within five weeks of each other. Their parents visited Reninge and found the collective grave containing the mixed remains of six airmen. At the time, the grave was being cared for by Yvonne Hermans, a resident of Brugge (twenty miles away) who attended on a regular basis to lay flowers. Reverend Campbell asked that the remains be moved to Adegem Canadian War Cemetery, as the men buried there were Canadians and continued care would be simpler. It appeared no locals in the Reninge area were caring for the grave, which had been placed out of the way up against a tool shed.

The request was initially turned down by the War Graves Commission, who responded: "Where so many relatives are concerned, there is bound to be some difference in the wishes expressed. Many applications for removal have been made, and had to be refused for it is necessary, even if sometimes difficult, for the Commission to follow a consistent line of equality to all. It is not a question of trouble or expense but simply adherence to a rule of action which is generally accepted, and the dissatisfaction which would result if different decisions were made in different cases can be readily visualised." However, the Commission also committed to launch an enquiry into the concern expressed by the Campbells, and stated that the grave would not be left in its present location if it was not possible to ensure a high standard of maintenance. Further action was indeed taken, as the remains of the six crew who were buried in Reninge military cemetery now rest in a collective grave in Adegem, the exhumation and relocation having taken place in 1968.

Though initially memorialized as *Unbekannt Fliegers*, the crew of Lancaster KB713 each left a legacy. Flying Officer Robert Roy Campbell was the aircraft's navigator and one of three sons to Reverend Harvey and Grace. Robert and his twin brother Grant were born on October 7, 1922, in Glengarry, Ontario. Robert left full-time education at Regina College to join the RCAF on December 13, 1941, requesting flying duties, preferably as a pilot but willing to fill other aircrew positions. At No. 2 Initial Training School, he did extremely well in all subjects, scoring 91.4 percent, and was highly recommended as having the ability and temperament to be a navigator. He was noted to be a "leading student in his flight." In July 1942, he began an air navigator's course at No. 3 Air Observers School in Regina, again scoring well in his exams. Robert was described by the chief instructor as having a "very pleasing personality and he gets along well with his fellows." He was awarded his navigator wings on October 23, 1942, and promoted to sergeant. It appears his twin brother Grant followed a similar trajectory. Grant also graduated from the BCATP as a navigator, and the two left together that December for the UK to finish their training. Given Robert's excellent record, he was probably diverted to an instructor's position, as he was only posted to No. 419 Squadron on March 16, 1944, to begin operations. In the interim, he had been awarded a commission and subsequent promotion. His death came on his third bombing mission, almost one month after his twin brother—also flying Lancasters with RAF 576 Squadron—was lost in another operation over France. The family in Ontario can only have been devastated at this latest news.

PILOT OFFICER Peter Dewar was born on July 1, 1914, in Lethbridge, Alberta, one of three siblings, to Thomas and Janet Dewar. Peter's parents had been born, raised, and were married in Stirling, Scotland, before moving to Canada. Prior to enlisting in July 1942, Peter had tried a variety of occupations: stenographer, clerk, ore sorter and carpenter's helper. Described as very quiet and with a sincere manner, Peter had been an athletic type who played hockey, baseball, and rugby. The general medical board was of the opinion that Peter would have trouble with studying as it had been eight years since he had left school. Nonetheless, he was assessed as potential observer material, with refreshment in mathematical subjects, and recommended for active duty as aircrew. He passed the air bomber's course on May 23, 1943, at No. 7 Air Observers School, although the chief instructor recorded that he could have applied himself better, was a little lax, and at times lacked self-drive. Arriving in the UK on his birthday in 1943, Peter spent most of the next year improving his skills before finally being posted for active service on March 16, 1944. His commission to the rank of pilot officer was received two days prior to his death. He left behind a wife, Kathleen Mary Dewar, whom he had married in June 1941, and two young sons, Thomas and Donald Dewar. His memorial stone is inscribed: "In memory of our dear Peter. 'Peace.' Wife and sons. Mother and dad, brother and sister."

THE AIRMAN manning the Lancaster's wireless set was Pilot Officer Roy Stanley Smith of Hamilton, Ontario. Born on October 11, 1922, to Violet and Blake Smith, Roy had three siblings: two brothers and a sister. He attended Hamilton Technical School studying industrial electrics, at the same time holding down a job as a delivery boy with Dominion Stores Ltd. After three years as a packer with Balfours Ltd., Roy became a machine operator with the Boston Insulated Wire and Cable Company while taking a machine shop course at Westdale Technical night school in the evenings. In March 1941, Roy offered his services to the RCAF. With an obvious interest and background in technical matters and machines, Roy first enlisted as an airframe mechanic, subsequently volunteering for flying duties towards the end of 1942. A reference from a previous employer stated, "I have known Roy Stanley Smith and his family for many years. His father was decorated for bravery in the last war and this young man has the same brave spirit of his sire. I can vouch for his honesty, trustworthiness and cheerful disposition. He is a bright and intelligent man, keen on mechanics and undoubtedly would be a great asset in any branch of the Royal Canadian Air Force."

Roy made it clear he had an interest in radio and had experience carrying out minor repairs, so wireless operator was the perfect aircrew trade for Roy. He was remustered accordingly and sent on course at No. 4 Wireless School in Guelph, his examiners rating him "above average." He went on to No. 2 Gunnery School in Mossbank, Saskatchewan, where he was again recognized to be "academically above average." His instructors also noted that Roy was "quite aggressive" in his approach and that he was a "hard worker."

On completion of his training in Canada, Roy was posted overseas and left Halifax, Nova Scotia, on July 16, 1943, to arrive at Greenock, Scotland, six days later. After honing his skills at No. 11 Radio School and completing the heavy bomber conversion course with No. 22 Operational Training Unit, Roy finally joined No. 419 Squadron on March 16, 1944. Only two days before he was killed, a promotion was issued to the rank of pilot officer. Roy left behind an English girlfriend. He was on his third operation when he was shot down.

FLYING OFFICER Joseph Alexander Webber was one of the Lancaster's air gunners, manning the small, cramped mid-aircraft turret defending the aircraft from attack. He was the oldest crew member, born on March 27, 1913.[28] Joseph was one of seven children of Joseph and Sarah Webber who raised their family in Calgary, Alberta. After leaving school, Joseph followed in the footsteps of his father as an apprentice paperhanger and painter. He was initially employed and taught by his father, working six years with him up until 1935. He then took employment with Crossland and Beale, a painting contractor business, until 1941. A family man, Joseph had three young sons and a wife Lillian, whom he married on March 13, 1937, in Sarcee, Alberta.

Joseph joined the RCAF in June 1941 as a security guard and was posted to the Penhold Manning Depot, carrying out general security duties. The following year, he applied to change to air gunner duties. He impressed his interview board; his record states "anxious to get in aircrew and should make a good air gunner." His personnel officer noted, "education suitable, class score very good. This airman might make observer or pilot with a short education course." Having passed the selection board, Joseph was assigned to a gunnery course with the No. 8 Gunnery School in Lethbridge on July 5, 1942. He was awarded the air gunner's badge on September 25, 1942. He clearly performed well, as he was then assigned to instructor training, followed by a position as a gunnery instructor at No. 3 Bombing and Gunnery School in Macdonald, Manitoba. It was not until December 1943 that he was finally posted overseas.

Following the heavy conversion course Joseph was sent, with his crew, to No. 419 Squadron for operational duty. Less than eight weeks later, he was missing. As did the relatives of so many of these airmen, his wife Lillian remained optimistic. In a letter to an RCAF casualty officer dated March 10, 1945, she wrote: "Dear Sirs, In answer to your letter for information concerning my husband, Flying Officer Joseph Alexander Webber, I have had no news concerning him and I wish to thank you for your kind sympathy in the past and now. I will not let my hopes down for his safe return until this fight is over. I am yours sincerely, Mrs. Lillian Webber."

FLYING OFFICER Harold Engman Oddan, the other air gunner on board KB713, was born in Manitoba on March 12, 1911, one of three sons to Ole and Mary Oddan. They also had six daughters. Like many of the young men who enlisted from the prairie regions, Harold had a farming background. He worked on his father's farm until 1935, then left to run his own farm in Chamberlain, Saskatchewan, until he decided to enlist in the RCAF in 1941. Harold was keen to fly, as either a wireless operator or air gunner. The selection board found him suitable for both trades, commenting: "Physical effi- ciency tests—fit. A quick acting and attentive chap... Sound rural type, keen intelligence, alert and mature." However, Harold strug- gled on the wireless operator's course which he started in Calgary in March 1942, especially with Morse code. He was soon trans- ferred to air gunner training and awarded his air gunner's badge on November 20, 1942. He would spend another year instructing before being posted overseas. His commanding officer at one course stated, "He has completed the No. 9 Gunnery Instructors (Aircrew) Course finishing 4th in a class of 12. A keen hard working pupil showing interest throughout the course. His armament knowledge is good and with further experience he will develop a good lecturing ability. He will make a good assistant instructor."

Harold was married to Adrianna on April 18, 1942, while in service, and it was not long before she fell pregnant with their first and only child. Sharon was born on September 7, 1943, only eight months before Harold was killed.

UNFORTUNATELY, LITTLE information is available about the crew's flight engineer, Sergeant John Robert Carruthers of the Royal Air Force Volunteer Reserve—the only non-RCAF member of the crew.

THE SKIPPER was a skilled and capable pilot, RCAF Flying Officer Burdel Frank Edwards—but he wasn't a Canadian. Born on Decem- ber 12, 1919, in Bloomington, a small village in Grant County, Wisconsin, USA, Burdel's parents divorced when he was a young boy, and he was cared for by his mother's parents. When he was six, his mother remarried, and he and his mother moved in with his new stepfather. Burdel graduated from twelfth grade at the Bloomington high school in 1937. That same year, he undertook a commercial pilot's course. On completion of the course, he became a flight instructor for the next two years and, in 1940, settled down as a crop-dusting pilot in Texas, with plenty of low-level single engine flying. When he applied for the RCAF, he already had seven hun- dred hours flying time and was an accomplished pilot.

Burdel impressed the interview board, a note stating that, with guidance, he would make "a bloody good pilot." It seemed, however, that he had difficulty with authority, and he mentioned to the interviewing officer that he was washed out of the US Air Corps for disciplinary reasons. The interviewing officer commented that Burdel appeared to have a lack of self control, a fast temper, and was hard to manage. Indeed, discipline issues would arise later in his short career. Throughout the October 1943 to January 1944 time frame while he was stationed at No. 24 Operational Training Unit, Burdel faced charges relating to payment of mess bills and loans to airmen with cheques that bounced when they were cashed. The total value was approximately $100. Burdel suffered a severe reprimand and forfeiture of seniority.

Burdel carried out his elementary flight training in Oshawa, Ontario. He was awarded his wings on March 5, 1943, on graduation from No. 16 Service Flying Training School in Hagersville, Ontario. Despite his experience, Burdel's flight training had taken longer than normal owing to a period of hospitalisation which forced him to be put back a course. Finally posted overseas, Burdel followed the usual posting sequence of advanced flying unit, operational training unit where he crewed up, and ending with a conversion course to the four-engined Avro Lancaster. On completion of his AFU training, Burdel's record noted, "average in his flying and preflight work. Rather slow starting the course but has improved a great deal. Good average Captain. He has carried out four day cross countries and six night cross countries at an average height of 14,000 including one Bull's-eye and one Pickle. Four details of fighter affiliation with Tomahawks and decompression chamber exercises. He will have no difficulty in converting to the four engined aircraft but may require a little more dual than average. A good pilot who at times appears to be overconfident."

Burdel had married Francis May Edward on November 22, 1942. She was left to mourn their brief time together when he lost his life on the operation to Louvain.

They are no longer unknown airmen; each of the members of the crew of Lancaster KB713 is remembered by those he left behind.

TOP, LEFT Burdel Edwards, RCAF, pilot. CVWM VIA OPERATION PICTURE ME

TOP, MIDDLE Harold Oddan, RCAF, air gunner. CVWM VIA OPERATION PICTURE ME

TOP, RIGHT Joseph Webber, RCAF, air gunner. CVWM VIA OPERATION PICTURE ME

BOTTOM, LEFT Peter Dewar, RCAF, air bomber. CVWM VIA OPERATION PICTURE ME

BOTTOM, RIGHT Robert Campbell, RCAF, navigator. CVWM VIA OPERATION PICTURE ME

OPPOSITE Roy Smith, RCAF, newly qualified wireless operator, and his obviously proud father, Blake Burton Smith, DCM. DIANE LORENZ AND DAVE THOMSON

No target was ever without its risks. Generally, though, attacking transportation links and flying bomb sites in northern France was considered less risky than a long haul to Berlin, or the intense flak of "Happy Valley"—the industrialized Ruhr. But danger stalked the men of Bomber Command wherever they flew, and even the most experienced aircrews could take nothing for granted.

10

A WILL AND A WAY

SEAN FEAST

S HORTLY BEFORE MIDNIGHT on June 6, 1944, the Komman-
deur of II/NJG4, Hauptmann Paul-Hubert Rauh, raced across
the tarmac at Chateaudun airfield to his aging Messerschmitt
Bf 110 night fighter. There had been high hopes for Willie Messerschmitt's twin-engined *Zerstorer* (Destroyer) before the war, but as a
day fighter in the Battle of Britain its flaws had been badly exposed.
Relegated to a nighttime interception role, however, it had excelled.
Although better aircraft had superseded its design, and huge anten-
nae and extra equipment had impacted its performance, in the right
hands it could be deadly. And with Rauh at the controls it was especially lethal.

His orders were clear: the British were causing havoc with the
ground radio control frequencies—the vital link between aircraft
and controller—so he was to fly a "freelance" sortie in the area of
Saint-Lô. And he was in luck. Heading towards him was a large formation of more than a hundred Lancasters on their bombing runs
to destroy road and rail links at Vire and prevent German reinforcements and armour from reaching the beachhead.

Carefully selecting his first target, Rauh eased his fighter into the
enemy's blind spot and opened fire, his canon shells tearing into the
moving shadow of a Lancaster in front of him. The heavy bomber
almost immediately fell out of the stream and headed crashing to

earth. Six of the seven crew members were fortunate enough to make it out of the stricken bomber, including its Canadian pilot.

Rauh was pleased with his fifteenth victory—Lancaster ME811 of RAF No. 576 Squadron—but his night's work was not yet done. Minutes later, he spotted another dark shape in the sky and identified it immediately as another Lancaster. Sliding once more into position, his thumb hovered over the gun button until his sights rested upon the aircraft's wings and its vulnerable petrol tanks. He opened fire.

Lancaster NE173 of RAF No. 103 Squadron was only moments from destruction; its crew, skippered by another Canadian pilot—Flight Lieutenant Wilfred Way—was on its final sortie.

RCAF PILOT Wilfred "Bill" Way had been a bank clerk before the war. Born in Brandon, Manitoba, on October 22, 1920, he had taken naturally to flying. He eased through service training on single and then twin-engined aircraft. Converting to four-engined Halifax at 1656 Heavy Conversion Unit (HCU) at Lindholme, Bill found himself in charge of a crew that was complete save for a pilot. He could not have hoped for a better group of men.

THE NAVIGATOR was Pilot Officer Derrick Hollingsworth who, like Bill, had been a bank clerk before volunteering for aircrew. Derrick was a Londoner, whereas the air bomber, and the third of the three officers in the crew, was another Canadian. Pilot Officer John Gallagher, from Port McNicoll in Ontario, had given up his studies to train for war.

The rest of the crew were non-commissioned men, two Englishmen and one Australian. The two Englishmen were both from Yorkshire: Flight Sergeant Roger Cooper, from Leeds, was the wireless operator; Sergeant John Jennings was the flight engineer. John, from Bradford, was the baby of the crew at only nineteen years of age. The oldest and final member of their band, the air gunner, was thirty-two. Flight Sergeant Leonard Zingelmann (RAAF) came from Boonah in Queensland, Australia.

The bulk of the crew, minus their pilot, had been together since Operational Training Unit (OTU). The young flight engineer had joined at the Heavy Conversion Unit (HCU) as a direct entrant after completing his training within six months of joining up. He had enlisted on his eighteenth birthday.

On February 9, 1944, with their training over, the crew was posted to No. 103 Squadron. Elsham Wolds, in Lincolnshire, had originally been established to help counter the Zeppelin threat in the First World War. By 1944, it was home to two Main Force Lancaster squadrons—Nos. 103 and 576—and part of No. 1 Bomber Group under the command of Air Vice-Marshal Edward Rice. By the time the Way crew arrived, the squadron had been stood down for several days as a result of the foul winter weather, much to the annoyance of the pugnacious Officer Commanding, Wing Commander Eric Nelson. (Nelson, who had boxed for the RAF between 1932 and 1939, later went on to achieve air rank).

No. 103 had already established a proud tradition of "pressing on" when others may have faltered, yet its casualty count was still within the realms of what would have been considered "acceptable." Only three crews, for example, had been lost in January although the weather had mercifully played its part in keeping those losses to a minimum.

As was customary with any new crew, they were not initially let loose on their own, but rather flew as part of a more experienced crew to learn their trade. Bill and the two Johns—Gallagher and Jennings—found themselves in the company of Pilot Officer Edgar Jones on the night of February 24/25 for their first taste of true operations, taking part in a thankfully uneventful trip to Schweinfurt. While all the crews reported the usual flak and searchlights and at least one had a run in with an enemy fighter, all returned safely. (Jones, who was coming to the end of his operational tour, was awarded the Distinguished Flying Cross at the end of the month.)

THE NEXT night, Jones was reunited with his usual crew, and Bill was given the chance to win his spurs. He and his colleagues were joined by a "spare bod" in both the rear and the mid-upper turrets (Zingelmann, although on the battle order, had been taken ill). The target was Augsberg, the squadron contributing nine bombers—a comparatively modest total—to an attacking force of almost six hundred on the first major raid to the city.

The attack was a stunning success, but the crew's first operation almost proved to be their last. On two occasions, both on their way in and on their homeward journey, they were attacked by twin-engined night fighters. On both occasions they were successful in fighting them off. Not so lucky was Flight Lieutenant William Eddy, DSO, who was shot down by flak, but managed a forced landing, saving himself and all his crew. Eddy even succeeded in evading capture and making it home. (Eddy later went on to add the DFC to his Distinguished Service Order, flying with 139 Squadron Pathfinder Force.)

No doubt buoyed by their success but equally disturbed by the attention paid to their aircraft by the German *Nachtjäger,* the crew (complete with the mid-upper gunner now fully recovered) had to wait another full month before they were again on operations, this time to the big city—Berlin—on what was to be the last major raid of the war on that beleaguered metropolis. Even to the more experienced crews, the mere mention of Berlin was enough to have them running to the nearest boys' room. The German capital was understandably heavily defended and a long way distant, especially from the hinterland of Lincolnshire, often necessitating an arduous and nerve-wracking homeward leg across the North Sea.

Their payload was substantial, a reflection of their air officer commanding's drive to deliver the heaviest payloads in all his squadrons' aircraft. The majority carried one 4,000-pound "Cookie" accompanied by six 1,000-pound medium capacity (MC) bombs and several 500-pound bombs. The remaining Lancasters carried primarily incendiaries, the intention being to blast the roofs from the Germans' buildings and set them ablaze.

Take off was shortly after 18:30 hours, Bill getting away at 18:51, one of the last of the squadron's sixteen aircraft to leave out of a total attacking force of more than eight hundred. Climbing out, the crew quickly settled into its routine. The bombers assembled over Mablethorpe on the coast to join the stream for the long outward leg. Although the crew did not know it at the time, strong winds were to play havoc with the attack, with almost disastrous consequences. Intense flak over the target and in a belt between Leipzig and Berlin was especially deadly; many aircraft were blown off course and found themselves over the strong defences of the Ruhr.

John Gallagher, the air bomber, dropped his bombs successfully on the Pathfinder markers at 22:51 hours and with bomb doors closed, navigator Derrick Hollingsworth gave his skipper the course for home. Almost immediately there was a call from the "spare bod" rear gunner, Sergeant Jones, to "corkscrew," an extreme evasive manoeuvre that put immense pressure on the airframe and crew alike. The gunner had seen what he identified as a Focke-Wulf Fw 190 while still some two thousand yards distant and alerted his pilot shortly before the single engine fighter opened fire with a long burst. In response, Jones squeezed his guns' triggers, but instead of the comforting sound of his four Browning machine guns and the reassuring smell of cordite there was nothing: his guns had frozen.

The mid-upper gunner, Leonard Zingelmann, had better luck, and fired off his own longer burst as the fighter came into his sights at five hundred yards. He had the satisfaction of seeing his tracer ammunition find its mark as the Focke-Wulf broke away to port. Any euphoria was shortlived, however; for some of the enemy's cannon shells had struck the Lancaster's starboard wing. Fortunately, the damage was not serious. Even so, the Lancaster did not make it directly back to base, the navigator preferring instead to direct his pilot to North Killingholme.

THE RAID on Berlin had been costly to Bomber Command. Seventy-two aircraft were shot down, the majority by flak. One was from No. 103 Squadron, flown by Squadron Leader Kenneth Bickers, DFC. Bickers, a flight commander and only twenty-one years of age, had been awarded the DFC for gallantry for fending off a determined attack by an enemy fighter in April the previous year. But the total loss figure in any raid did not always tell the whole story. Often aircraft would return damaged, with killed or wounded on board. Flight Sergeant Browning's rear gunner had been killed in a fighter attack, and the pilot did well to nurse his damaged aircraft back to crash land at Dunsfold.

Though their aircraft had been damaged, Way and the crew returned unhurt to Elsham Wolds in time for the squadron's next operation to Essen in the so-called Happy Valley—as the Ruhr was ironically named by attacking aircrews—on the night of March 26/27. It was yet another eventful night for at least three of the crews. The aircraft flown by Flight Sergeant Whitley returned early with engine trouble, and in the subsequent crash landing his aircraft caught fire. Pilot Officer Birchall and Warrant Officer Chase were both attacked by fighters but returned safely. The Way crew also once again found themselves on the wrong end of a *Nachtjäger*'s fury. Homeward bound, the Lancaster was still some two hours flying time from Elsham when Zingelmann, ever alert, glimpsed what he took to be a Messerschmitt Bf 210 some nine hundred yards away on the starboard quarter. He waited until the heavy fighter had closed to six hundred yards before calling for a "corkscrew" at which point the rear gunner opened fire. The Messerschmitt broke way and set off to look for easier prey, while the crew flew on into the night. They eventually landed without further incident at 01:22 hours.

The squadron operated next on the night of March 30/31, taking part in the dreadful slaughter over Nuremberg in which the RAF lost almost a hundred aircraft in the space of only a few hours. No. 103 Squadron lost two crews, those of Flying Officer James Johnston and Pilot Officer Robert Tate. The Way crew was not operating that night. They were next on the battle order on April 10, just when the might of Bomber Command was being redirected onto tactical targets specifically to support the coming invasion of Europe.

The target was Aulnoye, one of several railway yards identified for special attention. Twelve aircraft from No. 103 Squadron contributed to a total attacking force of thirty-two Lancasters and fifteen Pathfinder Mosquitoes. The raid was a success, with a good many locomotives put out of action, but again it came at a cost. Several crews reported fighter activity, and seven aircraft were shot down, including the crew of Pilot Officer John Armstrong RNZAF from Elsham Wolds.

Bill Way was luckier. Almost immediately after dropping its 14,000-pound bombload, Lancaster ME722 was attacked by a Junkers Ju 88, the enemy closing from dead astern. Both gunners—the established team of Jones and Zingelmann—opened fire, the pilot once again throwing the heavy bomber into a "corkscrew." Unusually, another Lancaster flying close by witnessed the attack and also opened fire just as the enemy aircraft broke away.

Over the course of the next few weeks, the pace of operations accelerated, and the targets varied. The Way crew flew seven further sorties in April to Rouen (April 18), Cologne (April 20), Düsseldorf (April 22), Karlsruhe (April 24), Friedrichshafen (April 27) and Maintenon (April 30).

The raid on Düsseldorf resulted in the deaths of Pilot Officer Thomas Astbury and his crew, who flew into the side of a hill on return to base, as well as the loss of Flying Officer J.W. Birchall and his crew over enemy territory (they would later turn up as prisoners of war).

The attack on Karlsruhe was also noteworthy for several reasons. The Lancaster of Flying Officer Thomas Leggett was hit by incendiaries from another aircraft and almost immediately became uncontrollable. The captain told his crew to prepare to abandon aircraft at which point the mid-upper gunner either left or was catapulted from his seat into the open sky. Leggett, however, managed to regain control of the Lancaster and fly home.

That same night, the Lancaster of Flight Sergeant Cecil Ogden was attacked by two Ju 88s over the target. The gunners claimed to have shot one of them down and forced the other away, but only after their own aircraft was hit and seriously damaged. The captain made for the emergency landing field at Manston with its extra-long runway but was obliged to ditch in the channel, the aircraft sinking in less than a minute. Remarkably, sixty seconds was sufficient time for the crew to make it out in one piece, and all were picked up safely by a local lifeboat.

Bill Way's already war-scarred Lancaster ME722 was this time hit by flak over the target area, but the crew and the aircraft made it home otherwise unscathed.

Two more crews were lost over Essen (Pilot Officer Frank Shepherd) and Friedrichshafen (Flight Lieutenant Maurice Cox AFC—a pre-war regular airman) to bring a busy month to a close. But worse was to follow.

THE RAID on Mailly-le-Camp on May 3/4 is known to virtually every student of Bomber Command history as being one of the most disastrous attacks of the war—not in terms of the destruction caused to the target, but rather to the attacking force who fell foul to a series of fatal mishaps. No. 103 Squadron put up fourteen aircraft and all—including Lancaster ME722 with Bill Way at the controls—got away safely, taking a route via Reading and Beachy Head to the target in central France. Mailly was an established military base with troops and armour in abundance and an attractive target.

Way arrived over the target at 00:26 hours, having first had to orbit the assembly point awaiting an instruction to bomb. The order seemed late in coming; problems with transmissions were primarily to blame, but the delay forced the bombers to collect over the assembly point and allowed German night fighters to find and infiltrate the bomber stream. Finally, with his own bomb doors closed and the aircraft relieved of all its heavy explosive (HE) load, Way headed for home. But behind him, several No. 103 Squadron crews were fighting for their lives. And losing.

Squadron Leader Jock Swanston, Pilot Officer John Holden, and an Australian Pilot Officer Sydney Rowe were all shot down, and Flying Officer Eric Broadbent was lucky to make it home after successfully fending off a determined fighter attack. Two other crews were obliged to land away from base. It was a poor night for the squadron, with a great many empty seats at the post-op interrogation. It was a poor night too for Bomber Command, having lost some forty-two aircraft in all in a tragedy that could and arguably should have been avoided.

But the squadron was not allowed long to lick its wounds. The aerodrome at Rennes—Saint-Jacques was the target for a badly executed attack on the night of May 7/8, even though the Squadron Operations Record Book (ORB) suggests differently. There was one early return. A comparatively "safe" mine-laying trip (known as a "gardening" sortie with the mines known as "vegetables") took place on May 10/11 with little or no opposition encountered.

The Way crew was itself an early return on the raid to the Hasselt marshalling yards on May 11/12 as the result of a faulty compass. It was a disappointing trip all round for the squadron, with several crews being obliged to bomb targets of last resort and two aircraft missing. One of those was piloted by a South African, Wing Commander Hubert Goodman, who had assumed command of the squadron only a few days before and who had already impressed the men with his press-on approach.

Two more mine-laying sorties followed, over Kiel Bay (May 15) and Aalborg Borg (May 23), the former being yet another frustrating affair that led to two of the crews being obliged to return home with the "vegetables" still in the bomb bay, and another aircraft shot down. Pilot Officer Kenneth Mitchell and his crew were all killed.

The railway marshalling yards in the historic city of Aachen were subject to two raids on May 24/25 and May 27/28. The former, a large attack comprising more than four hundred aircraft, did less damage than the raid that followed two nights later by a force less than half the size. No. 103 Squadron put up thirteen aircraft for the first and twelve for the second, the precise targets being the west marshalling yards and the Rothe Erde yards. The Way crew took part in both attacks without incident, despite many fighters being reported. Three aircraft were lost by the squadron over the two nights, those of Flight Sergeant Tate, Squadron Leader Ollier, DFC, AFM, and Flight Lieutenant Leggett.

AS MAY turned to June and the Supreme Allied Commander and his staff put the finishing touches to their invasion plans, the pace of bombing operations and the range of targets increased significantly. The major showpiece battles, however, gave way to multiple tactical raids involving smaller numbers of aircraft on precision targets: ammunition dumps, rail and road infrastructure, radar stations, and coastal gun batteries. But the attacks didn't only take place in the proposed invasion area of Normandy. It was critically important to deceive the Germans into thinking that Calais was still the preferred landing ground, and targets were chosen accordingly.

On June 2, No. 103 Squadron prepared fourteen aircraft for the short hop across the channel and an attack on a series of gun positions in northern France. The weather was poor, both on takeoff and over the target, with the crews struggling to see anything meaningful through the 10/10ths gloom. They had been instructed that if they could not see the markers, they were not to bomb.

Way had a distinguished guest on board for this particular flight, none other than the new officer commanding Wing Commander John St. John, DFC & Bar, who had been posted to Elsham Wolds from 1656 Conversion Unit on May 12. St. John had won his two DFCs with 101 Squadron, the first for bringing a seriously damaged aircraft safely home. He would later add the DSO to his list of decorations after completed three tours of operations.

History does not record whether St John was happy with what he saw—three of the squadron's crews brought their bombs back, and Way was one of eleven who completed the operation satisfactorily.

Yet another gun emplacement was singled out for an attack twenty-four hours later, this time in Wimereaux. The takeoff was once again encumbered by the unusually wet summer weather, but all fourteen squadron aircraft managed to get away on time; all returned to the UK after successfully bombing the target.

THE RELENTLESS bombing of tactical targets in northern France continued. Gun positions in Crisbecq were chosen for attention on the night of June 5/6. The raid was unremarkable, save for the return flight when many of the crews reported seeing large numbers of ships in the channel. The more astute among them realised at once that this was the invasion fleet, and their suspicions were confirmed not long after their return.

The Way crew was fast coming to the end of its first operational tour. They had flown eight operations in May and were on the battle order on June 6/7 for their third operation for the month. At that rate they could expect to have finished their tour within weeks—an exciting prospect. But they were not complacent. The odds of survival typically improved in direct correlation to the experience gained, but the fickle hand of fate could strike at any time. And fate would be unkind to Bill Way and his men.

Vire was the target. Way was once again in the pilot seat with his regular crew: Jennings, Gallagher, Hollingsworth, Cooper, and Zingelmann. The rear gunner was a "spare." Indeed, throughout their tour the crew had flown with a variety of different air gunners in the tail, including most recently Bill Donnahey, who had completed his second tour on the night of June 2/3. On June 3/4, they had flown with Sergeant Hunt; over Crisbecq with a Flight Sergeant Wollard; and for their final sortie, a nineteen-year-old Canadian—Flight Sergeant Joseph Duns, from Caledonia, Ontario—took the rear turret. Officially, Duns was on the strength of 576 Squadron who were also at Elsham Wolds.

At the briefing, the crews were told that they would be attacking two bridges that formed a vital link across the River Vire and could be used to rush German reinforcements towards the invasion area. No trip was ever without its risks, but operations to France were generally faced with less fear and trepidation than a long haul to Berlin or Stettin in the east, where the enemy was not only the Germans but also the weather and the reliability of your aircraft.

The flight out was uneventful, all of the squadron's eighteen aircraft getting away safely. Flight Lieutenant Way—in Lancaster NE173—left the ground at 21:40 hours. Assembling over base, the Lancasters headed for their first rendezvous point over Cheltenham and then on to Bridport before making for the Channel Islands and a straight run in to the target.

The raid was going very much according to plan. Despite heavy cloud, the Pathfinder Mosquitoes were still able to mark the target, some of the aircraft coming down as low as 3,000 feet to ensure the accuracy of their bombs. But flak and fighters were very much in evidence. Short of the target, Pilot Officer Frederick Knight of 460 Squadron was the first victim of the attack, the Australian's aircraft seen to explode in mid-air, showering debris in a wide arc over the French countryside. Then a second aircraft was seen to go down, that of Canadian Flying Officer G.E.J. Bain from 576 Squadron, who had the misfortune of being stalked by Hauptmann Paul-Hubert Rauh. Now Rauh was looking for more "trade," and soon after Lancaster NE173 was in his sights.

What happened next cannot be known with any certainty. Approaching the target at three to four thousand feet, Lancaster NE173 was seen to catch fire in both wings. It continued flying and completed the bombing run, dropping its payload on the target. It was then seen to make a slow, descending turn 180-degrees to port, flying against the stream. Steadily the aircraft began to lose height, the aircrew choosing—or perhaps being obliged—to stay with their aircraft. When the Lancaster finally hit the ground near Omaha beach, it did so at a shallow angle which broke off the tail, while the main section continued to speed along the ground, shedding burning wreckage, before finally coming to rest a few short yards from a remote farmhouse.

Perhaps Bill had been attempting to crash land. Perhaps he had dead or wounded on board. Perhaps he was himself wounded, and unable to give the command to leave the aircraft. No one can possibly know. Whether by necessity or design, what is known is that the crew stayed together until the very end and died together as a result.

All seven were taken from the aircraft the next day and buried close to where they had fallen. They were later reinterred in three separate cemeteries: Bill Way, Roger Cooper, John Jennings, and Leonard Zingelmann at Bretteville-sur-Laize Canadian War Cemetery; John Gallagher and Joseph Duns at Beny-sur-Mer Canadian War Cemetery; and Derrick Hollingsworth at the Bayeux War Cemetery.

OPPOSITE, TOP, LEFT Roger Cooper, RAF, wireless operator, and Derrick Hollingsworth, RAF, navigator. Friends in life, united in death. ANONYMOUS

OPPOSITE, TOP, RIGHT John Gallagher, RCAF, air bomber. ANONYMOUS

OPPOSITE, BOTTOM, LEFT John Jennings, RAF, flight engineer. ANONYMOUS

OPPOSITE, BOTTOM, RIGHT Bill Way, taking a break with his Lancaster. ANONYMOUS

ABOVE, LEFT Leonard Zingelmann, RAAF, mid gunner. ANONYMOUS

ABOVE, RIGHT Joseph Duns, RCAF, rear gunner. ANONYMOUS

Sixty-four years had passed since Flight Sergeant Jack Trend's Lancaster plunged into the ground in flames. Jack returned to the small village of Meerlo in Holland to be guest of honour at the unveiling of a memorial to RAF No. 15 Squadron Lancaster LM465, LS-U. It was a sad and poignant occasion for Jack; he was there to remember his six crew mates who perished on that fateful night of June 13, 1944.

11

UNLUCKY FOR SOME

HOWARD SANDALL

THE SOUND OF the skylark's song resonated across the airfield on the summer afternoon in Suffolk, England. Flight Sergeant Jack Trend sat at the edge of the airfield watching the activity from the ground crews making the four-engine Lancaster bombers ready for that night's operation. In the distance he could see small children messing about around the perimeter, hoping to catch a glimpse of a Lancaster on a test flight. At twenty-one years old, it had been but a handful of years since Jack himself had taken part in similar pastimes. He sat for a while briefly reminiscing about the innocence of that activity compared to what was expected of him as a wireless operator in Bomber Command. How times had changed! He felt anger towards the enemy for taking away his youth prematurely.

JACK'S JOURNEY began in October 1941 while he was serving in the Air Training Corps. He volunteered for aircrew and, after the initial aptitude tests at Euston House in London, was graded as suitable for training as a wireless operator. On January 1, 1942, Jack arrived at RAF Padgate in Lancashire for his initial instruction, followed a few weeks later by a posting to No. 2 Signals School in Blackpool for an intensive ground course. The next few months involved learning the basics of Morse code and gaining an understanding of the radio sets used by the RAF. Early 1943 brought a further posting to the

Radio School at Yatesbury in Wiltshire where he experienced his first flight training in de Havilland Dominie and Percival Proctor aircraft. Aircrew were expected to multitask, and Jack's secondary role would be as an air gunner. For this second part of his training, he was posted to No. 1 Air Armaments School at RAF Manby in Lincolnshire for a two-week ground gunnery course. This was followed at No. 3 Advanced Observer Flying School by an intensive course covering both wireless operation and air gunnery, flying in the Avro Anson trainer.

After what seemed to him like an eternity, Jack finally received his certification as a wireless operator/air gunner. Qualifications in hand, he was posted, in August 1943, to No. 82 Operational Training Unit at RAF Ossington in Nottinghamshire. It was there that he crewed up with four members of his crew, including pilot Carl Thompson, an American. Carl had grown up on a farm in Paris, Michigan, and tried to enlist in the US Army Air Force (USAAF) as a pilot but was turned down because of a leg deformity. Undeterred, he crossed the border into Canada and signed up with the RCAF on November 27, 1941, as a pilot trainee in the BCATP.

While at the OTU, the Thompson crew were introduced to the Vickers Wellington bomber. The unit's machines had seen considerable operational service earlier in the war, were war-weary, and suffered from poor reliability. Nonetheless, it was here that the crew learned to operate as a team, each one of them dependent on the others to fulfil their respective operational roles. The crew undertook cross-country bombing exercises, navigational flights and the obligatory "circuits and bumps" designed to assist the pilot to familiarise himself with the controls of a large twin-engine bomber. Then in early November 1943, the crew was posted to No. 1651 Conversion Unit at RAF Waterbeach and RAF Wratting Common for the next stage of their training. Now flying the larger four-engined Short Stirling, two additional crew members were needed. Tom Stubbs and Duke Pelham joined as mid-upper gunner and flight engineer, respectively.

Carl Thompson and his crew of seven soon mastered the idiosyncrasies of the Stirling of which there were plenty. Perhaps the most challenging was landing the aircraft with its notoriously poor undercarriage configuration. Heavy landings sometimes caused the undercarriage to collapse, with the inevitable results.

On December 27, 1943, the crew began the final stage of their training. They arrived at No. 3 Lancaster Finishing School at RAF Feltwell for conversion onto the bomber they would take to war. Compared to the more awkward Stirling, the Avro Lancaster was a dream to fly, and the crew became accustomed to the instruments and systems in double quick time. A mixture of cross-country navigation and bombing exercises honed the crew's skills. It was a short and intensive conversion course, and seven days later, on January 2, 1944, they finally arrived at RAF Mildenhall in Suffolk as part of No. 3 Group Bomber Command. No. 15 Squadron, to which the crew were posted, was a pre-war squadron steeped in history and the crew felt very proud to be joining such an accomplished unit.

Their arrival at Mildenhall coincided with the squadron itself converting from the Short Stirling to the Avro Lancaster. The early part of the month consisted of lectures on survival and escape and evasion, something at the time Jack did not realise would become very relevant to his cause. As an entirely non-commissioned crew, they were assigned a small, terraced house within the central confines of the camp, and took their meals in the sergeants' mess. The crew now consisted of three RCAF volunteers (including the pilot, Flight Sergeant Carl Thompson) and four RAF.

The other two RCAF members filled the navigator and bomb aimer positions. The navigator was Sergeant Roderick McMillan, from Vancouver. He listed his previous occupations in his service record book as a somewhat eclectic mix of "engineer, deck hand, student." He had an uncle in Scotland and identified his mother as next of kin. Bomb Aimer Sergeant Ronald Lemky was also from British Columbia, claiming Port Mann, near Vancouver, as his hometown. He graduated from Lord Tweedsmuir High School in Cloverdale with above average marks and good recommendations. He had worked in a box factory before joining the RCAF.

In addition to Sergeant Jack Trend in the wireless operator position, the other RAF crew members included: Sergeant Thomas Edward Stubbs from Brockley in London, mid-upper Gunner; Sergeant Richard Sidney Mobbs, from Cratfield in Suffolk, rear gunner; and, Sergeant Maurice Bernard Pelham, from Stamford Hill in London, flight engineer.

HISTORIANS CONSIDER the period from November 1943 to March 1944 as the Battle of Berlin, but throughout early 1944 Bomber Command's strategic bombing of German industrial cities also continued at an intense pace. The weather toward the end of January improved, and Carl and his crew found themselves on the battle order for their first mission to bomb the industrial heart of Augsburg as one of 594 bombers. They completed several subsequent missions in quick succession to heavily defended targets in the Ruhr Valley, including two trips to Stuttgart in early March and two to Frankfurt on March 18 and 22.

On March 23, Carl was commissioned to the rank of pilot officer in recognition of his skills; he would need all of them the following night. March 24 marked the final mission of the Battle of Berlin. Strong winds blew the aircraft off course on every stage of their route, scattering the bomber stream and pushing several bombers over heavily defended areas en route to the target and back. Like so many other pilots that night, Carl Thompson struggled to keep on course and overshot the target area. There was no alternative but to circle around and rejoin the bomber stream, an extremely dangerous manoeuvre with a high risk of collision and another opportunity to be picked off by the German defences. Once over the target, the bomb aimer was unable to see the target indicators and was obliged to release the bombs on the fires burning below. The time needed to keep the Lancaster on a steady course through intense flak to obtain the obligatory target photograph seemed like forever to the crew. Sergeant Lemky's confirmation that the photo had been taken was the signal for Pilot Officer Thompson to throw the bomber into a steep dive to clear the target area swiftly. But it was no escape. No sooner had the aircraft levelled out than they were attacked by a night fighter that sprayed cannon shells into the fuselage, damaging the ammunition ducts and rear elevator trim cables. Luck was with them; there were no further attacks, and LM465 was able to return to Mildenhall safely. Seventy-two bombers from the main force were not so fortunate.

This was a particularly unsuccessful period for Bomber Command. In the bright light of the moon and with cloudless skies, the German night fighter force reaped its revenge on the attacking crews. Berlin was at the outer limits for the bomber force, and the combination of adverse weather conditions and improved enemy night fighter techniques made for heavy losses that could not be sustained indefinitely.

Fortunately for the Thompson crew, April 1944 brought a new strategic direction for Bomber Command, with the focus switching to support for the Allied invasion. However, excursions into the Ruhr were still being detailed, interspersed among the French and Belgium invasion support targets. During April and May, Carl and his crew completed seventeen sorties against various heavily defended industrial cities including Aachen, Cologne, Düsseldorf, Karlsruhe, Essen, Friedrichshafen, Duisburg, and Dortmund as industrial city targets. Targets in support of the impending invasion covered Rouen, Cap Griz Nez, and Courtrai in France.

THE PRELUDE to D-Day began on the morning of June 5. Because of the strict secrecy surrounding the invasion, Jack thought it would be just another operation. At 08:00 hours the adjutant's parade took place, and the afternoon was taken up with two squadrons air testing their Lancasters. This usually involved a flight of twenty-five minutes or so to check navigational aids, guns, radio, electrics, and hydraulic system. Any faults were reported to the ground crew who would set to work immediately to rectify the problems.

Jack described the buildup to the operation and the day's experiences:

The briefing that day took place very late in the evening. We had a separate briefing to that of 622 Squadron who shared Mildenhall with us. As soon as the operational target was revealed all the aircraft were bombed up with 11 x 1,000 lb bombs and 3 x 500 lb high explosive bombs. In addition the ground crews put in 1,516 gallons of fuel. The meteorology Officer delivered his forecast as extremely cloudy with some drizzle. Our target was to be the German 105 mm gun emplacements situated between the Caen canal and the River Orme at Ouistreham. We later found out that it was essential to destroy the target to allow the first wave of troops onto the beaches.

With all the pre-flight checks made and our equipment collected, we were driven out to the dispersal point in darkness of the early hours of 6th June. The vital engine warm up began and at 03:45 hours, we left the runway behind and climbed to 6,500 feet following a course over Rochester, then Hastings. From here we set out across the English Channel towards Ouistreham on the Normandy coast. The run in to the target was timed for 05:00 hours. The cloud that night was up to 12,000 feet and we could clearly see the Pathfinder Mosquitos accompanying us. There was little if any *Luftwaffe* activity, but anti-aircraft fire and rocket salvos were considerable as we approached the target area. After our bombs had been released, it was a quick turn round before we headed back to Mildenhall to complete our E.T.A. at 07:00 hours.

Before we arrived back at base, I received a BBC announcement on the aircraft wireless as the breaking news about the D-Day invasion was being transmitted all over the country. The bombing offensive that we'd taken part in had been the start of the Allied landings in France. My heart begin to beat somewhat faster as I relayed this exciting but not unexpected news to the captain and the rest of the crew via the intercommunication system. For the remainder of the journey we were in an upbeat mood.

We landed safely and after the routine de-briefing we retired to bed, emotionally exhausted by our efforts. We were roused for lunch and informed that we would be operating again that same night. The target was announced at a joint briefing for 15 and 622 Squadrons because we would be attacking the same target. Our objective was to bomb specific military targets in Lisieux, the biggest town after Caen in the invasion area. Weather conditions were reported to be improving in the area, therefore at 23:40 hours thirty-three bombers took off for a return to the Normandy coast. As we approached the target we bombed on the red marker left by the Mosquito Pathfinders which were accurately placed. Our arrival above Lisieux coincided with a break in the clouds and we could see the town clearly laid out below. Once again there was little *Luftwaffe* activity and sporadic anti-aircraft fire.

We landed at Mildenhall for a second time that day at 03:00 hours, whereupon we were de-briefed and then thanked our lucky stars for having survived such a memorable day. Every single aircraft belonging to 15 and 622 Squadrons had fulfilled their missions that day and returned home safely.

Just six nights later, on June 12, 1944, the briefing room in the operations complex at RAF Mildenhall was full to capacity. Some of the one hundred and fifty assembled aircrew belonging to Nos. 15 and 622 Squadrons had to stand at the side or at the back. The usual simmering, rumbling undertone of conversation grew louder as the anticipation increased. It stopped in an instant as the two squadrons' commanding officers entered the room, immediately receiving the attention of the massed audience. Wing Commander Watkins, DSO, DFC, DFM, moved quickly to the front and up the few steps to the stage.

The instant coming to attention was not just a reaction of compliance to military tradition, but a demonstration of genuine respect for the respective squadron commanders. Most of the aircrew were non-commissioned officers (sergeants and flight sergeants) in those days, and they knew their commanders had operational experience.

Wing Commander Watkins was well respected among the crews. His Distinguished Flying Medal proved his courage and outstanding ability had been officially recognised when he also had been a sergeant—one of them!

Watkins motioned for his crews to be seated and when the shuffling had settled the high curtains parted to reveal large maps of East Anglia to southern Europe. There were some quiet gasps of disparagement! Even quieter short whistles, and from some just the word "Jesus" passed their lips.

Watkins spoke. "Gentlemen, the target for tonight is Gelsenkirchen, once again. We have bombed this industrial enemy giant before but its importance in the production of oil is already well known. Intelligence has it that in spite of previous bombing by us and the USAAF, production has not been materially reduced. It is indeed a committed German Industrial city. A force of up to three hundred Bomber Command aircraft will strike it tonight. As some of us know already, targets in this area of Germany are notoriously well defended and the mission will not be easy, no bombing mission ever is! The *Luftwaffe* will be our major concern as well as other bombers in such a large force. Extra care and vigilance will be necessary, even more so than usual. Good luck!"

The wing commander motioned with a partially raised finger and in a soft voice he asked the squadron leaders to step onto the stage. The station intelligence officer came forward, the first of the specialist officers, several of whom sat in the front row of easy chairs. Other leaders, flight commanders, navigation officer, engineering, signals, armament, and gunnery leader would follow. Station padres were always asked to be present and took a passive role. The presentation lasted on average thirty to forty minutes and there was always a short applause when the catering officer announced that chocolate and sweet rations should be collected from the officer nominated.

Finally, the noisy shuffling of chairs signalled the crews' departure to the locker clothing rooms to prepare for the night's flying and for final words from their specialist leaders. Then it was on to chat up the young WAAFs who had packed the parachutes. The women would hand over the parachute after a final check of the safety pin on this last piece of survival kit. Sergeant Jack Trend looked at his crew prior to leaving the briefing room and he realised that any initial doubts they might have had in each other's abilities had well and truly disappeared. This would be Jack's twenty-first mission and they had been assigned their usual aircraft, Lancaster LM465, LS-U. They were a proficient crew, professional once in the air and inseparable when on the ground. Their tour to date had not been entirely uneventful; on April 30, a violent swing forced their Lancaster off the runway, resulting in a ground loop and subsequent crash. All the crew walked away unhurt.

Roderick McMillan, now a warrant officer second class, and the other navigators now learned for the first time exactly the target and routes to be flown not only to the target, but also tracks to get back home. They would have to spend time on their charts and maps. Navigators usually needed help with all the "clobber" they had to carry in addition to a parachute. There was a large case with maps, rulers, computers, and manuals, and sometimes a larger canvas bag and heavy Plexiglas case containing a semi-automated sextant.

There was always an opportunity for a quick visit to the bathroom before jumping on the transport to the dispersal. There were no such facilities even remotely associated on the windswept isolated dispersals far from anywhere. The next opportunity might be as much as ten or twelve hours later—unless the brave used the frigid and quirky Elsan toilet on board.

Finally ready, the crews would be taken to the aircraft dispersals—often quite a distance—in aircrew coaches or, more often, in three-ton trucks. Each in turn proceeded with their parachutes in hand to have a quick word with their ground crews. The pilot and senior flight sergeant (chiefy) or warrant officer engineer would go over the engine servicing and any airframe or electronics issues and carry out a final outside check and inspection of the bomb load. Some crews took the opportunity to anoint their aircraft's tail wheel as part of their pre-departure "good luck" rituals. With all on board, the closing of the huge bomb doors with all four Merlin engines running was one of the last checks before the pilot formally accepted the aircraft's airworthiness state and signed the special RAF document known as Form 700.

AT APPROXIMATELY 23:15 hours on the evening of June 12, 1944, Pilot Officer Carl Thompson lifted LM465, LS-U off the runway at RAF Mildenhall, along with fourteen other Lancasters from No. 15 Squadron and seventeen from No. 622 Squadron. The bombers climbed towards the rendezvous point over Southwold on the Suffolk coast. German radar controllers were already plotting the estimated course and target of the aircraft; their only question was what the actual target was. Diversionary and spoof raids made it difficult for the German plotters to instruct the night fighters to join the bomber stream at a particular point.

Carl Thompson settled into keeping the Lancaster on a precise course heading as directed by Roderick McMillan. The crew crossed the Dutch coast at 00:53 hours on schedule, anticipating that the German night fighter force would have picked up the Bomber Stream some time ago and were planning their interception.

Silhouetted against the night sky, Unteroffizier Gustav Sarzio from 6 *Gruppe/Nachtjagdgeschwader* 1, manoeuvred his Me 110G night fighter stealthily underneath the British bomber. Rear gunner Sergeant Richard (Dick) Mobbs peered endlessly into the night sky, oblivious to the danger creeping ever closer below. Sarzio positioned his *Schräge Musik* gun configuration to fire in between the engines on the wing in an attempt to give the crew time to bail out. Approximately twenty kilometres northwest of Venlo in the province of Limburg, he fired his 20-mm cannon shells into the bomber's starboard inner engine and fuselage, instantly setting the wing alight in a mass of flames. Carl Thompson fought with the controls, knowing that the bomber was doomed to go down. With no alternative he ordered the crew to bail out.

Jack Trend recalled the night:

I was listening to the Group broadcast at 01:00 hours when we
appeared to be hit by cannon shells, the starboard inner engine
was on fire with a second fire near the SBA equipment, amidships.
Our pilot Carl Thompson was giving instructions to bail out and I
followed the bomb aimer Ron Lemky and Duke Pelham out of the
forward hatch. I observed what I thought was a river just before
landing, this turned out to be a road when I tried to dump my parachute. I eventually buried it on the other side of the road. I heard
the sound of what must have been clogs on tarmac, I didn't know
that a curfew was in force and realized that these people must
have been looking for me. I crossed the road again when all was
quiet and hid in a corn field until mid-afternoon. From my hiding
spot I heard and saw Germans with dogs searching the area but I
stayed hidden. I thought that there was a built up area on the east
side of the field possibly electrical installations or water plant. I
had previously checked that I was all in one piece, just a minor
nosebleed and a burning sensation on my face. I moved out onto
the main road, thankful to be able to stretch my legs, into the sun
and walked south.

Holland lay on the edge of the main route utilised by Bomber
Command to deliver its deadly cargo. The intensity of German
night-fighter activity in 1944 resulted in many aircrews being shot
down and on the run behind enemy lines in the Dutch countryside.
For each one of them, the mercy and courage shown by the local people was beyond measure. Holland is flat, open terrain, criss-crossed
by a labyrinth of dykes and waterways. Evaders often found themselves trying to cross a river when the only way was over a guarded
bridge. All these obstacles meant evading out of Holland was very
difficult indeed. The Dutch population was very sympathetic to
aircrew, even though anyone found assisting or harbouring enemy
airmen would face the penalty of torture, prison camp, or even death.

After walking a little way, Jack came across a farmer and by gesturing made him understand his plight. The farmer, fortunately, pointed him in the right direction. On the outskirts of town (now known as Meerlo), Jack was given shelter at a farmhouse. The farmer and his two daughters provided a meal for him and gave him civilian clothes in exchange for his revolver. The danger of discovery was ever present, so Jack rested in the chicken house. At 21:30 hours, he was introduced to a guide who took him over the River Maas on bicycle to the house of the burgomaster in Well. After some questioning to verify his identity, he slept the night at "Pop" Krebbers's house.

The morning of June 14 dawned bright, and Jack recalled that it was his twenty-second birthday. Any celebrations would have to be put on hold for the time being, however; he had to cycle with Pop Krebbers some thirty kilometres to Griendtsveen to meet other members of the Dutch resistance movement. Imagine his surprise when he was presented with a birthday cake, a tot of whiskey, and some cigarettes! The unexpected kindness shown by his helpers was brought to an abrupt end when he was asked, for security reasons, to sleep in the garden shed.

It was around this time that news of the other crew members reached Jack. Between the churches at Meerlo and Tienray, six aircrew bodies had been found near a crashed Lancaster. The Germans buried them in separate coffins in the local churchyard at Venlo. Some were found lying next to unopened parachutes whilst others were next to an open parachute. This news disturbed Jack tremendously; at least the two who exited the aircraft before him should have been able to jump successfully, even if the bomber had exploded soon after he escaped. In the end, the fates of his crewmates would never be known.

On June 15, Jack was given the opportunity to listen to BBC radio. The same day, he received a forged identity card describing him as Johann Pieters, a deaf and dumb pianist. A few days later Jack was introduced to a Polish evader. Together, they cycled to Lierop via Deurne-Someran and Asten. Near midnight, the two arrived at one of the out-of-the-way, hidden resistance camps, Denne Lust/ Stroubouw—also known as the "Sanitorium."

This camp and others like it were purpose built to help evaders like Jack. After the Normandy landings on June 6, Allied aircraft were striking targets of opportunity at will, especially railways, bridges and supply routes. The Germans were retreating in the face of the Allied onslaught, and the safe houses used by the Dutch Resistance were now being overrun on a frequent basis. The solution came in the form of hastily built camps in wooded areas that could not be attributed to any one or group of Resistance members. One such camp was Denne Lust. Jack remembered his first sight of it:

> Coming off the side roads we came to the usual fire tracks which split up this section of pine forest. We dismounted from our bicycles and walked into the wood up until we reached a clearing. There were a number of small straw houses built into the trees. In the distance I could see the offices and a large pit was obscured some way away.

At the camp, Jack met other evaders: a Canadian named Bob Punter and Eric Grisdale, an RAF pilot, both members of the same 626 Squadron crew. The days passed slowly for the camp residents. The highlight of each day was the arrival of the daily meal, usually a mixture of sandwiches, potatoes, and fruit. Otherwise, the days stretched on, with the evaders occupying themselves playing cards and teaching the young *Onderduikers* (Dutchmen) Morse code in exchange for lessons in the Dutch language.

TOWARDS THE end of June more evaders, namely Eddy Walker (RAF) and Harry Cooper and Bill Kinney (both USAAF), joined the group. Around mid-morning on July 8, Jack and the others left the camp by car. The journey took them to Crisis Hoevre, where the group was sheltered overnight. The following day their journey continued by train to Venray and then on to Sittard, where Jack parted company with the other evaders. He was destined for Nuth with two other aircrew, to be housed with Mr. Pinckaers in the Stationstrasse. The days passed uneventfully until July 20 when three additional evaders arrived. While at Nuth, Jack was presented with a new *carte identité*, identifying him now as René Joseph Colin, a coal miner at Jemeppe.

The passage of time was excruciatingly slow. Every day brought more anxiety about being discovered. Jack was desperate to get home and wondered if his mother had received the dreaded letter from the Commanding Officer informing her that he was missing in action, presumed dead. After what seemed far too long a time, Jack and the others were given a thorough briefing by his protectors and put on a train destined for Roermond. Jack's false documents passed inspection at the many check points and each time he settled into his seat, hiding behind a newspaper. On arrival, the entire group cycled across Maas Bridge, straight past a disinterested sentry. The journey continued by car on July 29 and then by boat to a place known as the "Shack," about one and a half miles outside the village of Roggel. Twelve evaders in total arrived and slept in huts suitable for six people. The next few days passed without incident, every day brought more anxiety and impatience to get home. On the morning of August 12 they were on the move again, for a long and uncomfortable car journey to Huntsvel orchard at Kelpen.

The resistance movement had built another camp in the woods at Kinrooi, just inside the Belgian border. The group of evaders arrived there on August 17. At first Jack slept in the open, but as the nights grew colder, he and his fellows turned to the nearby barn for some warmth. It was not entirely safe; one morning the whole party were woken early and warned about a German patrol approaching. They made a swift exit and escaped to the woods where they watched the suspicious Germans first inspect the barn, then destroy it with hand grenades.

On September 1, the group moved again, this time to Elen, another staging post on the route to freedom. Unbeknown to Jack, extensive plans were being made to avoid capture of the fugitives.

It was evident that the Allied advance was close by and they frequently witnessed German troops retreating along the roads. A few days later the party was on the move again, this time to Rotem where they met a group of partisans busy cooking an entire sheep in a large pot. Jack tried to sleep under a tree, but the rain and cold, damp conditions kept him awake. Just before dawn, four German troops routed the camp, and they all ran for their lives. Jack jumped into a ditch to hide. Without realizing at the time, Jack had dropped his identity card in the ditch.

It was now clearly unsafe to remain at the camp, so the party took over the ticket collector's office at the Rotem train station. The next day, the entire group returned to where they had been forced to flee by the German troops. Searching the area, Jack was fortunate to find his lost identity card. It was evident that the area was now overrun by the retreating German troops, so on the night of September 8, the group simply walked out of Rotem and kept going until they were exhausted. From a hidden vantage point a few days later, Jack spotted a vehicle with an American star on the side. Hopes raised, he followed some tank tracks until he came across an American advance party. The tension and anxiety Jack had endured over the last days, weeks and months ebbed away. The transition from being on the run to a position of safety and liberation would always make the date of on September 11 one of great significance for Jack.

The whole group was driven to the Intelligence Corps headquarters at Guitrode, an RAF Canadian Unit emergency aerodrome (TAF Unit). There, they were debriefed and enjoyed the American hospitality. On the morning of September 14, Jack was transferred to Brussels to board a Dakota transport aircraft destined for England. They lifted off the runway at 14:00 hours and touched down at RAF Hendon at 17:00.

It was around midday on September 16 when Jack arrived back in Brighton. The strain of what his mother had been through and her great relief at seeing him again were etched on her face during an emotional reunion.

IN 2008, Jack attended the unveiling of a memorial to his crew at the exact position the Lancaster crashed some sixty-four years earlier. He was the guest of honour that day with local dignitaries, the local mayor, veterans, and officials from No. 15 Squadron also attending the event.

The main panel of the memorial is made from a fragment of the metal skin of the Lancaster and inscribed with the names of the six crew members who lost their lives. As Jack stood next to the memorial, images of his crewmates returned in a moment of emotional remembrance. His thoughts ventured to a reported scene that he has visualised in his mind many times over the passing years: the wreckage of a Lancaster bomber burning in the distance with six young airmen lying motionless near their parachutes, under the shadow of a church. For Jack's six friends in his crew, the night of June 12/13 was a tragedy that would forever darken the lives of their families.

The passing years have not dulled Jack's memories. He takes great solace from the fact that his crew will be remembered for posterity. This story of heroism and terrible misfortune was the norm for many Bomber Command crews. To a significant degree their lives depended on a twist of fate. Ask any veteran of Bomber Command how he survived his tour of operations and he will tell you: a combination of teamwork and luck. For six members of Carl Thompson's crew, their luck finally ran out that night in June 1944. Unlucky for some.

TOP, LEFT Sgt. Jack Trend, RAF, on completion of his air gunnery course, 1943. J. TREND

BOTTOM, LEFT On arrival at RAF Mildenhall, crews were allocated quarters on the base. Back row from left: Stubbs, Thompson, Burch, Pelham. Front row: McMillan, Trend, Lemky. J. TREND

TOP, RIGHT April 1944. Crew poses next to their regular Lancaster LM465, LS-U. Back row: Thompson, Stubbs, Lemky, Burch (not on final raid). Front row: Pelham, Trend, McMillan. J. TREND

MIDDLE, RIGHT Lancaster LM465, LS-U, stands on the dispersal point in April 1944, ready to be loaded with racks of incendiary bombs. J. TREND

BOTTOM, RIGHT Evaders photographed while at Kinrooi camp in the woods. Rear, left to right: Eric Grisdale, Denis Walker, Robert Punter; front: Leslie Shimmins, Roger Gardiner, Jack Trend. J. TREND

TOP At the memorial service in 2008, Jack stands and reflects on the events of June 1944. With the unveiling ceremony over and wreaths laid, the Meerlo band played one last tribute to the fallen. A. WHEATLEY

BOTTOM No. 15 Squadron briefing room, April 1945. The large map of Europe was used to plot the route to the target and back, ususally with a silk cord. On the right are silhouettes of the latest German jet fighters, the ME262 and ME163 Komet. HOWARD SANDALL COLLECTION

OPPOSITE Map of evasion route taken by Jack Trend across Holland and Belgium. MARISKA AND HANS VAN DAM

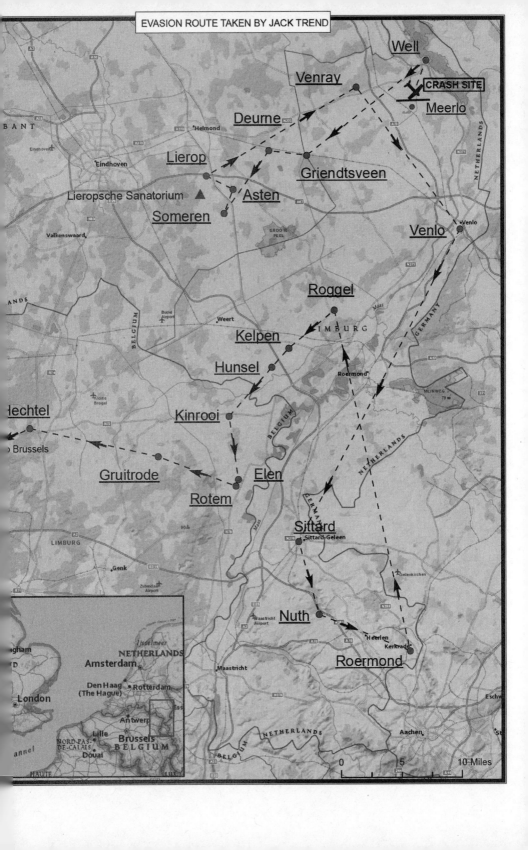

EVASION ROUTE TAKEN BY JACK TREND

A quiet French village named Siracourt in the Pas-de-Calais region housed one of many of the Third Reich's v-1 *Vergeltungswaffen* (vengeance weapon) flying-bomb facilities. On July 6, 1944, ops were on, and a total of 551 RAF Bomber Command aircraft took to the air. One of the targets was the large site at Siracourt, which had been subjected to a heavy bombing raid only a week previously and had already claimed several bomber crew lives. In the early hours of the morning of July 6, Flying Officer Bannihr and his crew of RCAF No. 424 Squadron were briefed for their target and made preparations for what would be their last flight. Ensuring they were properly laid to rest would be a challenge of its own.

12

THE SEVEN SOULS
OF SIRACOURT

MARC HALL

FLYING OFFICER BANNIHR had an experienced crew, most on their twenty-ninth operation and very close to completing their first tour of operations. They had been flying together for approximately seven months, having received a glowing report from No. 1664 Heavy Conversion Unit: "Above average pilot and good average crew. Competent navigator and bomb aimer, gunners above average." The flight commander also mentioned: "Above average pilot. Steady and reliable with good crew co-ordination."

Bannihr's crew roster normally included air gunner RCAF Flight Lieutenant Melborn Leslie Mellstrom, DFC, who had completed the conversion course with the other crew members. On the morning of June 6, 1944, Mellstrom was for unknown reasons not on board. He would survive the day, but sadly lose his life less than a year later, on April 10, 1945. By then Mellstrom was an experienced gunner with nearly fifty missions completed. Flying with No. 405 Squadron, he was lost in Lancaster ME315 when his turret was shot away by a German fighter. His body now lies in the Berlin war cemetery, while the remainder of his crew on that mission managed to return successfully to base in their heavily damaged aircraft.

This June day the Bannihr crew and their replacement gunner, RCAF Flying Officer Raymond Viau, would also fare badly. Liftoff from their base at RAF Skipton-on-Swale in Yorkshire was at 05:32 hours, with the expectation that they would be back to base in a few hours. The lumbering Halifax LW169 carried a full bomb load as it roared down the runway and slowly climbed into clear conditions. The pilot banked the aircraft for the heading toward the target in northern France—and the anti-aircraft fire that would soon shoot it from the sky.

Exactly what occurred on board in those moments will never be known. One report spoke of a direct hit by flak in the nose of the aircraft. Several other returning aircrews said that they believed they saw the doomed Halifax spiralling slowly downwards after being hit. Although it appeared momentarily to level out a short distance from the ground, the aircraft plunged to earth and exploded on impact. During the descent it was believed one of the crew escaped as a parachute was seen to open. The eyewitnesses could not confirm it was from Halifax LW169, but Bannihr's aircraft was the only one lost on the raid. The aircraft crashed at approximately 08:05 hours, leaving no survivors despite the parachute being observed. The crash site was located approximately two kilometres south of the town of Saint-Pol-sur-Ternoise, very close to the road that led to the town of Doullens, just seven kilometres from the target at Siracourt. Seven families were now left without husbands and sons.

Three months later, in September 1944, information was received via the Red Cross centre at Geneva confirming that the Halifax had been shot down with the loss of all of the crew. It showed that there was one unidentified airman, but that four others had been named, including May, Morrison, Viau, and Bannihr. No mention was made of the remaining two missing airmen.

The task of locating the missing airmen—with what sketchy information there was available—fell to Flight Lieutenant Milliard of No. 5 Section of the Missing Research and Enquiry Service (MRES). It proved to be a challenging case and required several visits to the military cemetery at Saint-Pol, with the initial visit in February 1945 by Flight Lieutenant Bugold. The mayor of the village was consulted, and he supplied a map of the cemetery containing all the burials for Allied personnel during the current conflict. The official records showed that five bodies of aircrew were laid to rest in the cemetery on July 6, 1944, four of which were not identified, but one having the number CAN.J22859 recorded. This service number belonged to Flying Officer Alan May. The remains were not recognisable and had been brought to the cemetery by a German warrant officer and two other ranks; the cemetery keeper was only able to obtain the one service number. It was known that the aircraft had a crew of seven and that one parachute was seen, but despite enquires with the local population and the Resistance, it was found that no Allied airmen had been assisted around that time.

The investigators made a further visit to the cemetery on April 18, 1945, and again the mayor of Saint-Pol was interviewed. He again confirmed that the entire crew had been killed by the impact. Flight Lieutenant Milliard was assured that the collective grave contained the bodies of the entire crew from the crashed Halifax, although not all were named in the records. It was also now asserted by the cemetery keeper that the Germans had recovered the bodies from the scene of the crash and handed them over to the cemetery completely stripped of all clothing and belongings, although this later proved to be unfounded. One other man also confirmed the bodies were from the crash site of Halifax LW169. This man had been arrested on October 8, 1944, and found to be in possession of a Ronson cigarette lighter which had belonged to Flying Officer John Morrison, a gift that had been presented to the airman by the No. 8 Air Observer School in training. The lighter was seized and returned to the Morrison family.

The cemetery held conflicting reports. Some showed that only five airmen were buried there, as per the initial visit. Further records suggested that three unknown airmen were buried on July 6, 1944, one of which was Canadian with the service number J22859 (Flying

Officer May), and the remains of three more individuals were buried on July 10, with a seventh, unknown, airman having no burial date shown. This now made up the crew of seven, but there was no further information about the parachute that the other aircrews had seen. Local members of the population confirmed that it was not usually customary of the Germans to bury the dead on the same day and that it could be days or weeks before the wreckage and crew remains were moved. In this case, though, it seems to have been partially cleared on the same day as the crash. The later date of burial for three other airmen on July 10 was accounted for as their bodies had been removed from underneath the wreckage of the aircraft when it was taken away by the Germans. The last body was found sometime later and buried on the spot by several local people. This was later revealed to be the remains of Sergeant Leonard Dawson.

The investigation was closed temporarily, until it was time for the airmen to be made ready for their final identification and registration. However, in December 1945, further information had come to light from Lance Corporal Edwards, the stepbrother of Sergeant Dawson. He stated that he had himself attended the cemetery and had dug up some of the graves for identification purposes without any formal permission. It was observed that some of the bodies were clothed and he thought he had confirmed the grave of Sergeant Dawson as the body had sergeant stripes on the arms, and Dawson was the only sergeant in the crew at the time the aircraft was lost. Lance Corporal Edwards maintained that the story given to the investigating officer regarding the bodies being stripped naked had been untrue and that he had carried out his own investigations prior to the first official visit of Flight Lieutenant Milliard. It was then that an official exhumation was requested at the earliest opportunity to formally identify the bodies.

On April 9, 1947, Flight Lieutenant Milliard and Captain Hillier of the 83 Graves Concentration Unit attended the military cemetery of Saint-Pol to exhume and identify the remains for their final burial.

After consulting the cemetery records further, they made their way to row three located in the centre plot. The collective grave was then cleared and gradually the team dug down with their shovels and opened the grave up to reveal the remains of five intact bodies buried side by side, although they were beyond recognition. Mixed up in among these were several individual bones and scraps of clothing that appeared to be what survived of a sixth airman, which was not quite evident at the beginning of the exhumation.

Starting from left to right, row three, grave one, the remains were positively identified as the pilot, a flying officer, having located a pilot's brevet and parts of a flying officer's braid and shirt. The second grave contained an airman identified by a laundry mark showing *859* on his clothing, believed to be last three digits of Flying Officer May's service number, together with an electrically heated flying suit and aircrew sweater. The third and fourth graves held the remains of two flying officers, and items found with them included flying helmets with headphones, parachute harnesses, and shirts. The fifth grave revealed an unknown airman, with scraps of clothing, and the sixth grave contained remnants of clothing together with several bones, which were assumed to be the remains of the sixth airman.

It was the opinion of the investigating officer that the first three remains, in graves one to three, would be positively registered as individuals, while the others in graves four to six would have to be located in a communal grave upon registration. The seventh member of the crew was not located in the cemetery; the body remained where it had been buried after being found by locals after the Germans had cleared the crash site. A witness advised the investigating officer that an envelope found near the body was addressed to Sergeant Dawson. After further examination Dawson's remains were removed and reburied inside the cemetery in his own grave. The remaining six aircrew were eventually registered and left as they were in a communal grave, with only Flying Officer Morrison and Flying Officer May having been positively identified. But in the end, these men deserved more than simple identification and a peaceful resting place; each had his own story leading up to this circumstance.

The skipper in charge of the crew, Robert "Bob" Huston Bannihr, was born on September 19, 1920, in Detroit, Michigan, and was the only American crew member on board the Halifax. His family had moved to Toronto, Ontario, when he was very young, and he spent his school years in that city. Robert, named after his father, was the family's only son but had three sisters, one sadly not living at the time he enlisted.

Robert had a colourful background. Before signing up with the RCAF, he had previously served with the US Navy Air Force as an aviation mechanic's mate for four years on board the USS *Lexington* out of San Diego, California. While there he was awarded a good conduct medal for his service. He had enlisted upon leaving his Toronto high school in 1937 and was honourably discharged in September 1941. The military lifestyle obviously agreed with him, for Robert volunteered in November 1941 in Toronto for active service with the RCAF. His enlistment documentation noted that he had previously received training on gunnery, flight engineer, and mechanic duties. It was further mentioned on his application form that he "can do anything around a plane, except fly one." The interviewing officer noted he was the "desirable type and above average American with a tall and slender build, clean, neatly dressed and pleasant manner." His ambition following the end of the war was to return to school to study aircraft design or to continue a career in aviation.

Robert was accepted as a trainee pilot and graduated with his pilot's wings in early 1943. He was posted overseas and joined No. 23 Operational Training Unit at Throckmorton, near Worcester. He again scored reasonably well in his exams, but he found instrument flying challenging. Although rated as an energetic captain who led his crew well, it was noted that slight distractions in the cockpit could divert his attention from flying. However, his overall performance, including his leadership skills, improved with further experience. At the end of December 1943, the skipper and his now fully qualified crew were posted to No. 424 Squadron for operations. He was killed on his thirty-first mission.

PILOT OFFICER Walter Harold Tomlinson, the wireless operator on the crew, was twenty-two when he lost his life. He was born on November 12, 1921, in Kingston, Ontario, to English parents. His father Walter, a former soldier, was from Leeds, and his mother Margaret from Burnley. Walter was their only child. He had a keen interest in model aeroplanes and amateur radio while growing up, as well as in rugby and sailing.

Walter hoped to get into active service as soon as possible after leaving school. He joined the non-permanent active militia and served in it for two years. He attempted to enlist with the Royal Canadian Engineers, but his service was cut short after less than two months when they discovered he was under eighteen. Undeterred, he joined the Royal Canadian Navy Volunteer Reserve (RCNVR) on June 17, 1940, and three weeks later, on July 9, 1940, was given permission to join the RCAF. The transfer was approved on the grounds that immediate active service could not be promised to him in the Navy. In November, the RCAF interview observed Walter to be "quick minded, accurate and with a mature personality for his age," summing him up as an above average candidate all round. Following completion of his initial training in drill, signals, and other core subjects, Walter was assessed by his commanding officer to be "a quiet airman who lacks dash and initiative. Reliable and dependable, although does not instil much confidence. Should improve with service and training." A year later, he enrolled at No. 3 Wireless School in Winnipeg, followed by a gunnery course. Walter arrived in the UK on June 4, 1943, and spent the next six months completing further training before finally being transferred for operational duties on December 28, 1943.

FLYING OFFICER Alan Edward May was the aircraft's navigator. One of two sons to Mabel and Edward May, he was born on June 5, 1922, in Winnipeg, Manitoba. On completing his schooling in 1939,

Alan took up temporary employment with a timber operator but left soon after to attend United College. He moved on to the University of Manitoba, graduating in 1941. Alan was big and strong, participating in the physical sports of boxing, wrestling, and rugby—team sports suited for the RCAF. After nine months in the Canadian Officer Training Corps he enlisted with the RCAF, on November 13, 1941, at the age of nineteen, with initial hopes of becoming a pilot. The interviewing officer was of the opinion that he suited the position of pilot or observer and was an "exceptionally fine student and athlete with a good appearance and nice personality."

The medical officer described Alan as "alert, intelligent, cheerful and poised to do a good job but with a fiery character due to his father's war wounds," his desire to enlist evidently having been influenced by his father's experience in the First World War. Alan's initial training began in March 1942 and went without a hitch—he was someone who had "surplus energy and was burning with enthusiasm," as stated by his commanding officer. But his pilot training at the elementary flying training school did not go to plan, and he washed out before going solo. Despite strong motivation and high intellectual capacity, he could not grasp the concept of flying an aircraft, suffering from poor coordination and being too tense when flying. His flight training ceased on May 23, 1942; his report read: "His overabundance of exuberance is perhaps one of his main faults. He flies as if every movement is something to be done forcefully and quickly—the idea that an aircraft might respond more readily to smooth and easy movements is one he finds impossible to put into execution. An excellent type of airman for any type of duty except precision work requiring patience." Alan was remustered to a ground trade as a radio mechanic, but he was determined to make aircrew in some capacity. Less than six weeks after leaving flight school, he enrolled on a navigators' course at Winnipeg, graduating in January 1943, having achieved high marks in his practical work in the air and on the ground. Alan became operational on December 28, 1943, and had flown twenty-nine sorties at the time of his death at the age of twenty-two.

FLYING OFFICER Raymond Gerald Viau was born on September 29, 1921, in Greenfield, Ontario. Raymond was somewhat suited for the role of air gunner, having been raised on a farm and hunting game since the age of twelve. His parents, Albert and Armancia, had a large family of eight children, with Raymond being one of the oldest siblings. He enlisted with the RCAF in the late summer of 1941, specifying ground duties, which are only shown on his service record as general duties. However, as the demand for aircrew increased, Raymond applied for remustering to aircrew. His interviewing officer described him as "confident with a sincere manner, but quiet with an unassuming determination," sending him on for training in June 1942.

Raymond joined his gunnery course at No. 6 Bombing and Gunnery School in Mountain View, Ontario. The chief instructor commented that "his air firing results were below average, but he had no trouble in the classroom and should make a good NCO." Raymond passed his final exams and, having qualified on September 25, 1942, was promoted to the rank of sergeant. Despite his quiet demeanour, Raymond did land himself in trouble on a few occasions while serving, including being caught with others gambling in the classroom and breaking out of barracks just two days into a seven-day sentence of being confined to barracks. For these he received forfeiture in pay and further days in detention. After completing his course in late October 1942, he was posted overseas for further gunnery training on air exercises around the UK. It would be many months before he would see active service on operations when he took up his final posting with No. 424 Squadron in November 1943.

FLYING OFFICER John Houseal Morrison was the oldest member of the crew at age twenty-six. Born on August 16, 1917, he was one of two sons of Bernard and Anna Morrison. John enlisted in Halifax, Nova Scotia, in June 1939, noting on his application form: "My ambition is to remain in the armed services and serve my country as best I can." Upon enlistment, he became a clerk but later transferred to begin flying training as a pilot.

Despite his hard work, he struggled at the elementary flying training school. He would fly the aircraft by instinct rather than by the rules, causing his chief flying instructor to comment that he "lacked air sense and reacted too slowly to changing circumstances in the air." On July 7, 1942, John was reprimanded for crashing an aircraft on his first solo flight after he raised the landing gear instead of the flaps. He realized the writing was on the wall and requested that he be allowed to discontinue pilot instruction to train as an air bomber. He qualified for this role on January 22, 1943. In their remarks his supervising officers said he "tried hard" and was "keen and interested at all times," a "clean cut, bright worker, with good leadership qualities, and officer type material." At the time of his death, he was an experienced airman; he had flown twenty-nine sorties over enemy territory and was almost at the end of his first tour and set to enjoy a long period of leave away from operations.

PILOT OFFICER Stanley James Queen was the rear gunner on Halifax LW169 this unlucky day. Born in Colchester, Ontario, on April 9, 1921, he was one of two sons and a daughter to James and Mable Queen. Sadly, by the time he volunteered to go to war, his sister Marjorie was his only remaining next of kin. In his RCAF Service Book, Stanley identified her as a resident of Essex, Ontario, and claimed his pre-enlistment occupation as farming.

In the spring of 1942, Stanley made an application to the navy for the position of ordinary seaman. In September of that year, he was discharged at his own request in order to join the air force to train as a pilot. He claimed he wanted to be actively involved in the war, but the navy was too slow in processing his application, so he volunteered his services to the RCAF for the duration of the war. There is no record that he underwent any pilot training—the trade shown on his official documents is "air gunner" only. In this, Stanley excelled, coming third in his class of 122 trainees. On completion of his gunnery course in Trenton in June 1943, he was identified as a suitable candidate for gunnery instructor should the position arise.

The chief instructor commented that he "displayed initiative and applies himself diligently," and that he had a "sound knowledge of his trade; should make an excellent crew member."

Stanley avoided being diverted to a career as an instructor and was instead sent to the processing depot in Halifax for the journey to the UK. Once there, he was crewed up and spent time with No. 23 Operational Training Unit and No. 1664 Heavy Conversion Unit before finally being posted to RCAF No. 424 Squadron on December 28, 1943. On his death, he left behind his sister and his wife Stella, whom he had married just a year previously in July 1943 at Windsor.

THE FLIGHT engineer on board this Halifax was Sergeant Leonard Bert Dawson, the only RAF member of the crew. Like too many who sacrificed their lives for something in which they believed, he left few records, and little is known about him beyond his assessment during training as an accomplished and very keen student, working well, with good results as a crew member. He was clearly an integral part of an ill-fated team.

THE INSCRIPTION on Flying Officer Alan May's headstone in St. Pol cemetery in Pas-de-Calais perhaps expresses best the sad fate of May and his crewmates on Halifax LW169. It records: "A gallant youthful heart who died valiantly for freedom and home."

OPPOSITE, TOP The Bannihr crew. JANE WILSON

OPPOSITE, MIDDLE, LEFT John Morrison, RCAF, air bomber. NATIONAL ARCHIVES OF CANADA VIA MARC HALL

OPPOSITE, MIDDLE, RIGHT Walter Tomlinson, RCAF, wireless operator. CVWM VIA OPERATION PICTURE ME

OPPOSITE, BOTTOM A well worn picture of one of the crew's Handley Page Halifax bombers. GRANT BAILEY AND ANDREW MORRISON

ABOVE, LEFT Robert Bannihr, RCAF, pilot. JANE WILSON

ABOVE, MIDDLE Raymond Viau, RCAF, air gunner. CVWM VIA OPERATION PICTURE ME

ABOVE, RIGHT Navigator Alan May (left) and Air Gunner Stan Queen (right) in 1943. GRANT BAILEY AND ANDREW MORRISON

Halifax LW436 of RCAF No. 434 Squadron, based at RAF Croft, south of Darlington, was detailed for a sortie late morning on August 4, 1944, to attack the supply dump at Bois de Cassan, believed to be storing V-1 flying bombs. The target site was inside dense woodland and consisted of numerous bunkers and storage facilities, with strong accompanying air defences. On this day, 291 aircraft of Nos. 6 and 8 Bomber Groups departed their bases to attack Bois de Cassan and the Trossy St. Maximin site. The weather was clear over the target areas, and the raids were successfully carried out, with the loss of four Bomber Command aircraft. The crew of Halifax LW436 had roared into the sky at 10:29 hours that summer morning and would be one of those fated not to return home.

13

YOU DID YOUR DUTY...
MY BROTHERS IN ARMS

MARC HALL

WITH THE AIRCRAFT and crew long overdue, enquires were made to see if Halifax LW436 had landed elsewhere. The next day, however, telegrams were sent to the next of kin advising them that their relatives were missing in action. This was all the news they would receive until the end of September 1944, when further details became available and the Red Cross were able to inform four of the families that their loved ones had indeed lost their lives. Nothing further was heard regarding the remaining three airmen, but after the war's end, a tale of struggle and survival would emerge.

Following the end of hostilities, the Missing Research and Enquiry Service (MRES) set about locating and laying to rest the fallen airmen who had not come home. By then, the three hitherto unaccounted for aircrew of this Halifax were known to be safe and well. It fell to Squadron Leader Wood and his team from the No. 6 Section of the MRES to locate the four other airmen, investigate the crash, and undertake the grim task of exhumation. The team located the graves in the parish cemetery in the small village of Drosay, a quiet farming community situated near Pays de Caux, some twenty-five miles southwest of Dieppe. The account of M. Herbert, the secretary of the church at Drosay, supported the statements from the survivors that the aircraft had exploded over the area after being hit by flak. Three bodies had been named from their personal identification discs, and the fourth, that of Sergeant Raymond Bruegeman (from Hanover, Ontario), by a process of elimination. The Red Cross had previously advised the Allies via a telegram, quoting German information, that Flying Officer Jack Kelly (Toronto) and Flying Officer George Perkins (St. Catharines), along with one non-RCAF airman and one unknown—later identified as the only RAF member of the crew, Sergeant Norman Marley—had indeed lost their lives on the afternoon of August 4, 1944. French locals had recovered the deceased and buried them side by side with crosses made from pieces of the crashed aircraft. The graves were well kept with flowers, the local people taking pride and great care to honour the airmen. Following their identification, the Graves Registration Unit were handed the case and the deaths recorded for official purposes, enabling some closure for the families. Today the four young airmen rest in the same churchyard at Drosay, along with six other Allied airmen not affiliated with the Halifax's crew.

THE YOUNG crew were only on their third operational sortie when tragedy struck. Their Halifax aircraft had reached the target area and was positioned for the bombing run, flying through a thick flak barrage. Large puffs of black smoke from exploding shells rocked the aircraft as it pressed on. As it came over the target, a nearby flak burst sent shards of hot metal into the airframe and shredded the port elevator and rudder, critically damaging the Halifax. The pilot, Flight Lieutenant Robert "Bud" Lang, later recounted that the aircraft was becoming increasingly hard to control but the crew carried on and successfully bombed the target at 16,000 feet before making a swift exit to the northwest in the direction of the French coast. The skipper continued to battle with the controls to get his severely damaged aircraft and its crew back to base. Nearing the Channel, the crew discovered that two bombs had failed to release from their

racks and remained hung up in the bomb bay. With the pilot struggling to steer the aircraft, their luck was about to run out, as German
anti-aircraft batteries continued to hound the fleeing bombers.

Twenty miles from the coast and near Rouen, the aircraft took
a direct hit in the starboard wing. The fuel tanks were torn open,
the contents spilled out over the hot, running engines and ignited
instantly. With fire now raging, Lang took immediate action to
shut down the starboard outer motor and feather the airscrew. The
British flight engineer, Sergeant Norman Marley, activated the
fire extinguisher and fuel cutoffs; the fire died back until it was no
longer visible from the cockpit and appeared to have been extinguished. But by now, Halifax LW436 was in a critical state. Lang
later reported: "Owing to very little port elevator and rudder control
and only one starboard engine, I had to close the throttle on all of
the remaining engines so as to keep the aircraft under control. We
could not hold our altitude, so I gave the crew the order to prepare
for ditching."

The Halifax was now heading for the cold, uninviting waters of
the English Channel, but it didn't make it that far. Without warning
the aircraft exploded violently, breaking into a barrage of large parts
and abruptly ending four lives. The three survivors—who had their
parachutes when they were thrown out of the aircraft—suddenly
found themselves falling through the sky. All landed safely. In his
statement given following his return home to the UK, Robert Lang
recounted: "Then the fuel tank exploded and the next thing I knew
I was out of the aircraft and had pulled the rip-cord on my parachute.
All of this happened at 13:30 in the afternoon. I was picked up by
Dr. and Madam Aureille at Cany-Barville, Seine Inferieur [*sic*],
France, a mile from the crash. The bodies of four of the crew were
found near the crash: Flying Officer George G. Perkins [mid-upper
gunner], Flying Officer Jack H. Kelly [navigator], Pilot Officer Raymond G. Bruegeman [bomb aimer], all from Ontario; and Sergeant
Jack Marley [flight engineer, RAF] from England. They were buried in
the church yard of Drosay, Seine Inferieur, a mile from the crash site."

LANG LANDED, injured, in a farmer's field. The two other survi-vors, wireless operator Sergeant Gerald Donovan and tail gunner Sergeant Nelles, landed close to one another and met up, crawl-ing into a ditch. After two days in the open, they began to look for food before finally being taken in and given shelter by a sympathetic farmer. They would eventually return to England. Some letters and accounts survive, giving further detail of the tragic loss of the air-craft and the events that followed. The first is from Madam Eva Aureill, written to the Bruegeman family:

28 October 1946

Dear Madam:

I received your letter this morning and with the sincere hope of easing your mind and making you a little happier I am answering you by air-mail.

It was about half-past one in the afternoon of the 4 of August 1944, that a Halifax plane exploded and crashed near Drosay a few miles away from Cany where I live. I was absent at the moment but on my return at six o'clock and hearing about the accident, I went immediately to the place to see if we could do anything and help escape any of the boys if there were any still living, but all we found was the wrecked plane and a newly dug grave beside it. We searched until dark and began again the next morning at four o'clock as soon as day broke and this time we were fortunate enough to find the pilot Robert Lang severely bruised all over and hiding in a wheat field and it was through having been given the description of the body found beside the plane that we knew it was Raymond Bruegeman. The explosion was so sudden that he was thrown out of the plane without having the time to open out his parachute, he was killed instantly and was not even disfigured, so please let your mind rest at ease, everything happened so quickly that it was already over before he knew even that they were in danger. Two days later he was taken from his temporary grave, put into a very nice coffin, and was buried this time in the cemetery beside the church at Drosay after a very touching burial service. The next day the bodies of the other three poor boys were found and were also buried in the same cemetery beside your son, they had all been killed immediately. Robert Lang explained to us that coming back from the target near Paris, they were crossing Rouen when the flack made a small hole in their right wing, the hole must have got bigger and bigger and at last broke off (it was found about 3 miles from the plane) at the same moment the plane exploded into 5 or 6 pieces. Robert said that they were all so far from thinking that something could happen that some of them had not even put on their parachutes. That Robert Lang has not written to you or been to see you, does not astonish me in the least. We are very disappointed in him for we risked our lives to help him and hid him a month in our house with the Germans coming in and out every day until we were liberated, and yet not one simple word of thanks have we received from him. He left us in September 1944 and was flown back to England and when I went to England myself in April 1945, I moved heaven and earth to find out what had happened to him since the commanding officer had come to our house to fetch him, at last found him and learnt that he had even been home to Canada on leave and had come back again, it was then that I gave him the photos, he promised me faithfully then to write a letter to my husband, who as you can imagine was not very pleased with him, but we are still waiting for the letter and will probably wait a long time. Of the twelve air men I helped to escape he is the only one who has shown such rank ingratitude. Yesterday a Mrs. Michel-Taboulet came to see me saying that you had written her, asking news of your son. I gave her some photos of the church and the other boys' graves to send you, I hope you receive them safely. I again assure you Madam that your son died instantly and without even being disfigured that he was buried like a Christian and his grave is always well kept. Perhaps one day you will come and visit it yourself.

You have suffered terribly also by the war and my heartfelt sympathies goes with you and will you please give my deepest sympathy to your daughter and daughter-in-law.

My sincere best wishes to you all. Eva Aureille

On November 20, 1946, a relative of Flying Officer Kelly wrote to Mrs. Bruegeman. "Bud" was the nickname for the pilot, who had apparently been in touch with the family of at least one other crew member:

Bud was fortunate that he came down near the French couple of whom you speak, and of whom we all got snaps. He tells us his French is anything but good but she was an English lady married to this Frenchman who was probably actively connected with the French underground. At any rate, they hid Bud for several weeks. He tells me the Germans followed the usual procedure of going out to examine the plane and take anything valuable from it and from the bodies of our boys, and any who were alive would be brought out of the wreck as prisoners. That is why Bud, also the lad from the Maritimes, seemed so sure none of the boys in the plane when it reached the ground, were still alive. The Maritimes boy said in his letter, that the blast from the explosion was so terrific the boys would not survive it, and Bud said if they had been alive, even though hurt, the Germans would have lined them up. He also assured me the bodies were not burned at all, the boys died in the air as a result of the explosion before ever they hit the earth. After the Germans have looked over the wreck thoroughly, they tell the French people—bury them or do what you like with them, we don't care. The French people are very good and the boys were all buried (at) the little church nearby. Bud was not permitted to attend, as this would have been very foolish, even in rough working clothes the Germans would have noticed a young man around who was not familiar to them and would have asked questions, so he was hidden in a barn a short way down the road, from which he could see the funeral procession. All the time he was there, which must have been several weeks, the French people from nearby kept fresh flowers on the graves of the boys, every day. Bud said he had only a little French money on him and when he was finally able to leave, he offered it to the lady, and she refused to even touch it, saying they were only too glad to be of any service. So he left it with her to buy flowers for the grave, or to repay in some small way the poor people who had been so faithful in taking care of the boys' graves. Immediately on his return to England, he made his report to the proper authorities, telling of the boys being buried and that he saw the funeral service, etc.

A French law student, Madam Evelyne Michel, whose father was the local mayor of the village during the German occupation, contacted the Bruegeman family after the war with further information of what had occurred to their son's aircraft and to his crew mates. She informed them that the priest had located Raymond Bruegeman in a cornfield, close to parts of the aircraft, the priest mentioning the wreckage having broken into five or six parts, with a wing being found three miles from the main crash site. Madam Michel said:

When we found Raymond we buried him the same day at the place he was lying, but two days later we put him in a beautiful coffin and buried him in the church cemetery at Drosay. We had splendid obsequies; all the men of the village who had fought in the 1914– 1918 war were present with all the French and Allied flags, and all the people of the village and surrounding country... Raymond's grave was covered with flowers, several people gave me money for me saying masses for him. The day after his funeral we found two other Canadians and one English lad. They were buried in the cemetery too. We did everything we could for them, but their obsequies were not quite like Raymond's.

The wireless operator, Sergeant Gerald Donovan, had his own tale to tell after spending many weeks on the run and in hiding before finally being liberated by the advancing Canadian Army. A letter describes how he became a crew member and relates their last sortie. Then a short story, which was published several years after the war, details his escapades with the rear gunner, Sergeant Nelles.

October 22, 1945

Dear Mrs. Bruegeman,

This is the first time I have had a chance to write you, and I am afraid I am not much of a letter writer. It sure is good that the wars are over but you poor people can never forget Ray, nor shall I, those four very fine boys that were killed in our aircraft. I first met Ray in the later part of April at OTU (operational training unit). He came to our billets one evening asking for a wireless operator for a crew, I don't know how it happened but I was the first to speak to him and so from then on we were the very best of pals. We had plenty of work to do and plenty to learn, but all the boys were anxious to make a success of it.

The later part of June we had two weeks leave, and Ray and I spent it together in London and Edinburgh, and a very enjoyable time we had. Then came Conversion Unit, now we started to fly in the Halifax and there was plenty more to learn but it only lasted a month, and we were ready for the squadron. It was the Bluenose squadron and again we were flying in the Halifax. We had made two very successful trips both over France and we were more or less a little more confident in ourselves and each other since we had actually flown over enemy territory and had more idea of what it was like. Then when our third trip came along we listened very closely and wanted to make sure there were no mistakes. Equipment etc. was checked and rechecked as before. We reached our target, dropped the bombs, or at least Ray did, and were on our way home again. Everything was going fine when we were hit in the wing, the most vital spot, by enemy ground defences. Fire started immediately and we did what we could to put it out and it did seem to be out when there was a terrible explosion.

Just what happened after that I do not know too much about, however I do remember putting on my chute and the next thing I was on my way down. I have no idea how I left the aircraft. Finally I reached the ground not far from our rear gunner, so we were together from there on and he didn't know any more than I did except that the aircraft had broken in two and he had managed to get out of the rear part. We hid in a ditch very near to us for two days; at the end of that time we asked a French farmer for food and also where we were. Starting the second night we walked in a southerly direction getting bread and cider from the good French people when we could, until the eighth night when the farmer we went to for food was with the underground and he hid us away in his barn until more of the underground came with civilian clothes, false passports etc. and took us away in a wagon to a place where we were to stay until the Allied army came along. At our last place at Caudebec en Caux we had the very best of everything except we had to stay upstairs in the house and run to the attic if the Germans came around, which they did many times. However, the army came along and we knew we were free and safe.

It was about six weeks later that we met Lang in England and he told us that the other four boys had been killed. I do not believe that he even knew what happened to them, if they were hurled out without their chutes or just what may have happened. But if anybody knows it would be him because I am sure I do not know. Ray's position in the Halifax was quite well up in the nose of the ship, the navigator Kelly was very near. They worked at the same little table. I was next and the pilot Lang was directly over me, in all we were not over six feet apart. I was about seven or eight feet from the very front end.

I do remember Ray speak about some English friends of his and I believe at least one of them was killed or missing before we were reported missing. As for crew pictures, we did have some taken but they were at a studio being developed but I do not know where. Lang said he was going to try to find them if he could but I have not heard from him since March. I do hope that Ray's wife can carry on with the Business course, it will help her a lot to brave it off, Ray used to speak of her so often that I almost think I know her. Mrs. Bruegeman, if there if anything else I can tell you I would be glad to do so but I believe I have answered at least the questions you asked.

So long for now and my God bless you all.
Gerald Donovan, Canterbury, New Brunswick

After the war, Donovan recorded his further recollections of the event, writing them in the third person:

They were flying above the clouds, great cumulus billowing puffs which blotted out all the view of the ground, but occasionally there was a glimpse of Paris out to the left. It was not long after they had left the target approximately 10,000 feet or so above some dense cloud when Gerald felt a heavy jar through the aircraft, which was in fact the impact of parts of an anti-aircraft shell through the starboard wing outer engine which had exploded nearby to the aircraft. Pieces of flak caused the fire in the motor and the extinguishers were activated, which appeared to have the effect of putting out the fire. Gerald informed the skipper that the aircraft was on fire and he replied: 'If the fire is out, we'll try to make it home.' They were over the French coast just then and there was only the English Channel to cross. As Gerald watched, the fire flared up again, and he shouted: 'Skipper, the whole right wing is on fire.' In reply, the pilot spoke into the bomber's intercom. 'Prepare to ditch,' he said. Enemy radar got them just when they believed that they were safe. Almost immediately after the fire flared up again the second time, there was a terrific explosion as if the gas tanks out in the wing had exploded. The right wing blew right off ripping a big hole in the side of the bomber right near Gerald's position. He grabbed his parachute just as the plane broke in two. Actually, Gerald believed that the bomber broke into three pieces because he just caught a glimpse of the tail breaking away with the tail gunner still in it. He was flying away all by himself, but Gerald noticed that the tail gunner was cranking the machine gun blister around to get his parachute. Later he told Gerald that he just grabbed his chute and fell out. While still struggling with his own parachute, Gerald fell through that big hole in the side of the bomber. As he was falling the pilot gave him a good solid kick in the forehead above his eye. He only got one snap fastened and kept struggling to fasten the other snap hook and so there he was hanging horizontally on one hook. Looking up he saw that his parachute was just barely hooked on the support bar above him, and he prayed that it would hold. Although now free of the doomed bomber he was now in grave danger of dropping free from the parachute and risked falling to earth without it. Then he reached up, fearing that his parachute would break free of the bar securing it to his body, and pulled the rip cord. It had to be done. The chute opened with a snap and his loose-fitting boots flew off, but the fastening on the bar held. Looking down towards the ground he was drifting towards the uninviting waters of the English Channel; however, as he became lower he noticed ploughed fields and fortunately landed sideways in one of these, shoulder and head first due to the way he was suspended in the harness. A sudden and sharp pain convinced him he had broken some ribs but there was no medical aid to hand.

As he gathered up his parachute, he saw another member of the bomber crew land over in a field some distance away. That fellow immediately fell down and couldn't get up so Gerald knew that the other airman was hurt. He kept looking around for more of the crew, and at the same time wary of the presence of Germans. It was then he spotted one of their fellows running towards him and immediately recognised him as the tail gunner and, with a river of adrenalin flowing, the tail gunner took both parachutes over and hid them in the scrub. They both moved into the bushes and took stock of the situation and what they had, which was a small emergency ration and some survival equipment. All day they hid in those bushes and eventually they saw some Frenchmen attend the area and go over to the third airmen they had seen approximately four hundred yards away who was struggling to move or get up. The Frenchmen came back for him later on and removed him to a hiding place.

Every hour the soreness in Gerald's head and chest increased. After dark they began to walk westwards as they had been taught in training. They walked all night, staying off the roads to avoid the Germans who were always moving. It was very rough on his feet without shoes as he had lost his flying boots when the parachute had snapped open. They hid in the bushes all of the following day and walked all of the next night. The tail gunner with him was very nervous and jumpy as he kept remembering flying all alone in that gun blister after the tail broke off. The two flyers had life jackets on under their parachute harness and on the third morning, they took all of that stuff off, and buried it. Gerald found out that he had quite a bad cut over his right eye and it was very sore and as such felt that he was in bad shape.

The next night as they hid they noticed several French people coming near to them and their actions told the two Canadians that the Frenchmen knew that they were there. After dark one of the Frenchmen went over to them and explained that he wanted to get them into civilian clothes as quickly as possible. Gerald told him that he needed boots. After a while, he brought a pair of boots over, but they were too small. The next day they hid in a straw stack out in the field, but some young children came to play around the stack. They were afraid that the attention would draw notice to them so they decided to move on in order to get away from the children's activity. The day after this the pair took up their hiding positions among some stacked corn stocks out in a field but a farmer then came over and hauled most of the corn stocks away. Upon his return he parted the stocks and saw the two Canadians but immediately covered them back up again and left. In the daylight he again returned but stayed well away from the two airmen as being caught with them by the Germans who were everywhere would likely end up with them all being shot. The following day another man returned to their place of hiding and removed them to a barn where he then questioned them and informed them that the French underground wanted to speak to them.

On the eighth day after they were shot down, a civilian came to them and he could speak perfect English. He questioned them to find out who they actually were, giving them a long examination, all about Canada. He asked Gerald dozens of details about New Brunswick where he came from, then he asked the tail gunner all about Alberta where he came from. Questions were asked all about the rivers, the industry, the farming, many of the local places, and he knew all of the answers. After a while he seemed satisfied that they were who they said [they] were.

Then they were taken to another house where they were put up on the third floor in what was believed [to be] the attic. Although the French people had barely enough to eat themselves, they were able to find food for the two Canadians. At night they could go out into the fields and walk around. Up in their part of the attic hidden behind the bricks of a fireplace was a radio which they used to listen to, especially the BBC newscast about the war. It was from this they found out the Allied developments and the progress of the war.

Later, the men came to the two Canadians and invited them to attend a sabotage patrol with them. They went along walking up the road, five or six abreast, all ages, with some as young as sixteen and seventeen. There must have been about seventy-five of them all together. Gerald and his buddy did not speak French and so had no idea what they were supposed to do or where they were going. In fact he believed that they were just in the way. They

shot up a bridge that night, but Gerald didn't know what damage was done. On another day, the two flyers watched as Allied
fighter bombers attacked a nearby bridge with a number of Mosquito planes destroying it.

A visit was made to the mayor's house where everything was
spoken in English but, nevertheless, not knowing what was going
on, they were always nervous, and being tense and ready to run all
of the time was very tiring. The village where the mayor resided
was on the bank of a river and they soon discovered it had some
secrets. The Canadian army had advanced and they were on the
bank on the other side of the river, meaning rescue was now so
near. The French told Gerald that they should cross the river to
the Canadians. At first Gerald didn't even know that the Canadians were there and of course they didn't trust anyone at any time.
It was then they learned that the village was also hiding about a
dozen other Allied personnel, most of whom were Americans and
they had been right in the village all of the time, but their presence was of course kept secret all of the time. Two of them took a
canoe and paddled over to the Canadian army where they were
met by an armed soldier from a Highland regiment. He kept his
rifle aimed right on Gerald and his companion and upon crossing
he challenged them in a determined manner. The prisoners were
then informed to go back across the river and wait. Some of the
Americans had been hiding in that village for weeks, and all were
excited about getting across the river. The next day the Frenchmen got a boat and all of the flyers got into it and crossed over
to the Canadians again and it was from there they were taken to
the French coast and put on a ship bound for England. That was
a happy trip. In England they were immediately sent to a centre
for returned prisoners of war and they were given a medical and
clothing that fit. Those needing care and treatment were tended
to. The escaped flyers had arrived in old clothes and boots which
were too big or too small for most of them and they were glad to
throw them away. They were confined to one barrack block and

there was a constant guard on the place. They were all extremely nervous and Gerald had lost fifty pounds in weight from his experience. With the guards and all, it wasn't as if they were really free, or back with friends. Of course the authorities had to find out who they really were. The military police kept them in that special barracks for about a month and all that time Gerald was most anxious to get word back to his parents to tell them that he was all right and back in England. They were told that they were confined to barracks and that there were no phones. However, one guard was sympathetic and he made it easy for Gerald to get to a phone to call home.

During his medical, Gerald's extreme nervousness showed, and it was concluded that his flying days were over and so he was declared unfit for aircrew duty. Gerald Donovan spent over a month in hiding and running and said that it was very stressful and risky most of the time. 'There never was enough food and the food was barely enough to sustain us and we all lost a lot of weight.'

A while after the war Gerald was in Moncton in a restaurant with a couple of friends and suddenly heard a commotion. A fellow had jumped up onto a table and he came running towards them, right across the top of all of the tables. Glasses and dishes went flying. In amazement Gerald recognized his old pilot, the one who had injured his back when he landed parachuting into France. He had last seen him on the ground way out in that field. They grabbed one another, hugged and slapped each other, both talking and laughing at once. Gerald had thought that he was dead. Of course the police came and arrested both of them despite them paying for the damages but Gerald remembered that he knew the magistrate and so following a phone call and having explained everything the pair were released. It was a very happy day. Gerald settled back into civilian life as the owner and operator of a small men's clothing store.

LEFT Ray Bruegeman, 1942. MARILEE MAGDER AND FAMILY, MARY AND RUEBEN

RIGHT Jack Kelly, RCAF, navigator. CVWM VIA OPERATION PICTURE ME

LEFT Gerald Donovan, RCAF, wireless operator (survived). MARILEE MAGDER, JESSICA DONOVAN, RONALD PERKINS, CARL DUIVENVOORDEN AND FAMILY

RIGHT George Perkins, RCAF, mid-upper gunner. 434 SQUADRON ASSOCIATION

At half past three on the morning of August 27, 1944, the residents of the small Danish village of Åstruplund were awoken by the sound of an intense air battle taking place in the night skies above their homes. Those who gazed into the night had their faces illuminated as a fireball flashed overhead, plummeting into a field outside the village. The fireball was an Avro Lancaster manned by four British and three Canadian airmen. The Royal Air Force heavy bomber disintegrated in a ball of flame in the field of farmer Svend Andersen, who, later that morning, made his way to the crash site, which was guarded and cordoned off by German soldiers. Svend persuaded one of those serving in the army that occupied his country to allow him closer to see if there had been much damage to his crops. The horror of what he saw remained with him for the rest of his life.

14

LOVE AND REMEMBRANCE
LAST FOREVER

STEVE DARLOW

MANY THOUSANDS of Canadians answered the call to take up arms and fight a distant war across an ocean in Europe. Tens of thousands of those who put their names forward for duty with the Royal Canadian Air Force went on, after training in Canada, to serve with RAF Bomber Command in the air offensive against Nazism. Those left at home followed the progress of the war via the national press and the radio, and some may even have recognized familiar faces on the news reels. The personal details of husbands, sons, and brothers, however, usually came via the written word, often taking weeks if not months to arrive. However, some of the unwelcome correspondence would arrive more quickly.

The letters of John Ernest Fitzgerald are typical of those written by young Canadian airmen serving with RAF Bomber Command in the United Kingdom. They reflect his keenness to contribute to the cause for which he signed up in January 1943, just before his eighteenth birthday. Having already served with army and air cadets before enlisting, "Jack" left his home in New Westminster, BC, to begin basic training under the BCATP and completed the Canadian portions of his course at No. 3 Bombing and Gunnery School at Macdonald, Manitoba, in November of that same year. On February 19,

1944, Jack was in the final phases of training as an air gunner and wrote to his mother and sister Ruth from Britain and described his frustrations with the delays he was experiencing in getting into an operational role.

> For the last three days I have been trying to get in a little flying time but everything seems to be against me. Either my pilot's sick or the aircraft is unserviceable. It is starting to get me down because I'm just itching to get flying again . . . For the last three days I haven't done a thing except sit around and clean the occasional gun. This monotony is beginning to get me down. As you can plainly see I can't think of a darn thing to write about, but I guess you will be glad to know that I am still alive and kicking at everything and everybody . . . One of these days I will write a decent letter that is if anything exciting ever happens that I can write about. Well I will sign off now.
>
> Lots of Love, Jack.

Jack wrote again on what he thought was May 1, opening that letter. "My Dearest Mother & Sister. Hello sweethearts how is my two best girl friends coming along?" He went on to mention a visit he had made to Westminster Abbey, which he describes as "an immensely high place."

> It must be around three hundred feet from the floor to the ceiling. Inside it smells musty as though a lot of books were slowly crumbling into dust. There are statues of famous artists and there [sic] work all over the place and the actually coffins of the people. Under the floor are graves of people who did a few famous deeds in their life. I didn't notice any Fitzgeralds or Mills there though. Probably we were there under an assumed name though. About the most striking place of all was the grave of the unknown soldier, it impressed me deeply for some reason or other . . . we went for a walk in St. James Park near the Buckingham Palace. It was a swell place and what I liked was the fact that they had Mallard ducks

tearing around the place. It sure reminded me of the good old days when I used to go hunting with Uncle Frank. I would have liked to have the old trusty 12 gauge and made our fine feathered friends a nice roast duck. All I could see when I saw them swimming around was one of your good old roast duck dinner on the hoof.'

Because Bomber Command was by now fully engaged in operations directly supporting the build-up to the Normandy invasion, many sorties were of shorter duration over French and Belgian territory than the more distant German raids. Bomber Command began to record these as less than a full operation in terms of contributing to the main force tally of thirty operations for a complete tour.

Commander-in-chief of Bomber Command Air Chief Marshal Sir Arthur Harris dispatch, 8 March 1944.

The risk, fatigue and strain in respect of operations carried out against short range and lightly defended targets in France, and short range mining operations where fighter defence is practically nil, is nowadays in no way comparable to those associated with long range targets in Germany. Under present arrangements those entirely different types of operation count as one sortie. The result is that some aircrews must inevitably finish their operational tour having experienced far less risk and strain than others, which is obviously undesirable. In addition, with the large amount of bombing of targets in France and occupied territory now being or about to be undertaken, crews will finish their operational tours too quickly, and the crew strength of squadrons cannot possibly be maintained . . . In view of the above I consider it essential to differentiate between the two entirely different types of operation, and to institute two separate methods of assessing operational sorties. I have therefore given instructions that bombing and minelaying operations which are carried out in an area W of 7°E and N of 53°N, and W of 6°E between 53°N and 46°N should each be counted as one third of a sortie only.

Such a policy, unsurprisingly, did not go down to well with aircrew. As of May 18, Jack was yet to take part in main force operations, and mentioned the new Bomber Command policy in a letter.

My Dearest Mother & Sister

Well Mom I feel pretty low for not writing more often. But I have really been working for the last few weeks. When we got off leave we went right on to an advanced gunnery school and they worked us twenty-four hours a day. But it was really worth it. Cause we were really taught some good stuff. My mid upper gunner and myself both made 89% in our final exams, which I think is pretty good.

That raid I had over France. I don't know whether it counts or not. Some say it does and some say it doesn't so I don't know what to think. By the way Gene has now made 18 trips which is pretty good in a way and pretty lousy in a way because he has been doing these targets in France and each trip consists of only ⅓ of a op. which is silly because if you go over there and get killed you don't get only ⅓ killed.

Jack

Posted to RAF No. 166 Squadron in the middle of June 1944, Jack and his crew flew their first operational sortie on the night of June 27/28, an attack on the V-1 flying bomb launch site at Château Bernapré. Since mid-June hundreds of flying bombs had flown low across the English Channel, fired from launch sites in northern France and aimed at London. The toll of civilian casualties had steadily risen. Bomber Command had been tasked with lowering the V-1 launch rates, attacking the launch sites and the supply and storage organization. These were short raids, but there was still danger. On the night of June 27/28, the No. 166 Squadron Lancaster of Pilot Officer Hunt, DFC, was lost, with no survivors.

Jack continued to play his part in the V-1 counteroffensive, with raids to Domleger (June 29 and July 2), Oisemont (June 30) and then to the V-2 rocket site at Wizernes on July 20. In between there were raids supporting the Normandy land battle, notably on Caen on July 7 and Sannerville on July 18, Bomber Command having been called in to blast an opening for the Allied land forces attempting to push ahead through the front lines. Bomber Command also maintained its attacks on rail targets bringing supplies to the German forces; Jack was involved in raids to Orleans on the night of July 4/5 and Revigny on July 12/13 and July 14/15. Twenty Lancasters were lost on these raids, including five from No. 166 Squadron on the Revigny attacks. Then there were the continuing attacks on German industrial targets: Scholven/Buer oil plant on July 18/19, Kiel (July 23/24) and Stuttgart (July 25/26 and 27/28). Against the last of these raids the following was recorded with reference to Jack's crew in the squadron diary: "Very quiet trip except for one fighter attack, enemy claimed as damaged." A mine-laying mission was assigned on July 26/27 off Heligoland, the squadron diary recording against Jack's crew: "Severe electrical storms and St. Elmo's fire along fuselage, wings, and propellers."

At the end of July and into August, the intensity of operations continued with attacks on the enemy navy at Le Havre (July 31 and August 2), the v-1 launch site at Le Belle Croix les Bruyeres (August 1, when poor weather hindered the attack), and the oil storage depot at Pauillac (August 4 and 5). On the latter daylight raid, there was particular tragedy for No. 166 Squadron. The squadron diary recorded:

> No enemy opposition was encountered, but the operation was marred by a collision between J2 and V, whilst flying at 450 ft. over the sea. As a result the tail unit and rear turret of J2 were broken off and fell into the sea. The aircraft then turned on its back and plunged into the sea and it is feared that the impact caused the bombs to detonate. The aircraft disappeared from view immediately and no survivors were seen. The mainplane of 'V' was very badly damaged and the aircraft had to abandon the mission and return to base. The remaining 21 aircraft successfully bombed the primary target but had to land away from base owing to unfavourable weather conditions.

Indeed, there were no survivors from Flight Lieutenant Holman's crew. With no known grave, their names are now etched on the Air Forces Memorial at Runnymede.

Jack's crew must have been given leave prior to their participation in a mine-laying operation on the night of August 16/17 to Stettin Bay. Jack's combat report records the action that night. (The combat report mentions "Fishpond," an airborne radar device to give early warning of approaching German night fighters.)

COMBAT REPORT

No. 166 Squadron	Night 16/17th August 1944
Lancaster III K2 PD 153	Fishpond Serviceable. Operator trained
03.00½ 11,000, 236T, 55.46½N. 07.25E	Homeward. Off track. 3–4 miles port of track
No cloud. No moon. Vis. starlight. Very dark	No flak, flares or other activity
Rear gunner Sgt. Fitzgerald. J.E.	
150–200 rounds. 150 yards 50 yards	
4 stoppages (link and ammo. stoppages)	

Soon after laying mines in the Stettin area Lancaster K2 of 166 Squadron received a warning on Fishpond of an A/C approaching fairly rapidly from slightly below almost dead astern. About 2–3 second later the R/G obtained a visual on a Ju 88 boring in from fine port quarter at a range of approx. 150 yards. The R/G immediately opened fire at the same time ordering a corkscrew port and observed smoke and flame pouring from both engines of the E/A. Firing another burst the R/G then observed E/A break away on fire about 50 yards away in the direction of the starboard beam. The M/U gunner was never able to get in a burst due to his G.F.I. coming into operation but confirms that the Ju88 went down in an almost vertical dive well alight. The E/A/ never opened fire at any time during the attack.

Comment by S/Ldr. Cox G.G.L.

Suggested that the claim of 'Probably destroyed' be made rather than 'destroyed', as the E/A was not seen to hit the sea and explode.

Jack's next letter home, written the day after this combat, reflects the intensity of the operations he had recently been experiencing.

Aug 17/44

My Dearest Mother & Sister

Hello Mom & Ruth I am sorry I haven't written before but it has been absolutely impossible to write we have been operating steadily with no time in between flights except to sleep. We are on now but there is a time between take off so I can dash off this letter.

I believe the last time I wrote my total of ops. was 9 well it has jumped up to 22 now and if every thing goes okay we ought to be finished pretty soon. So far we have been attacked by fighters twice and both those guys will never fly again. Last night I went on a trip and was attacked by a J.U.88 I opened up and set the guy on fire and watched him go down in flames and hit the sea and explode.

We have been doing a few battle front trips and it was really a pleasure to do them. I was talking to a Canadian officer in the army and he was telling me it was worth going over there just to see all the kites going over and knocking the living daylights out of Jerry.

What is the idea of saying I was in a Halifax bomber. Now that is an insult to us 'Lancaster!' boys and there is a sore point between the Hally & Lanc squadrons. So don't make the mistake again cause we are in aeroplanes and not flying Jalopies (Hallies).

With All my Love
Jack

After a raid to Reime on August 18, it was a week before the crew were next operational. The night of August 25/26, 1944, is noteworthy in that Bomber Command aircrew set a new record, flying 1,311 sorties, attacking Rüsselheim, Darmstadt, Brest, and various smaller operations: diversions, mine-laying, Resistance support, small de Havilland Mosquito raids and patrols, and radio countermeasure flights. Losses totalled twenty-five aircraft, with eight more aircraft written off in crashes on return to England. Once more John Fitzgerald was in the thick of the fighting.

COMBAT REPORT

No. 166 Squadron	Night 25/26th August 1944
Lancaster III N2 LM 694	Fishpond Serviceable. Operator trained
0113½ 18,000 Ft, 230T, 5000½N. 0737E	Homeward on track.
No cloud. No moon. Starlight.	Coned few mins prior to attack. No flak indiscriminate flares

Rear gunner Sgt. Fitzgerald, M/U Sgt Schafer.

Soon after leaving the target area after bombing Rüsselheim the M/U of Lanc N2 of 166 Squadron saw tracer fire from astern and slightly above. Searching the source of the trace he saw a twin engined A/C which he was unable to identify diving down from slightly above. Before he was able to bring his guns to bear in the E/A it suddenly burst into flames and dived steeply out of control. No tracer fire was observed entering the E/A from any direction. No damage was sustained by the Lancaster.

COMBAT REPORT

No. 166 Squadron	Night 25/26th August 1944
Lancaster III N2 LM 694	Fishpond Serviceable. Operator trained
4.00.48 18000 Ft, 327T, 4923N. 0357E	Target on track.
No cloud. No moon. Starlight.	Distant S/Ls. No flak

Rear gunner Sgt. Fitzgerald, 40 Rds.
Sgt Schafer.J. 50 Rds

Just prior to making their bombing run the M/U of Lanc N2 of 166 Squadron observed tracer fire coming from the Port Quarter Up. He immediately identified a Ju88 at about 250 yds diving down to the attack from an angle of about 20/30 degrees. Ordering a corkscrew Port the M/U opened fire at 175 yds and was joined by the R/G who had also sighted the E/A. The E/A immediately broke away down and was not seen again. Strikes were observed by both gunners and the E/A is claimed as damaged. Two mins prior to this attack the Lanc had been attacked by an ME109.

Comment by S/Ldr. Cox G.G.L.

The fighter was allowed to approach to within 250 yds range without being sighted; in fact the first indication of an attack was fire from the Hun. The gunners' search would appear to be not of the best. I consider that the claim of damaging the E/A is not justified.

There was little rest for Jack and his crew, detailed for operations the very next night—another large-scale operational night for Bomber Command. From the 844 sorties carried out, 28 aircraft were lost. Jack Fitzgerald was to fly on a mine-laying operation to the Bay of Danzig. RAF Flight Lieutenant F.J. Dee, flying Lancaster Mk III LM694 AS-M2, lifted his four-engine bomber from the runway at RAF Kirmington at 20:45 hours. The squadron diary identifies the rest of the crew: RAF Sergeant Jack White, flight engineer; RCAF Flying Officer James Russell (from Toronto), navigator; RAF Flying Officer George Palmer, air bomber; RAF Sergeant William Holt, wireless operator; RCAF Sergeant Jacob Schafer (Kingsville), mid-upper gunner; and the third RCAF crewman, nineteen-year-old Jack, flying in the rear gunner's turret.

Next to the list of names, the squadron diary later recorded that terrible comment: "Failed to return. Nothing heard after takeoff." In fact, 186 airmen failed to return from operations that night. 186 "regret to inform" telegrams were dispatched to next of kin. LM694 was not the only 166 Squadron aircraft to be lost. The No. 166 Squadron Lancaster of RCAF Flying Officer R.G. Bradley was also lost on the night of August 26/27, 1944, coming down into the sea with a total loss of life. Only the bodies of the pilot and one other member were found.

IN THE early hours of August 27, 1944, Flight Lieutenant Frederick Dee's burning Lancaster smashed into the ground near the village of Åstruplund and exploded. Some local people, initially transfixed as the fireball passed overhead, rushed to the crash site. One man recovered a parachute; his wife would appreciate the silk. Later that morning, with the area cordoned off, Svend Andersen, the owner of the field, approached, concerned about his crops. With permission granted, Svend neared the scene of devastation. He would never recover from what he then witnessed. Scorched pieces of wreckage and the horror of charred human remains were strewn across his field. Svend's nose filled with the acrid fumes of burning wheel rubber mixed with the stench of burnt flesh. With ammunition occasionally exploding, German soldiers gathered up body parts using whatever tools they had at hand, secreting them in paper bags. As the day went on more locals would regret making a visit to the scene of the crash.

That evening the body bags were taken away. Three days later, on the morning of August 30, German soldiers sealed off all access to the churchyard at the town of Gammel Rye. Here the entire crew were buried, without dignity. The gravedigger and another local man had quietly gained access to the church tower and they later told how, with no vicar present, the soldiers kicked the bags into the graves. A few days later the Germans erected a white wooden cross.

For two weeks the Germans maintained a cordon around the crash site. Much of what remained of the Lancaster was recovered, anything of use to be sent back to Germany. Outside the cordon, Svend had noticed a piece of the spar, and his farm hand, Rasmus Due Andersen, surreptitiously placed it at the bottom of a cart, covering it with animal feed. A German soldier followed Rasmus home—the Dane was unsure if he had been seen—but shortly before entering the farmyard the soldier went his separate way. The spar was stashed away in a loft, and after the war Svend tasked a local blacksmith with turning it into a memorial cross.

After the war, on February 5, 1946, Svend received a visit from a Captain Adams and two RAF officers who were investigating the details of the crash. It was now possible to expand upon the "reported missing" information that relatives of the seven airmen had previously received.

Shortly after this visit, Svend found out that a local person had the dog tag of one of the airmen, Jack White. This was sent to his mother, and she passed on information about the names of the other airmen lost that night and addresses of relatives. The memorial cross was engraved accordingly, photographed and copies sent to the relatives.

Over the years, Svend maintained contact with the relatives, many of whom paid him a visit. In June 1976, Jack White's mother and sister came to Denmark. Svend's grandson, Anders Lund, remembers it well.

> A visit that made a great impression on me was when Mrs White and her daughter, the mother and the sister of Jack White, visited my grandparents. The mother, Mrs. White was 82 years old, and her last wish was to see her son's grave. For 30 years, she had, in letters to my grandfather, expressed a wish to see the last resting place of her son. It was very emotional to see Mrs. White pause by her son's grave. The visit had a strong effect on both my grandfather and Mrs. White and her daughter. At the request of the Whites, my grandfather received a Royal Air Force coat of arms in appreciation for his work with the memorial cross. Today this coat of arms, received by him in 1976, is hanging in my home, in my best room.
>
> My grandfather was not a member of the Resistance or in any way active in the war. His war effort was to contact the surviving relatives of the crew. As he would say, "We, having been most closely involved, will never forget it. They spent their lives so that we could live in a free country."

ADDRESS REPLY TO:
THE SECRETARY,
DEPARTMENT OF NATIONAL DEFENCE FOR AIR,
OTTAWA, ONTARIO.

OUR FILE R215210 (R.O.)
REF. YOUR
DATED

ROYAL CANADIAN AIR FORCE

OTTAWA, Canada, 27th June, 1946.

Mrs. J.E. Fitzgerald,
2317 Maple Avenue,
New Westminster, B.C.

Dear Mrs. Fitzgerald:

A report has been received from the Royal Air Force Missing Research and Enquiry Service on the Continent giving the results of their investigations concerning the fate of your son, Flight Sergeant John Ernest Fitzgerald, D.F.M., and his crew.

The report states that at 3:30 A.M. on the morning of August 27th, 1944, the aircraft in which your son was flying was observed amongst a number of others in combat at a low altitude and was seen to crash over the estate of Mr. Svend Anderson at Traeden, Denmark. The local inhabitants were prevented from approaching the scene of the accident but saw the Germans recover the bodies of the crew which they transported to Gamle Rye Cemetery.

Due to the severe nature of the crash, however, Pilot Officer White was the only member of the crew who could be identified and the entire crew were interred in a communal grave and it is numbered Row 9, Plot 11, Grave # 14, a photograph of which is enclosed.

The reverent care of the burial places of all who served in the Forces of the British Empire is the task of the Imperial War Graves Commission. Already eminent architects are at work, planning the construction of beautiful cemeteries and each individual grave will be supported and sustained by the nations of the Empire. I hope that it may be of some consolation to you to know that your gallant son's grave is in sacred care and keeping.

May I again extend my most sincere sympathy.

Yours sincerely,

R.C.A.F. Casualty Officer,
for Chief of the Air Staff.

R.C.A.F. G. 32B
200M-2-43 (8112-3199)
H.Q. 88-G-32B

OPPOSITE, TOP F/L Dee's bombing picture, taken during the August 4 raid to Pauillac. ANDERS LUND

OPPOSITE, BOTTOM Post-war letter to Jack Fitzgerald's mother confirming the fate of her son. FITZGERALD FAMILY VIA THE CANADIAN IMAGES AND LETTERS PROJECT

TOP, LEFT James Russell, RCAF, navigator. CVWM VIA OPERATION PICTURE ME

TOP, RIGHT Jacob Schafer, RCAF, air gunner. CVWM VIA OPERATION PICTURE ME

BOTTOM John "Jack" Fitzgerald, RCAF, air gunner. FITZGERALD FAMILY VIA THE CANADIAN IMAGES AND LETTERS PROJECT

Throughout the last few months of the Second World War, the Bomber Command campaign continued unabated. Although the *Luftwaffe*'s effectiveness declined sharply through lack of both experienced crews and fuel, Allied day and night raids over enemy-held territory remained highly risky for the bomber crews—right to the very end. Men continued to be lost, and veteran Jack Bromfield vividly recalls the signs back at base that highlighted someone had failed to return. "What used to get me was breakfast the next morning. You'd expect to see seven blokes sitting at a table and they weren't there. Then you sat around for a while, wondering if they had landed away from home. By dinner time you knew. These memories are still there. They're there all the time. You can go, maybe, two weeks and think nothing; there's a little snippet in the paper or on the television and suddenly it all starts to wind up again. Or somebody mentions a name, you've forgotten about him for years, and suddenly you remember."

15

LOST OVER HANOVER

STEVE BOND

O N THE NIGHT of January 5/6, 1945, Bomber Command launched its first large-scale raid on Hanover since October 1943, with a force of 664 aircraft, of which, 23 Handley Page Halifaxes and 8 Avro Lancasters were lost. One of these was Halifax III MZ432/NP-Q of No. 158 Squadron, based at RAF Lissett in Yorkshire. The crew comprised skipper RCAF Flying Officer Arthur "Robbie" Robertson from Stony Mountain, Manitoba; navigator RAF Flight Sergeant Tom "Jock" Laurie from Auchinleck, Ayrshire; bomb aimer RCAF Flying Officer Gar Cross from Vancouver; wireless operator RAF Flight Sergeant Jack Bromfield from Bletchley Buckinghamshire; flight engineer RAF Sergeant George Dacey from Liverpool; mid-upper gunner RCAF Warrant Officer Gerry Marion from Lethbridge, Alberta; and rear gunner RCAF Flight Sergeant Ed Rae from Ottawa.

This was the crew's twelfth operation, their first having been a daylight raid on November 16, 1944, to attack German troop concentrations at Julik. As Jack Bromfield recalled: "That frightened the bloody life out of me! I've never seen so much flak in all my life. But we gelled as a crew, except with the flight engineer, who always seemed to be on the outside looking in. Then we went to Mannheim, Cologne, Koblenz, Sterkrade, when we went after the oil refineries, you know, the usual run-of-the-mill targets."

On the fateful January night, they were flying with a replacement flight engineer who was joining them for the first time. The
regular flight engineer was from London, and according to Jack,
"He didn't go that night, he'd disappeared, and we don't know where
he went, or what happened to him. When I asked the skipper where
he was, he just said, 'He isn't coming.' After I eventually got back to
England in the summer of 1945, I bumped into him at Cosford, but
only got 'Hello, goodbye,' as quick as that."

For all seven men aboard "Q-Queenie," the takeoff at just after
17:00 hours would be the last time they would see RAF Lissett.
Just over two hours later, as the bomber stream was approaching
Hanover from the northwest, Robertson's Halifax was attacked by
a night fighter, which the rear gunner spotted and identified as a
Ju 88. The fighter was flown by Hauptmann Heinz Rökker, Knight's
Cross with Oak Leaves, based with *Nachtjagdgeschwader* 2 at Twente
in Holland. The Halifax was hit twice, with each attack following the
usual approach from below the bomber so that the *Schräge Musik*
upward-firing cannons could be used. The rear gunner was lucky
to have seen it at all. Jack continued:

> There was a hell of a lot of bangs and thumps and crashes, and
> then a fire started in the bomb bay... there were bits flying off
> here, there and everywhere. I didn't know until some days after-
> wards that I'd been shot on the outside of the foot, but my feet
> were so bloody cold I didn't feel it. Anyhow, things went from bad
> to worse, but the aircraft didn't do anything strange, it was just
> losing height. I looked past my curtain at the pilot, and he looked
> at me and pulled the control column backwards and forwards and
> said "I've got no control," so he said "Right, time to go." It was
> only a shallow dive, the aircraft was still quite steady on its feet, it
> wasn't rolling or whatever. But there was no point in staying with
> it if we put the fire out, because it just wouldn't come out of the
> dive. So out we went.

After a considerable struggle with the latching mechanism, Jack was eventually able to open the escape hatch between himself and the navigator where the navigator, bomb aimer, and wireless operator would go out. The wireless operator also had the job of giving the pilot his parachute, because it was stowed next to his on the starboard side, and the pilot would then follow the other three out. The mid-upper gunner and the flight engineer would go out of the rear door, while the rear gunner, who had a fighter-type parachute, just turned his turret to one side and rolled out backwards. However, at the time, the crew thought that George Dacey, the new flight engineer—at thirty-five, the old man of the crew—had not got out. The last Jack saw of him he was standing in mid-fuselage, and he did not subsequently turn up with the rest of the crew in captivity.

Having successfully abandoned the aircraft, Jack remembered hearing the Jumo engines of a Ju 88, perhaps the one that had shot them down. He then had to think about his landing. "I went through two lots of cloud and then it was white, just a white-out on the ground."

I could see the target burning, and I could see flares going down, so I knew we weren't far, but the bombs were still on when we left her; we hadn't bombed. Anyway, I couldn't steer this bloody thing (the parachute), so I thought well, training, turn the buckle and hit it. I did, and I fell out of the harness, straight on my arse in the middle of the road. It was a very wooded area, so I buried my 'chute and harness, and having seen the direction of the target, I knew which was south east and which was west, so I just buggered off in a westerly direction, thinking I might bump into somebody, but I didn't see a soul. I didn't see another 'chute, I didn't see anything at all. I had eight days on the run, and I thought I was doing quite well, hiding up in the day and walked at night. But I gave that up after two days because I got fed up of tripping over tree roots and falling down ruddy ditches in the dark. About the third

242 FAILED TO RETURN

or fourth morning, I was walking just off a road in the woods, and I heard voices; I could understand what they were saying. I thought, 'Some other members of the crew', but I'll be cagey, just in case it isn't. I got towards the edge of the wood and looked down the road, and there's two blokes with shotguns and three blokes standing with their hands up. They were Americans, you could tell by their flying boots; they were funny little things they used to have compared to ours. So, discretion being the better part of valour, I went deeper into the woods and just kept on walking and never saw anything of them again.

On the eighth day, Jack was following a single-track railway line going west, and by now he was getting very hungry. He saw a field that looked promising as a possible source of food and started scratching about in the soil to retrieve what looked like swedes (rutabagas), not very appetising but better than nothing. Suddenly he felt something in the middle of his back, and a voice said "Hände hoch!" He put his hands up and turned round—there was a man in a railway uniform who had seen him from a small station hidden behind the trees. Soon after, two *Luftwaffe* men came along in what Jack described as a clapped-out Beetle and took him away.

CANADIAN MID-UPPER gunner Gerry Marion had also successfully abandoned the doomed Halifax, leaving by the rear door. He too parachuted onto a road but was almost immediately captured, wounded with a broken leg caused by gunshot, roughed up, and taken to a guardhouse. The next morning, he was taken by car, with two guards, on a two-hour drive to another guardhouse. There he spent two weeks in solitary, the only POW there, with no one to talk to. He left on January 19 with a German officer and met another guard and a burnt American flyer and guard at Kassel. They then spent two days on a train to Frankfurt, with lots of problems, arriving on January 20. Gerry described his experience:

We then went to the air force interrogation centre (sweat-box) at Dulag Luft. Later that month I went to Hohemark Hospital by truck for medical treatment; my leg was in bad shape. There were 15 to 20 other POWs there. Then, still in January, I had to endure a forced march and boxcar ride with 15 POWs and five guards to Nürnberg [Nuremberg] POW camp, Stalag XIIIC, with approximately 2,000 POWs. Then in February, the camp was evacuated and we were marched to another camp at Moosburg, Stalag VIIA. At both Nürnberg and Moosburg we slept in tents.

The remaining crew members also successfully exited the doomed Halifax but, like Marion, were quickly rounded up by the Germans and spent the rest of the war in captivity. However, nothing was ever seen of George Dacey, and for many years the survivors believed that he had simply failed to get out of the burning Halifax. Certainly, no body was ever found, and Dacey is commemorated on Panel 274 at the Air Forces Memorial at Runnymede.

MANY YEARS after the war, it was Gerry Marion (who had been held in a different POW camp) who finally contacted other members of the crew with some information concerning George's fate. Sometime after his capture, Gerry had met an American airman who had been injured and taken to a German hospital. There the American met George Dacey, who had been quite badly injured when he bailed out. It seems that George decided that, if he was going to escape, doing so from a hospital was likely to be far easier than from a POW camp. When he attempted to do so, he was shot, and more than likely he was hurriedly buried in the vicinity.

The surviving five crew, including Jack, were finally liberated from Stalag Luft 1 at Barth in northern Germany on the Baltic coast.

One night we heard these bangs, and thumps, and somebody said "That's the Russian guns." When we got up next morning, there were Russians in the compound and there was a lot of conversation going on outside between the commissioned types in the camp and the Russians, and then they cleared off and just left us to our own devices. Then suddenly this hoard of B-17s appeared and landed, and that's what I flew home in, landing at Ford down near Littlehampton.

Gerry Marion had been held in Stalag VIIA at Moosburg in southern Germany, the largest of all the German POW camps; at the time of its liberation there were approximately forty thousand men in a camp designed to hold ten thousand. "We were released in April by American Army General Patton. I was flown back to Reims, France, then to army hospital in England. There was nothing first class on this trip."

Following their release and demobilization, the surviving members of the crew returned to their hometowns. Robbie Robertson returned to Canada to continue his career with the RCAF. On October 17, 1947, he was pilot in command of a 413 Squadron B-25 Mitchell that had been converted for photographic missions. After departing Calgary, the aircraft disappeared in filthy mountain weather near Rossland, British Columbia. The wreckage remained unfound for five years. After all that time in wild country, only very limited remains of the nine souls on board could be found; those that were, were laid to rest near the crash site. After surviving the challenges of war and captivity and returning home to continue his flying career in Canada, Robbie Robertson's luck sadly ran out, only a few short years later.

Both Jack Bromfield and the man who shot down his aircraft survived the war. In July 2004, the two met at the Oldenburg, Germany, home of Hauptmann Heinz Rökker to share their respects and memories. Rökker ended the war with sixty-four victories as the seventh-highest scoring *Luftwaffe* night fighter ace. That fateful night of January 5/6, 1945, Bromfield's Halifax was one of two aircraft shot down by Rökker, his forty-seventh and forty-eighth victories.

The author was fortunate to accompany Bromfield to this encounter. He observed wryly that "they got on like a house on fire," as did many former combatants who had the opportunity to meet in more peaceful times.

OPPOSITE, TOP No.158 Squadron, RAF Lissett, 1944. Left to right: Jack Bromfield, Gerry Marion, Gar Cross, Tom Laurie. JACK BROMFIELD

OPPOSITE, MIDDLE, LEFT The Robertson crew. From top: Robertson, Cross, Laurie, Marion, Bromfield, Rae. JACK BROMFIELD

OPPOSITE, MIDDLE, RIGHT F/O "Robbie" Robertson, No.21 OTU, RAF Moreton-in-Marsh. JACK BROMFIELD

OPPOSITE, BOTTOM In 2004, Jack Bromfield met the man who shot down his Halifax, night fighter ace Hauptmann Heinz Rökker (Knight's Cross with Oakleaves). STEVE BOND

ABOVE No. 21 OTU, RAF Moreton-in-Marsh. Left to right: Gar Cross, Tom Laurie, Gerry Marion, Jack Bromfield, Arthur Robertson, Ed Rae. JACK BROMFIELD

Jack Styles had managed to navigate his heavily damaged bomber back from Germany, but now his skipper, Joe Talocka, was fighting hard to control their RCAF 426 Squadron Halifax VII and land safely. They were returning from an attack on the Wanne-Eickel oil refinery, during which NP819 OW-B had been hit by flak, ripping up the starboard aileron and puncturing holes in the wings and the fuselage. With the ordeal nearly over, Talocka twice had to pull out of a landing, as the RAF Manston runway was not lit. Those on the ground tried desperately to make contact with the crew. It is thought that the aircraft hit a slip stream and went into a steep bank. The controls locked and the Halifax plunged to the ground from about five hundred feet. The wireless operator managed to bale out in time. The rest of the crew did not.

16

DEAR MOM

STEVE DARLOW

JACK STYLES was born in Midland, Ontario, in 1925 and, like so many of his peers, volunteered in 1943 to join the Royal Canadian Air Force. Throughout his training and operational flying, Jack kept in regular contact with his mother. A letter from Jack, addressed from London, Ontario, in October 1943 records the excitement of Jack's first flight.

Dear Mom

Boy was it wonderful. We got all dolled up in our flying clothes (I wish you could see me) which are much too big... The crotch of mine is halfway to my knees. When we put our parachute on it pulled all the slack up making a big bulge to front and rear where there shouldn't be a bulge. We then went to briefing where we get our orders... to sit in the plane and watch the passing scenery and if we got sick we were to use the paper bags supplied and instead of bombing some poor unsuspecting church goers with them, to bring them back and place them in the nearest garbage can. We then went to our plane and took our seats. Since there was one more man than seats... I sat on the floor. The pilot then tried to get in touch with the control tower by radio but the damned radio wouldn't work. Fine!! Then he tried the motors and one wasn't working well. Swell!! We then all piled out of the plane and into another one (again I sat on the bloody floor) ... we went to the edge of the runway and started down it. I was sitting there wondering when we would reach the end of it when I happened to look out of the window. There was the ground only it was about 1,000 feet below us. Wow!!

We started to fly along about 3,000 feet and I started to enjoy myself. You look out and you see a little mist pass you. That was a cloud. You look down and you see a lot of little squares (the ground) with little lines (roads) and blue curved lines (rivers). Then you look at your map which has roads, rivers etc. on it and you try to find out where you are. Not finding it you decide you must have brought the wrong map. However on checking with the lucky so and so's in the seats you find that you have the right map but are looking at the wrong corner of it (you are never near the centre, that would be too easy). You look out again and you see what looks like a thin wood (that's a town) and so on ... Then you put your map down and start to watch the scenery (against orders). The plane hits a pocket and your stomach feels funny after falling through the air. You decide you had better work than sit there thinking of those paper bags and what they are for. So you pick up your map and look out the window to try to find where you are. This being hopeless you ask the pilot. On locating yourself you find that there is supposed to be a racetrack somewhere under you but you can't see it through the wing so you tell the pilot. He gives the wheel a turn (stick to you) and tells you to look out again. You look out and the wing is gone but the racetrack is there. Thinking that you have lost a wing you look around for the one on the other side. It is there standing straight up in the air, then you decide that you are on your side. You hastily tell the pilot that you have seen the racetrack and everything goes back on even keel. Right then and there you decide never again to ask him to let you see something ... Fine, you decide you have a strong stomach by now so you commence to look around you ... after about an hour you see something and venture to ask if that is London airport. Hurra, you are right this time (now a veteran, never wrong) . . . the wing is gone again and that damn place starts to come right up toward you. That feels nice on your stomach . . . then the wing comes back up and the ground comes up faster until it is right under you. Bump you are down . . . [you see] the Interrogating officer who asks you who was sick. He seemed awfully sad when we said no one was. Then we went to dinner with our chests out and our heads held high. We were now veterans. We had flown. Boy oh boy. I am not kidding, it is swell . . .

This may not tell you much but it will give you an idea of my first flight in a flying box car, an Avro Anson.

Your loving son
(who didn't get sick) Jack

It is clear from Jack's letters that he had a close relationship with his mother, catching up on her welfare and sending money and flowers. On January 17, 1944, he wrote, "Sure you are lonesome, so are about a million others. Chin up and I'll be home before you know it."

IN THE early months of Jack's training, there was not much for him to report. In fact, boredom was the enemy.

MARCH 1944. No 1 AGTS, Maitland, NS: God what a hole. There is nothing to do here except sleep whenever you have spare time. Brother . . . I am going to increase my assignment to $90 per month soon. Do you think you can manage on that? Please write me. I have had no word from anybody yet & boy am I bored. They have the prettiest red mud around camp. However we went for a route march this morning and the mud was the usual colour farther away from camp. Yesterday afternoon we had the afternoon off & since the tide was out we walked out the shore for about a mile. Then it started to come in so we walked back in. Some excitement eh? . . . Brother, to think that I might spend 8 weeks or more here. Boy oh boy am I disgusted.

When Jack finally shipped out to the United Kingdom, he wrote two letters expressing his appreciation of his new surroundings.

APRIL 1944. Well here I am I didn't get seasick although I wasn't feeling well for a while. Boy oh boy, now I see why the RAF fellows wanted to get home. We saw some of the country, the grass is a lovely green, everything is in bloom... Nothing but the best for us here. We have swell quarters etc. so we are perfectly happy. I wish I could have seen you before I left but maybe it is just as well. You know how I am at saying goodbye... Right now the sun is out and I want to go for a walk.

MAY 1944. I had a wonderful leave. I was up at Windermere in the Lake District. Boy it is beautiful country up there it reminds me a lot of Muskoka district in Canada. I spent my leave lounging around, rowing, riding a bike, fishing etc. The fellow where I was staying owns 3 small lakes which he stocks with rainbow trout, speckled trout etc. Boy, that's fishing.

The day following the invasion of Normandy, Jack wrote home again, still chafing for action.

7 JUNE 1944. The invasion starts & I am not even on course yet. Most of us are mad because we are starting to wonder if we will see action or not. I wonder? Personally, knowing what we still have to go through, I doubt it... This English beer is horrible the fellows all want to give it back to the horses. However we can't complain. Well I still haven't seen the inside of a plane over here but I might sometime I hope.

16 JULY 1944. Well here we are again. About those flying bombs, don't worry we never see them. We are on a beautiful station now. The hut I'm in is about 2 miles from water, except what's in the mud, but then you can't wash in that can you. We have a swell crew here Pilot - Joe Talocka (Polish origin), Nav. yours truly, Bomber

Chuck (oh hell I never can remember his last name), Wag - John Davis, Air Gunner Al (Major) Bradley, and 'Nookie' Chisamore. As far as flying goes, don't worry, we are the best crew around (so we claim). Seriously, the pilot is an F/O who has been flying for quite a while & knows everybody's job. He's better in some parts of nav. than I am. They told me that I am an above average nav. (Please quit laughing, I'm serious) Chuck is an F/O too. The Wag and A.G.'s are sergeants.

The fledgling crew continued training, although there were some changes.

3 AUGUST 1944. What a life. I moved barracks the other day & am now sleeping in a single room with a bureau, table, chair etc. Some class I'd say... We had a change in our crew. We lost Chuck our Bomb Aimer & got Arlotte from Toronto.

21 AUGUST 1944. We lost our WAG today. He was put on charge for smoking on parade & so we will have to get another fellow. He was damn good too.

17 SEPTEMBER 1944. By the way we could use some canned fruit etc. now that you have a can opener. Please note that I said we. Whenever anyone in the crew gets a parcel the whole crew gangs up on him & there goes another parcel. But we all have fun anyway. I wish you could meet the crew. They are a swell bunch. Joe (the pilot) is a real gen boy. You can't catch him on the questions on flying. He lands these big crates as if he were carrying eggs... We have been looking forward to this leave for quite a while and it promises to be quite a blowout. And how. Our little mid upper doesn't drink so he will keep us in hand. I sure wish I could see you again soon. Maybe I will be able to. This war can't last long.

28 SEPTEMBER 1944. Then we came here, our new station. I have just finished fighting for two hours with the fire in my room

to get it to burn. Then I gave up. What a place. A second Maitland.
However it won't be too bad. We won't be flying for about a month
again so you can breathe easy for that long anyway... Edie sent
me some hot chocolate & oxo in hers but we have no place to make
it so I had to give most of it away to the batwoman. We haven't got
any here. What a life.

On October 2, 1944, Jack wrote to his sister telling her of some
of the sights he had seen on leave. It was not going to be something
he wrote home to his mother about.

All you can do in this country is go out & get drunk. I had a leave
last week in London & had quite a time. You walk along the street
dodging the Piccadilly commandos (Eng. type of lower class of
Montreal so & so girl.) Boy are they thick around there. They
charge anything from £2 (9 bucks) to £5 (about $22.50) Some girls.
You should see some of them.

By now, the war was shifting heavily to the advantage of the
Allies, and the losses to Bomber Command were diminishing significantly. With reduced demand for replacement crews, the BCATP
was beginning to plan the process of winding down. However, for
those men who had already completed most or all of their training,
the result was the kind of delay Jack and his crew experienced in
getting operational. As the nights lengthened and the war entered
a sixth winter, Jack kept his mum posted of his frustrations and further details of his crew.

8 OCTOBER 1944. Well here is your son Flying Officer Styles writing again (that sounds nice doesn't it). Still disgusted with your
homeland. What a country. As far as heating goes they haven't got
a clue. They stick a little stove in a huge room & everyone freezes.
Then when they have a very small room they stick a huge stove in
it & everyone sweats. Boy oh boy they haven't got a clue. Back at
school again... Always in school.

12 NOVEMBER 1944. Did I tell you about our engineer, he is an English fellow, and very keen. He knows the Halifax inside out ... His name is Graham Needham, I am going to give you his number soon, when I get it, & you can try to send him cigs. By the way, I haven't got any cigs for quite a while now. Try to send a thousand next time will you?

1 DECEMBER 1944. Well I finally have some pictures for you. They are pictures taken in Manchester and a couple here. I am sending a few now and some copies of the ones from Manchester later so that you can send some to Norma & Grandma.

There is one very good one of the whole crew, all sober etc. The one of Red and myself is pretty good. Red is another Nav. that I know. He is getting married over here soon.

In Manchester there were only five of us and we took the pictures. So most of the pictures only have five of us in them. (Sensible isn't it)

By the way, if you notice a queer look on my face don't blame me. I was trying to smile through a hangover or something. Some fun. I like the picture of Joe with the whole crew rather than his alone. It looks more like him. Chis of course looks very serious, don't let it fool you he usually isn't so serious ... They are a swell bunch.

18 DECEMBER 1944. This is quite a place. At last we are out of Nissen huts. In fact it is swell.

3 JANUARY 1945. Well here it is 1945, & still a war on. Oh well maybe it will stop soon. At last I can try to do my bit instead of doing nothing.

12 JANUARY 1945. Don't get too much of a surprise, I know that I haven't written for a week but I was on leave, you know, a holiday. We had a swell leave, went to Glasgow (in Scotland you know) ... That was my first trip to Scotland & it was swell. The people are swell.

I went up with our mid-upper 'Brad' who also went to see his friends ... We spent a very quiet leave, I only had 3 (THREE) pints (or maybe four but no more) in a week, but we still had fun. 'Brad' doesn't need any drinks, he is crazy enough as it is.

... I'm glad you liked the snaps. I was afraid you wouldn't get them. You like the crew eh, so do I, hope you can meet them sometime, they are a swell bunch of fellows. By the way Joe's number for the interested parties is J35641 F/O J.P. Talocka and he says that he will answer all fan mail personally. Seriously if you or anyone else write him for heavens sake no mush ...

You wish I could be home by summer, so do I. Keep your fingers crossed and for heavens sake try not to be too lonely. I want you to be happy ... Your loving son, Jack.

At the end of January 1945, Jack and his crew finally took part in a large raid in the Stuttgart area and on the night of February 1/2. Jack was one of 340 navigators entrusted with directing his crew to Mainz. The following night Bomber Command sent 323 aircraft to attack the oil refinery at Wanne-Eickel, which proved ineffective owing to difficulties with cloud cover. Owing to the extensive flak damage to their Halifax, Joe Talocka had tried to land at RAF Manston. The station diary recorded "A Halifax of 426 Squadron crashed while making wide circuit with controls shot away. All attempts by Police, NFS, and our own ambulance parties to find aircraft fail. One survivor who baled out thinks the aircraft crashed in Minster Marshes. 11 Group lay on land and sea search for this aircraft." The following day, the diary recorded, "Halifax of 426 Squadron, which crashed last night is located, but there are no further survivors."

Canadians Joe Talocka, Joseph Chisamore, Sidney Arlotte, Allan Bradley, and Jack Styles were all buried at Brookwood Military Cemetery. Graham Needham was taken back to his hometown and buried at Scunthorpe (Brumby and Frodingham) Cemetery.

F/O Joseph P. Talocka, originally from Winnipeg, had worked at the Malartic gold mines near Val d'Or, Québec. He enlisted in

August 1942 and was twenty-six when he died. P/O Joseph A. Chis-amore, from Port Arthur and one of the two air gunners on the Halifax that day, was twenty. Twenty-four-year-old F/O Sidney G. Arlotte, air bomber, had studied at Western Technical School in his hometown of Toronto before he enlisted. P/O Allan G. Bradley, also from Toronto and the second air gunner on the aircraft, must have signed up almost immediately he was eligible to do so; he was only nineteen at the time of the crash.

Jack Morris Styles was twenty.[29]

The handwritten letter reads, in part:

July 16/44

Dear Mom:
Well here we are again. About those flying bombs, darn it every we *never* see them. We are on a beautiful station now. The hut I'm in is about a mile from water, about which (on hush hush business) when you can I'll wash them so I can you. We have a swell crew here. F/O—Joe Talocka (Phil origin)—Now yours truly, Bomber cheese (oh hell I never can remember his last name) Way. John Davis, air gunner. Al (major) Bradly, & Norke Chessman. As far as flying goes, don't worry, we are the best crew around (so we claim) Seriously, the pilot is an F/O who has been flying for quite a while & knows everybody's job. He's better in some parts of nav. than Sam. They told me that I am a man above average now. (I have quit laughing) I'm serious) ...

ABOVE, LEFT Jack Styles's letter, dated July 16, 1944, in which he describes the rest of his crew to his mother. STYLES FAMILY AND THE CANADIAN LETTERS AND IMAGES PROJECT.

ABOVE, RIGHT Jack Styles and "Red" MacLean. STYLES FAMILY AND THE CANADIAN LETTERS AND IMAGES PROJECT.

ABOVE, LEFT Jack Styles's letter, dated July 16, 1944, in which he describes the rest of his crew to his mother. STYLES FAMILY AND THE CANADIAN LETTERS AND IMAGES PROJECT.

ABOVE, RIGHT Jack Styles and "Red" MacLean. STYLES FAMILY AND THE CANADIAN LETTERS AND IMAGES PROJECT.

OPPOSITE, TOP, LEFT An RCAF 426 Squadron Handley Page Halifax at RAF Linton-on-Ouse, winter 1944–45. It was an identical aircraft to the one in which all but one of Joe Talocka's crew died while trying to land at RAF Manston after being heavily damaged during a bombing raid on the night of February 1/2 that same winter. LAC 4476985

OPPOSITE, TOP, RIGHT An early portrait of Jack Morris Styles, from training days. Jack had been promoted to flying officer by the time his aircraft crashed at Manston. CVWM VIA OPERATION PICTURE ME.

OPPOSITE, BOTTOM View from the bomber stream of a Halifax, captured in the middle of a daytime raid over Europe. Exploding bombs and previous damage are clearly visible below—a scene that would have been familiar to the Talocka crew. LAC 4002568

R 2 5 4 7 2 4 1A5 7 0 5

POSTSCRIPT

THE YOUNG MEN who are central to these brief stories were, without exception, devoted to doing a difficult and dangerous job. Each had his own reasons for taking on this responsibility, but at the heart was common cause to risk all for something in which they believed deeply. None knew or would have believed the missions described here would be, for most of them, their last—that they would fail to return. Only a small number were fortunate enough to come home at all, often after months of hardship on the run or years in captivity.

Their comrades remain in the scattered cemeteries or dark waters of Europe, from Berlin to the pastoral countryside of south-western France, from the Baltic Sea to Dutch villages, and in the now peaceful ground of the country for which they came to fight, England itself. Their graves are kept by governments and by local villagers, in appreciation and recognition of the scale of their sacrifice. The ones who died are only a few of the nearly ten thousand young Canadian men who joined Bomber Command and, ultimately, gave their lives for a cause they believed was worth the risk. No matter whether they encountered their fates during training, as they flew in the heaviest operations against Germany, or in the last fading moments of the war in Europe, their sacrifice demands no less than that their names and stories be kept alive when they are gone. We will remember them.

ACKNOWLEDGEMENTS

WORKING ON THIS book presented special challenges during a period in which travel and communication was limited, so the support I received was especially appreciated. I owe a particular debt to Doug Rollins and the volunteer staff at the library of the British Columbia Aviation Museum who were always happy to dig in their piles of books in pursuit of the most arcane facts, always appropriately masked, disinfected, and physically distanced, of course. Steve Darlow of Fighting High Publishing in the UK began this important project of remembrance and kept it going through the Failed to Return series published in that country. It was originally his thought that stories highlighting the considerable Canadian contribution to Bomber Command deserved standalone recognition. Peter Celis, author of *One Who Almost Made It Back*, the story of S/L Teddy Blenkinsop, has been very helpful with information and photographs, as was Teddy's cousin, RCAF Brigadier General (ret'd) John Neroutsos. The folks at the British Columbia Archives gave me hands-on access to their collection of historical material relating to the Blenkinsop family, including Teddy's flying logbook. I also received enthusiastic support and a much-appreciated willingness to share material from Dave Birrell at the Bomber Command Museum of Canada at Nanton, Alberta, and from Greg Sigurdson at the Commonwealth Air Training Plan Museum in Brandon, Manitoba. My sincere thanks to the others who contributed intriguing

bits and pieces as the project came together, including Gary Bou-
dreau, John Brehaut of the Commemoration Division, Veteran's
Affairs of Canada, and the many friends and relatives who allowed
the use of the photos of their loved ones so that a face could be put
to their stories.

Finally, but definitely not least, I offer my appreciation to my life
partner, Francine, for her great patience while I "hogged the computer" for so long. She has always been my best and most important
supporter, whether she knows it or not.

NOTES

1   "The President [Roosevelt] wished to send a message of congratulations to
    Mr. King on the third anniversary of the British Commonwealth Air Training
    Plan, a project in which Canada now took a great and justifiable pride. I was
    surprised when a friend on the White House staff, ignoring all rules of diplomatic
    propriety and without telling the State Department anything, asked me whether
    I would be kind enough to do a draft of the message for the President. I did. So
    on 1 January 1943 the Prime Minister of Canada received a very impressive letter
    lauding Canada as the 'aerodrome of democracy' drafted by me but signed by
    the President of the United States!" — L.B. Pearson. *Mike, The Memoirs of the
    Right Honorable Lester B. Pearson* (Toronto, University of Toronto Press, 1972),
    208.

2   "Bomber Command's Losses," Bomber Command Museum of Canada website,
    assessed May 25, 2020, www.bombercommandmuseum.ca/bomber-command/
    bomber-commands-losses/.

3   Brereton Greenhous, Stephen J. Harris, William C. Johnston, and William
    G.P. Rawling, *The Crucible of War 1939-1945: The Official History of the Royal
    Canadian Air Force Volume III* (Toronto: University of Toronto Press, 1994), 13.

4   F.J. Hatch, *Aerodrome of Democracy: Canada and the British Commonwealth Air
    Training Plan 1939-1945* (Ottawa: Department of National Defence Directorate
    of History, 1983), 5.

5   The precise numbers were difficult to determine, at least partly because
    Canadian citizenship was only created as a distinct category as of January 1,
    1947, under the Canadian Citizenship Act. Until then, native born Canadians
    and naturalized immigrants were classified as British subjects.

6   Hatch, *Aerodrome of Democracy*, 21.

7   In 1942, Leckie transferred to the RCAF.

8   Allan Todd, "No. 1 Manning Depot – Toronto 1941 March 1941," *British
    Commonwealth Air Training Plan* (blog), assessed May 25, 2020, bcatp.wordpress.
    com/category/no-1-manning-depot/.

9   The Anson quickly became obsolete as an operational aircraft when the war began and was assigned to training and communications roles, which it successfully carried out in extended post-war service. A number were shipped from England to Canada in the early days of the BCATP. Eventually, more than 2,470 were built in Canada, mainly for use in multiengine pilot and navigator training.

10 Towing drogues was a dreaded assignment for graduates of flying training. Some of these pilots had been assigned as instructors and complained loudly about not being sent overseas to an operational squadron. The penalty for the loudest and worst offenders was a posting as a drogue pilot, which quickly and effectively reduced the number of complaints.

11 In April 1943, 405 was assigned to become the RCAF's only Pathfinder Squadron—that is, one of the elite squadrons in the newly formed No. 8 Group (PFF) whose outstanding records for accuracy meant they were tapped to lead bombing raids, marking targets and directing raid activities over the target.

12 Fauquier would later begin his third tour of operations as Commanding Officer of 617 Dambusters Squadron, an appointment for which he took a demotion from his (then) air commodore rank.

13 As reported in the *Hamilton Spectator* dated January 4, 1943: "Veteran Canadian Raiders Go into New Bomber Group."

14 Canadian House of Commons Debates May 12, 1942, quoted in Hatch, 196.

15 CB—Confined to Barracks.

16 This was the codename given to the rotating bomb especially designed for the Dams Raid by British engineer Barnes Wallis.

17 The spotlights were precision mounted so that they would converge at a predetermined height above ground. In the case of the Dams Raid, the height required for proper functioning of the Upkeep bombs was exactly sixty feet above the water.

18 To simulate night flying, the aircraft windows were covered with orange plexiglass. The trainee pilot wore blue tinted goggles. Everything inside the aircraft was seen as having a blue tint, but there was no visibility outside the aircraft. The instructor simply saw the outside view with an orange tint.

19 Also referred to as "touch and go," where the aircraft would land and take off again from the same runway without stopping.

20 Not Mercier, as reported in the original account.

21 Peter Celis, *One Who Almost Made It Back* (London: Grub Street Publishing, 2008), 28.

22 Letter from Teddy to his parents dated May 12, 1941, quoted in Celis, 51.

23 Path Finder Force.

24 Celis, 129.

25 Celis, 160.

26 From report of 1 War Crimes Investigation Unit, May 28, 1946, held in National Archives of Canada. Quoted in Celis, 171.

27 On May 2, 2019, Stuart Leslie's ashes were interred, according to his express wishes, with the remains of his crew comrades in the cemetary at Oudenaarde, Belgium.

28 There is some discrepancy in the available records as to Webber's age when he died. His memorial headstone records his age as 37, as does the Library and Archives Canada website. The latter site, however, notes his date of birth as March 27, 1913, which would make him 31 when he died. Either way, he would have been the "old man" of the crew.

29 Many thanks to Dr. Stephen Davies, Project Director at the Canadian Letters and Images Project, and to George Lord.

BIBLIOGRAPHY

General History and Context:

Allen, Kenneth R. *405 Squadron History*. Winnipeg, MB: Craig Kelman & Associates, 1986.

Allison, Les, and Harry Hayward. *They Shall Not Grow Old: A Book of Remembrance*. Brandon, MB: Commonwealth Air Training Plan Museum Inc., 1992.

Bashow, David L. *No Prouder Place: Canadians and the Bomber Command Experience 1939-1945*. St. Catherines, ON: Vanwell Publishing, 2005.

Chorley, W.R. *Royal Air Force Bomber Command Losses of the Second World War*. Trowbridge, Wiltshire, UK: Redwood Books, 1997.
(NB—there are 6 volumes in this series of books, published between 1992 and 1998, each covering one year of the war.)

Dunmore, Spencer, and William Carter. *Reap the Whirlwind: The Untold Story of 6 Group, Canada's Bomber Force of World War II*. Toronto: McClelland & Steward, 1991.

Dunmore, Spencer. *Wings for Victory: The Remarkable Story of the British Commonwealth Air Training Plan in Canada*. Toronto: McClelland & Steward, 1994.

Greenhous, Brereton, Stephen J. Harris, William C. Johnston, and William G.P. Rawling. *The Crucible of War 1939-1945: The Official History of the Royal Canadian Air Force Volume III*. Toronto: University of Toronto Press, 1994.

Hastings, Max. *Bomber Command*. Minneapolis, MN: Zenith Press, 1979.

———. *Chastise: The Dambusters*. London: William Collins, 2019.

Hatch, F.J. *Aerodrome of Democracy: Canada and the British Commonwealth Air Training Plan 1939-1945*. Ottawa: Department of National Defence Directorate of History, 1983.

Milberry, Larry, ed. *Sixty Years: The RCAF and CF Air Command 1924–1984*. Toronto: CANAV Books, 1984.

Richards, Denis. *The Hardest Victory: RAF Bomber Command in the Second World War*. London: Hodder & Stoughton, 1994.

Books Documenting Personal Experiences:

These books are a small selection from the many collections or full-length accounts of the experiences of men who participated in the air war. Their experiences were as varied as the men themselves, and this list is intended as nothing more than a representative sample of the many accounts that exist. Some, like Peden's *A Thousand Shall Fall*, are recognized as classics of the genre. Most are simply an effort to remember and document the momentous and unique events in which the individuals participated; they all open the door to a better understanding of the bloody human cost of war.

Bond, Steve et al. *Bomber Command Failed to Return*. Stotfold, Bedfordshire, UK: Fighting High Publishing, 2011.

——. *Bomber Command Failed to Return II*. Stotfold, Bedfordshire, UK: Fighting High Publishing, 2012.

——. *Bomber Command Battle of Berlin Failed to Return*. Stotfold, Bedfordshire, UK: Fighting High Publishing, 2017.

Celis, Peter. *One Who Almost Made It Back*. London: Grub Street Publishing, 2008.

Cothliff, Ken. *Four Who Dared*. Victoria, BC: Heritage House, 2019.

Darlow, Steve et al. *D-Day Bomber Command Failed to Return*. Stotfold, Bedfordshire, UK: Fighting High Publishing, 2014.

Harvey, J. Douglas. *Boys, Bombs and Brussels Sprouts*. Toronto: McClelland and Stewart, 1981.

Hewer, Howard. *In for a Penny, In for a Pound: The Adventures and Misadventures of a Wireless Operator in Bomber Command*. Toronto: Stoddard Publishing, 2000.

Owen, Robert et al. *Dam Busters Failed to Return*. Stotfold, Bedfordshire, UK: Fighting High Publishing, 2013.

Peden, Murray. *A Thousand Shall Fall—The True Story of a Canadian Bomber Pilot in World War Two*. Toronto: Dundurn Press, 2003.

Pyves, Richard R. *Night Madness: A Rear Gunner's Story of Love, Courage and Hope in World War II*. Markham, ON: Red Deer Press, 2012.

Thompson, Walter. *Lancaster to Berlin—The True Story of One Canadian's War Against Germany*. Don Mills, ON: Totem Books, 1987.

Wilson, Kevin. *Bomber Boys—The RAF Offensive of 1943*. London: Orion Publishing Group, 2005.

———. *Men of Air—The Doomed Youth of Bomber Command*. London: Orion Publishing Group, 2007.

———. *Journey's End—Bomber Command's Battle from Arnhem to Dresden and Beyond*. London: Orion Publishing Group, 2010.

Online Sources:

Canadian content in the RAF
- legionmagazine.com/en/2005/01/canadian-content-in-the-raf/

Canadian Military Records—general list of sources
- familysearch.org/wiki/en/Canada_Military_Records

Commonwealth Air Training Plan Museum
- airmuseum.ca/

Commonwealth Air Training Plan—Veterans Affairs website
- veterans.gc.ca/eng/remembrance/history/second-world-war/british-commonwealth-air-training-plan

Canadian Virtual War Memorial Project—Veterans Affairs Canada
- veterans.gc.ca/eng/remembrance/memorials/canadian-virtual-war-memorial

Canadian Warplane Heritage Museum Aircraft Details
- warplane.com/aircraft/collection/details.aspx?aircraftId=4

Commonwealth War Graves Commission
- cwgc.org/find-records/find-war-dead/

Find a Grave
- findagrave.com/memorial

International Bomber Command Losses Database
- internationalbcc.co.uk/history-archive/losses-database/

Imperial War Museum
- iwm.org.uk/history/life-and-death-in-bomber-command

Library and Archives Canada Service Files
- bac-lac.gc.ca/eng/discover/military-heritage/second-world-war/second-world-war-dead-1939-1947/Pages/files-second-war-dead.aspx

RCAF Squadron Operations Record Books
- heritage.canadiana.ca/view/oocihm.lac_mikan_135766

"Robbie" Robertson (Ch. 15)
- bamf.be/Dispersals/Dispersals_Nov_2018.pdf

"Teddy" Blenkinsop (Ch. 7)
- tracesofwar.com/persons/42224/Blenkinsop-Edward-Weyman.htm
- bombercommandmuseum.ca/chronicles/teddy-blenkinsop-the-montzen-raid/
- findagrave.com/memorial/15245784/edward-weyman-blenkinsop
  sites.rootsweb.com/~nbpennfi/penn8b2Blenkinsop_EW.htm
- archives.victoria.ca/blenkinsop-family-fondsweb.archive.org/web/2008050
  1194702/
- lancastermuseum.ca/s,blenkinsop.html

UK Archives Squadron Operations Books
- discovery.nationalarchives.gov.uk/browse/r/h/C112128

INDEX

ABOUT
THE AUTHORS

KEITH C. OGILVIE is a former aerospace engineer who worked on Canada's space program in the 1970s and '80s, before moving into the field of international development, supporting governance and economic development projects. He is also a former pilot (who owned an ex-RCAF trainer), a sailor, an explorer, and the bestselling author of *The Spitfire Luck of Skeets Ogilvie*.

DR. STEVE BOND served in the RAF for twenty-two years as an aircraft propulsion technician, before moving into the civilian aerospace industry, and subsequently joining City University London as a senior lecturer. Now a freelance lecturer, Steve's main interests centre on military aviation from the Second World War onwards. He is the author of numerous works including *Heroes All, Wimpy,* and *Special Ops Liberators*.

STEVE DARLOW is a military aviation author, publisher, and documentary consultant with twenty-one books to his name, including *Five of the Few, Five of the Many, D-Day Bombers, Victory Fighters,* and *Flightpath to Murder*. In 2009, Steve founded Fighting High Publishing, which seeks to publish books focusing on human endeavours in military situations.

LINZEE DRUCE has been researching Second World War aviation losses since 1999. Combining her love of the outdoors, Linzee visits crash sites and endeavours to piece together what happened using official records, eye-witness accounts, and family documents.

MARC HALL developed an interest in aviation at an early age and gained a commercial pilot's licence. Marc's research into RAF Bomber Command is ongoing, and his books *Operation Hurricane* and *Missing Presumed Murdered* were met with critical acclaim.

SEAN FEAST works in public relations and advertising and is an acclaimed Bomber Command author. Sean has authored and co-authored numerous books, including *A Thunder Bird in Bomber Command*, *Missing Presumed Murdered*, and *The Lost Graves of Peenemünde*.

DR. ROBERT OWEN is an aviation historian and the official historian of the No. 617 Squadron Association. A trustee of both this association and the Barnes Wallis Memorial Trust, he has contributed to numerous publications and television documentaries, including authorship of *Henry Maudslay Dam Buster* and a commentary in the recent republication of Leonard Cheshire's *Bomber Pilot*.

HOWARD SANDALL is the No. 622 Squadron historian and the author of the squadron's history, *We Wage War By Night*.